GW00322540

THE PANIC OF '89

Also by Paul Erdman

The Billion Dollar Killing
The Crash of '79
The Last Days of America
The Silver Bears

The Panic of '89

Paul Erdman

ANDRE DEUTSCH

First published 1986 by
André Deutsch Limited
105-106 Great Russell Street London WC1

British Library Cataloguing in Publication Data

Erdman, Paul
The Panic of '89.
I. Title
823'.54 [F] PS2555.R4

ISBN 0-233-97957-3

Phototypeset by Falcon Graphic Art Ltd,
Wallington, Surrey
Printed in Great Britain by
St Edmundsbury Press, Bury St Edmunds

This book, which is set in the future, is entirely fictitious. Though a few real names have been used, there is no suggestion that these persons have acted or will act in the way described.

‘Words ought to be a little wild for they are the assault of thoughts on the unthinking.’

John Maynard Keynes

PART I

Chapter 1

It was the first week of December and the weather in Georgetown was chilly. It was not, however, just the first blasts of winter air that were causing some of the more prominent residents of that élite community to shiver when they got out of bed that Tuesday morning. In this year of 1988 it was also the growing mood of apprehension that had begun to grip Washington since the first week of November. The fear that had been mounting during those thirty days was that everything would start to unravel – soon – and that the United States in 1989 could find itself dumped into a situation where the economy, the dollar, the banks, Chrysler and, yes, even IBM would all go into a dive, one after the other.

The troubles had been gathering since the beginning of Reagan's second term. But since he was the luckiest man to hold the office of presidency, they never got to him. He was like a quarterback who had never been sacked during eight years in the National Football League.

But the Gipper was going to be gone on January 20th of '89.

Paul Mayer, one of the more prominent of Georgetown's residents, was thinking just such thoughts as he skimmed through the papers in the upstairs bedroom of his house at 3514 Dent Place. They included the *Washington Post*, the *New York Times*, *The Wall Street Journal*, the *Financial Times*, the *Neue Zürcher Zeitung*, the *Handelsblatt* of Düsseldorf, and, to round things out, *Le Monde*. Then he picked up the TV remote control from the table beside his bed and tuned in to Channel 20, which carried the Financial News Network most of the day, to see what the markets were doing. He didn't bother to turn up the volume since he was interested in the numbers on the screen, not the commentary. All this took an hour, which brought Paul Mayer up to 9 a.m. on that Tuesday, December 6th, 1988.

The maid knocked on his bedroom door, as she was instructed to do at that time every morning when he was home, and entered with her tray bearing a silver coffee urn. She placed it on the bedside table adjacent to the IBM PC that Mayer kept there – just in case he needed it in the middle of the night or at the crack of dawn. She filled Mayer's cup, then added a touch of cream, all without saying a word. She had come from Puerto Rico; she was twenty-four, she was five feet two, and cute, and, when she bent over to pour, her more than generous bosom became more than half visible. However, her curves, analogue in nature, seemed out of place in Mayer's high-tech, and thus digital, bedroom.

'Anything else, sir?' she asked. Her Spanish accent added to her cuteness.

Paul Mayer just kept watching the FNN numbers on the screen.

'Ja,' he answered. 'Make sure my smoking is pressed for this evening.'

His accent was not so cute, since it was vaguely Central European.

'Smoking?' she asked.

'Tuxedo,' he now said. That is what they called it in Amerika. 'Smoking' is what they called it in both Stockholm and Zurich. Every now and then Mayer still reverted to his Swedish-Swiss origins, although he had lived in America for fifteen years now. Not that people seemed to mind. Around town he was known as a cross between Henry Kissinger and

Paul Volcker. The Volcker thing arose because Mayer was both a banker and six feet four; the Kissinger side related to their similar accents and origins, and the fact that Kissinger and now he were both professors at the School of Foreign Service of Georgetown University, and fellows at the Georgetown Center for Strategic and International Studies.

The next move that Mayer made was to pick up the phone and push the button which automatically dialed his private answering service. They had instructions to intercept all pre-10 a.m. calls, no matter what. Mayer did not want to talk to *anybody* until he was up to speed on what had happened in the world during the time he had wasted sleeping.

There were two intercepts: the first call had come from Sergio Dobrovsky, one of his colleagues at the Center for Strategic and International Studies. Dobrovsky, who headed the Center's Terrorism Studies Program, asked that Mayer drop into his office in the afternoon, if he had time. The other call was from George Pace, Chairman and Chief Executive Officer of Bank of America, the world's second largest. He had left no message; just a phone number in London, one that Mayer immediately spotted as not being that of any of B of A's branches in that city.

As Mayer found out later – much later, and some said *too* much later – the reason that the messages had been left was that the two callers were simultaneously just beginning to sense the emergence of the same ominous phenomenon: Dobrovsky the still very murky cause; George Pace the initial, faintly visible effect.

Mayer, not sensing that anything out of the ordinary was astir despite the general feeling of 'malaise' that was in the air in Washington in these pre-Christmas weeks, chose not to break his morning routine for either call, and instead took his usual fifteen-minute shower. That was the place and the time he planned his day.

This day would start with his eleven o'clock seminar at the

University. Next to Henry Kissinger's lecture series, Mayer's seminar was the hardest course to get into at the School. The seminar was limited to fifteen, and you had to be an honors student to qualify, all of which gave the whole thing prestige. But it was not prestige that had the students fighting to make the cut at the beginning of the seminar: it was greed. When word had gotten out in August of 1988 that Dr Paul Mayer was joining the faculty, it became instantaneously known that he had connections – *active, ongoing* connections – in the highest echelons of banking, connections that were unmatched on the face of this earth, connections which, if 'networked' by the chosen few among the Georgetown graduating class, could be parlayed into untold riches. For it was said that when Mayer spoke, the Rockefellers listened – and the Rothschilds, and the gnomes of Zurich, and the merchant bankers of London, and Merrill Lynch, and the gold and silver and currency speculators in Hong Kong, Los Angeles and Abu Dhabi.

The kids at Georgetown figured that if anybody could help them get a job after graduation, starting at, ideally, say $60,000 a year, and requiring at least two trips a year to Europe and one to Asia, it would be Dr Mayer. Dr Kissinger's lectures might help one get into the Foreign Service, and maybe a posting as vice-consul in charge of stamping passports in Lagos in a year or two. Mayer's seminar, however, strategically emphasized on a résumé, could land a job immediately with Lazard Frères, or Paribas, or Crédit Suisse, in, say, the foreign loan syndications department, which could mean a Porsche, lunches at the Four Seasons, lodgings at the George V, vacations at the Mauna Kea!

At least that's what the kids thought. Nobody actually knew for sure, since Mayer, like Kissinger, didn't particularly like college kids and stayed away from them to the greatest degree possible.

Mayer's house was seven blocks from the Georgetown campus, and he inevitably enjoyed the walk to it. It always seemed to awaken some thoughts that had nothing to do with professional matters. On this particular morning it was Beaconsfield that was evoked. Mayer had spent a couple of years as managing director of the Swiss National Bank's syndication operations in London, and had chosen to live out in Buckinghamshire. Every morning he had walked to the train which brought him, thirty minutes later, to Marylebone station, whence he had always taken the tube to the City. The cobblestones, the red brick houses, the slightly unkempt little yards, the dull, damp cold . . . that was his memory of Beaconsfield in December. That was also Georgetown now. How nice it is, he thought, to know and love two small towns, three thousand miles apart and separated by an ocean, towns that had barely changed from what they had been in 1888 or 1788.

He entered the campus at 37th and O, turned right on the walk that led past the landmark Healy building and then approached the modernistic Intercultural Center which housed the School of Foreign Service. The 'courtyard' in front had been built with red bricks; the students, inevitably, had dubbed it Red Square.

'Hey Paul!' The greeting came from the tall, handsome man just emerging from the building still twenty paces away. It was Dr Peter Krogh, the Dean of the School of Foreign Service, and the closest thing to a 'pal' that Mayer had encountered so far at the University.

'Got a message for you,' Krogh said, as they met in the middle of Red Square. 'Big stuff, as usual,' he added, grinning.

'Really?' Mayer replied. 'As you know, Peter, I don't usually go for big stuff. Unless she . . .'

'Sorry to disappoint you. No she. By "big" I mean Bob Reston. He wants you to return his call right away.'

Robert Reston was Chairman of the Federal Reserve Board.

Mayer grunted. Then: 'May I use your office?'

'Sure. Got time for lunch today?'

'Why not. Where?'

'How about the Metropolitan Club. At 1.00? I'll sign for it.'

'In that case I'll see you there.'

Krogh's office was all wood paneling, Persian rugs, and *objets d'art* from places as diverse as Egypt, Finland, Jordan and India – gifts from their governments to the world's leading educational institution devoted to the training of diplomats. From the Dean's office one had a commanding view of the huge atrium, or galleria as it was known on campus, that was surrounded by classrooms and offices of the School of Foreign Service, and topped by a roof densely packed with photovoltaic cells. It was one of the most advanced 'solar' buildings in the world, an example of the high technology which symbolized America's revived leadership of the international community of nations. Solar energy, Kissinger, Mayer – they were all now part of the power which Georgetown projected.

The Dean's secretary got the Chairman of the Fed in less than a minute. 'Appreciate your getting back so quickly, Paul. Say, could you by any chance find time to drop by this afternoon?'

'Of course. But look, I'm lunching at the Metropolitan Club at 1.00, with Peter Krogh. You know each other, don't you?'

'Sure. He lives two doors down from us on Q Street.'

'Then why not join us?'

There was a moment's hesitation. Then: 'All right. Although it's pretty touchy stuff I want to discuss. You might mention that to Peter.'

'Will do.'

'I'll be bringing somebody with me too,' the man from the Fed added. He then mentioned the name of the man who ran the Federal Deposit Insurance Corporation, known affectionately to all Americans who kept their money in a bank as the FDIC; affectionately because the FDIC was the governmental agency which insured their bank deposits up to $100,000 – free of charge!

'It looks like a real power lunch,' Mayer muttered to himself, as he hurried down the stairs to join his fifteen awaiting students. But he could not help but admit that he was greatly looking forward to it. Not that he regretted having left the lofty position of Managing Director of the International Monetary Fund, where he had had tens of billions of dollars at his disposal, and the fate of dozens of nations in his hands, for 'just' a university professorship. Because at Georgetown one was not necessarily 'just' a professor. Kissinger had certainly proven that. As had Brzezinski. There were a dozen others, ranging from James Schlesinger to Jeane Kirkpatrick, who had done the same. Hardly a day went by when some high government official, American and foreign, did not call upon them for advice. If, in 1988, the United States had a corps of 'grey eminences', it existed under the aegis of Georgetown University. And Paul Mayer knew that at lunch he would be 'officially' joining its ranks.

But his teaching came first. Mayer's seminar was conducted under the vague umbrella of 'International Finance: Problems and Potential Solutions'. The problem this week was Third World debt. His star student presented a paper summing up the situation: their debt as of mid-year 1988 was over a trillion dollars. Much of this was owed to American banks. None of it was being repaid. In fact, the only single instance that he had been able to track down of *any* repayment of principal by a Third World nation since 1982 was $250 million – the 'illion' starting with an 'm', i.e. not a 'b', much less a 'tr' – that Mexico, for some unknown reason, had made on December 3rd, 1985.

The solution? Well, none was in the offing, his student had concluded. But so what? Maybe none was needed. The problem had been there, and rapidly growing, for ten years now and nothing drastic had ever happened. The borrowers in Latin America periodically threatened default. They then demanded that the terms of the *old* loans which had now come due be renegotiated. Otherwise . . .

Their bankers inevitably caved in and extended a period of grace of two or three or five years and, that done, granted new loans to their debtors south of the border enabling them to pay the interest on the now-no-longer-due-for-repayment old loans. In the end everybody was happy. Argentina and Brazil and Mexico and Venezuela kept getting more and more money from Bank of America and Citibank and Chase Manhattan and the World Bank and the International Monetary Fund and could thus keep their economies going. On the other hand, the financial institutions of the developed world – private and governmental – could maintain the myth that the $250 billion, then half a trillion, now $1,000,000,000,000 in Third World loans outstanding on their books was 'good' since, after all, the interest on them was always paid more or less on schedule. Having demonstrated that, the private sector banks then proceeded to book the interest which they were paying themselves as income. Net result: they recorded record profits year after year.

'In my judgement, there is a complete mutuality of interest among the debtor nations of the Third World and the bankers of the developed world,' the student stated. And then he concluded, reading from his paper, 'There is no reason that this process cannot continue indefinitely, provided that all of the principal players continue to play the game.'

The other fourteen students in the seminar all seemed to agree, except one José Martinez of Caracas, Venezuela, whose sneer – his normal facial expression – was first replaced by a derisive grin, and then by a malevolent smile when he heard his fellow student's concluding words. If Paul Mayer had been following the Latino's silent commentary, he might have caught on to what was about to happen in the world since José Martinez's father, José, Sr, was the finance minister of Venezuela and his uncle the oil minister and Co-Chairman of OPEC, the Organization of Petroleum Exporting Countries, which had been founded at the instigation of his country, and was primarily designed for one purpose: to screw the United States. But at Georgetown José Martinez, Jr was just one of the large contingent of Latinos who had been in evidence for decades on the campus overlooking the Potomac – a place where Latin American generals parked their sons, dictators their grandsons, and in one recent instance, where the President of Bolivia had parked his nineteen-year-old mistress, all in the hope that they might grow up some day.

Few did. And thus they were not taken very seriously. Likewise José Martinez, Jr. However, Professor Mayer did take seriously and also seemed highly pleased with the paper that his star student, an eager beaver from the Midwest, had delivered, so much so, in fact, that he awarded him an A. Then, after looking anxiously at his watch, Mayer hurriedly ended the seminar and fled the building before any patronizing student could nail him with some asinine question.

Dean Krogh was waiting for him in the entrance hall of the Metropolitan Club, and they immediately took the elevator up to the dining-room on the 2nd floor. They shared the elevator with the Undersecretary of State for Economic Affairs, who had the Swiss Ambassador in tow. All knew each other; all mumbled to one another that they must lunch together one of these days. Then the two parties went their separate, conspiratorial ways: at the Metropolitan Club weighty matters were always on the agenda. Beer was seldom drunk; baseball was rarely discussed.

The man from the Federal Reserve Board arrived on the next elevator accompanied by the man from the FDIC. Both appeared almost too young for the positions they held within the financial power structure of the United States. It has often been said that the head of the Federal Reserve Board is the second most powerful man in the United States, and thus the world. Probably both Mikhail Gorbachev and George Bush would dispute that, despite the fact that neither of them could do what Robert Reston could do, namely create money – dollars, the currency which literally made the entire world go round – out of thin air.

The man who ran the FDIC was hardly in that league: nevertheless he ranked way up there among the power élite because it was he who, along with the Fed and the Comptroller of the Currency, supervised the nation's 14,700 commercial banks. In the decade of the 1980s, however, circumstances had occasionally required that he and his staff go beyond simple 'supervision' and step in directly to prevent financial calamities. It was, in fact, due to the direct intervention of one of his predecessors, William Isaac, that Continental Illinois was still among America's top eleven banks in 1988. For in the spring of 1984 a run had started on that bank, a run that had developed so rapidly that it came within a hair of forcing the collapse of what had up to then been assumed was Chicago's safest financial institution, an event that could have triggered the biggest monetary crisis in the United States since the 1930s. For at stake was not just the Chicago bank itself, all $40 billion of it. The critical nature of the situation had been compounded by the fact that 250 smaller banks in the Midwest used Continental Illinois as *their* bank, meaning that if Continental went belly up, most of them would probably go under too as word of their exposure in Chicago led to bank run after bank run in Peoria and Moline and Springfield.

Where the dominos would ultimately have stopped falling, nobody knew. So the then Chairman of the FDIC saw no alternative but to exercise his power in an unprecedented fashion. He fired all of the bank's top management, forced its Board of Directors to resign, and moved part of his Washington staff to Chicago to take the place over – thus putting the full faith and credit of the United States behind every deposit in that bank, from the very smallest to the very largest. In other words, he nationalized the Continental Illinois.

It worked.

But everybody in the banking business knew that it had been a close call. From the worried looks on the faces of both the new Chairman of the FDIC and the man from the Fed as they ate lunch at the Metropolitan Club on that Tuesday, December 6th, 1988, a suspicious mind might have surmised that another close call was in the making.

Paul Mayer, who had such a mind, had been surmising just that. And after coffee had arrived, he let it be known. 'Somebody in trouble?'

'Yeah,' the Fed man replied.

'Who is it this time?'

Bob Reston looked over at the man from the FDIC, and then at Dean Krogh. 'Peter,' he said, 'this has got to stay among us girls. OK?'

'No problem, Bob,' the Dean replied, and, putting on his stern face added, 'you've got my word.'

'OK,' Reston then said. 'It's B of A. The rumors started yesterday afternoon.'

'I've heard nothing,' Mayer stated. Now *he* looked worried. Normally Mayer missed *nothing*.

'Where's it coming from?' he then asked.

'Zurich and Frankfurt. It's been very muted so far.'

'What's the substance?' Mayer asked.

'We hope there is none.' The answer this time came from the Chairman of the FDIC. In 1984 that Continental Illinois fiasco had cost his agency a lot of money. Three years later, the one involving the First National Bank of Texas had cost the FDIC another $3 billion. It too had been caused by bad energy loans. After the price of oil took its first big dive, from $31 to the low-water mark of $10 in 1986, they had started plugging wells in Texas rather than drilling them. The result was that those

First National customers which had borrowed most heavily – independent oil producers in Midland, developers of shopping malls around Houston – were forced under, one by one. In 1987 the loan losses had caught up with the bank. The bailout had cost the FDIC almost a quarter of its capital.

'No, you misunderstand me. What's the substance of the *rumors*?' Mayer now asked.

'That Bank of America is going to have to take a big, big hit. They say the biggest hit of all time. Like $2 billion plus.'

'Why? And why now?'

'The second question's the pertinent one I would say,' answered the man who ran the FDIC. His name was Roger Wells. He was an accountant by training and a pedant by nature. In Washington social circles he had already made his mark as a man you definitely did not want to be seated next to at a dinner party. He continued: 'Like every other money center bank, B of A's had its problems for years now, as you know full well, Paul. But maybe it's somewhat unique in that it's got non-performing loans almost everywhere you look, both inside and outside the country. They've loaned billions up and down the central valley in California, and at least another billion north of San Francisco in the wine country.

'The problem is,' and at this point the head of the FDIC appeared to be lecturing the Dean, 'that American farmers collectively owe the banks more than Brazil and Mexico and Argentina combined, and, collectively, they are not any more solvent. Then there are still those energy-related loans. Every time the crude oil price goes down another notch, another couple of hundred loans in Denver and Houston and Midland go sour. On top of that there's real estate. God knows how many condos they've financed in LA and everywhere else in California, and we all know what's been happening to the value of condos and to the people who financed them with 15 per cent down. They are starting to walk away from them in droves leaving B of A and almost every S&L in California holding the bag. And finally there's Latin America: collectively the banks and the governmental agencies have half a trillion dollars' exposure down there, and growing. And B of A is the lead lender to Mexico and Brazil and Venezuela.'

He paused as if waiting for some comment from the Dean. Since the Dean did not appreciate being lectured to, there was none, so the Chairman of the FDIC continued.

'Sure, it is today an accepted truth that there is nothing to worry about down there, that those loans can be rolled over forever. But if we go into recession next year, and if the recession proves to be either a deep or a prolonged one, or, God help us, both, then that Third World debt issue is going to surface like a wounded whale. Add up the writeoffs that are going to have to be made in fiscal 1989, rumor now has it, and B of A will be out that $2 billion plus I already mentioned. If this situation gets out of hand we at the FDIC are going to have to step in, and it's going to cost us a packet.'

Now he was ignoring the Dean and addressing Mayer and the Fed.

As Mayer listened he thought that maybe he should have given that student an A−. Or, if the worries of the man from the FDIC proved correct, an F.

'So what's been the response in the markets so far, Bob?' Mayer then asked, addressing the Chairman of the Fed.

'So far it's been barely perceptible. But starting this morning in London, the Europeans started demanding one-quarter of 1 percent premium from B of A on their jumbo CDs. And B of A is going along with it.'

Reston then turned to Dean Krogh. 'That probably doesn't sound like much to you, Peter, but believe me, it's significant.'

'Why?' asked the Dean, who was becoming more than a little pissed off at being lectured at from all sides just because he was the only one at the table who had never been a banker.

'Because it's the first vote of non-confidence. What the market is saying is that the risk of depositing funds with Bank of America for a month or three months is now higher than it is at the other big banks. "We want a premium in terms of interest to compensate for that risk; otherwise we will take our money elsewhere" is what they are telling B of A.'

'Well, if one-quarter of 1 percent more interest is all they want, it would seem to me that nobody's exactly panicking,' the Dean responded, finally getting a return shot off.

'You're right,' the man from the Fed replied, 'but once these processes start, the one-quarter of 1 percent becomes a half, then a full hundred basis points and then . . .'

'Then the withdrawals start,' Mayer interjected, and then asked: 'Have they started?' directing this question at the FDIC.

'No,' was the immediate response. But then: 'At least we don't think so. One of our staff made a discreet call this morning to San Francisco to one of the bank's directors. He came back to us just before I came over here, and said no – no withdrawals. But we really can't be sure that he is fully apprised of the situation. Management does not exactly bend over backwards to inform the Board when there's trouble brewing, be it in banking or any other business.'

Mayer nodded his agreement to the last remark. Then he added: 'And you can't exactly go in and take a look, can you?'

The FDIC Chairman answered, and answered emphatically, 'Absolutely not. The next regularly scheduled audit – and, as you know, Paul, it will be the Comptroller of the Currency conducting it, not us, since B of A is a nationally chartered bank and we only audit those with a state charter – doesn't come up until April. If it was even *hinted* that the government, especially the FDIC, was suddenly taking a special interest in the bank before that time, who knows what response it would precipitate.'

He paused to let the import of that sink in.

Then Roger Wells continued: 'I don't know if you fellows remember the details of the Continental Illinois débâcle in

1984, but I do because I've been reading some of my predecessor's files this morning. The rumor that Continental was in serious trouble started in London on a Thursday morning, their time. Six hours later Continental's headquarters in Chicago was open for business and in the first hour alone the Europeans yanked out over $3 billion. A few hours later the Japanese got the word and before the day was over they had yanked out another billion and a half. Before the week was over, we – meaning we *and* the Fed – directly and indirectly had to put up $17 billion to keep Continental's doors open.'

The FDIC's acknowledgement of the Fed's help had obviously come grudgingly. For although the FDIC and the Comptroller of the Currency and the Fed were the three chief regulators of the banking system in the United States, everybody knew that it was the Fed that really ran things.

'So if you do something, you run the risk of precipitating a run. And if you don't . . .?' Dean Krogh asked.

'If we do nothing,' Roger Wells answered, 'and something really goes wrong, Congress will come down on us like a ton of bricks.'

'But don't people know they're covered by you no matter what happens to the bank?' the Dean asked.

'They do and they don't. They know it, but a hell of a lot of them don't believe it and follow the "rather safe than sorry" approach. Of course, the big depositors are *not* covered by federal deposit insurance. That's why they're so flighty, especially the foreigners. And once the big guys start to yank out their deposits, the little guy figures that they must know something that he doesn't know. That's when all the lemmings start to line up at the withdrawal window. Isn't that right, Bob?'

The Chairman of the Fed nodded his agreement and said, 'That's why we bailed out everybody who had money on deposit at Continental, big or small.'

'But will you guys do it again? That's the big question, isn't it?' Paul Mayer now asked.

'Sure it is,' answered Reston. 'But *you* know we'd have to; *I* know we'd have to. Only *they* don't. And you can understand their thinking, I guess, because they cannot be 100 percent sure since we, and by "we" I mean at least technically the FDIC,' and this time it was the man from the Fed who acknowledged the existence of the FDIC by glancing in the direction of Roger Wells before continuing, 'are not *legally* bound to cover any deposit above that $100,000 limit. We cannot even imply what you and I know – that we would *have* to cover them since there is no way that we would let a money center bank go belly up – because if we did there would be a hue and cry that would never end about the American taxpayer providing a free ride for the world's fat cats.'

'What percentage of B of A's funds are generated in the money markets?' Mayer then asked.

'Not as much as with most big banks,' Reston answered, and it was becoming obvious that he was increasingly asserting the Fed's dominant role as the conversation progressed. 'They have a hell of a broad deposit base in California. But my guess would be that probably 40 percent at least is outside of FDIC coverage.'

Then: 'Look, we keep talking about FDIC coverage protecting the depositors at the Bank of America. That's one issue, but in *our* judgement at the Fed, not the key one. We're worried not just about a bank but about the banking *system*. Nobody in Europe or Japan is exactly excited about the Democrats taking over on January 20th. They equate Democrats with inflation, and they equate inflation with a deterioration in the value of the dollar. Some, maybe a lot of them, may decide to park their money in some currency other than the dollar until they see what the new administration plans to do. Then we'd have double trouble: not just rumors about a big American bank in trouble – which could lead to a run on that institution – but fears that the dollar is going to get into big trouble – which could lead to a run on the currency. If we got hit by a double whammy like that, with fear of one compounding fear of the other, the whole banking system could start to run out of liquidity. Remember: foreigners now have a trillion and a half dollars of assets in the United States and almost a trillion of that is in the form of short-term deposits with our banks – deposits which are eminently yankable. If just 10 percent of that should leave the country abruptly . . .'

After Reston's voice had trailed off, silence set in at the table for a while.

Then the Chairman of the Fed continued: 'Look, we all know that we can't do anything about what's going to happen after January 20th. But maybe we can do something about the B of A situation. In fact, that's the reason I asked to see you, Paul. Why *we* asked to see you.'

'All right, I'm listening,' Mayer replied.

'You're close to George Pace, aren't you?'

'I guess you could say so. I knew him long before he became Chairman of B of A. He was in charge of their Swiss operations for years, you know, and at that time I was running the Swiss National Bank's operations in Basel, so naturally we did a lot of business together. In fact – and there are never coincidences in this world, as we all know – he left a message with my answering service this morning asking me to call him back.'

'He's in London, isn't he?'

'Yes.'

'Would you mind going over to talk with him?'

It was now Paul Mayer's turn to pause before he spoke.

'I guess not.' Then: 'When did you have in mind, Bob?'

'Soonest.'

Paul Mayer thought it over again. 'This week?' he then asked.

'Tomorrow if you can work it out. Or better yet, this evening.'

Another pause. Then: 'All right. If you feel it's that urgent. What approach do you suggest I take with Pace when I get to London?'

'Just level with him. Tell him that I asked you to go see him.' Robert Reston did not bother to include the FDIC this time. 'Tell him that I felt it urgent because of what we've been hearing. Ask him if there's anything to this story about the $2 billion plus writeoff. If there isn't, find out if he knows who's behind all the rumors. And why.'

'What if he needs help?'

'Our position is very clear: He'll get whatever help he needs from the Fed, no questions asked. At least for now.'

'I can tell him exactly that?' Mayer asked.

'Yes. If he wants it in writing, he'll get it.'

'You mean that if he wants a telex to that effect, say the day after tomorrow, he can have it?'

'Not quite. After Continental Illinois, and that fiasco in Texas, we have to proceed in an orderly fashion. Quick but orderly.'

'What's that mean?' Mayer asked.

'That means that first we get *your* report. Then he gets *his* telex – if he needs it. Which we fervently hope he doesn't,' Reston added.

'You agree, don't you?' Reston then asked the Chairman of FDIC.

'Absolutely. If you have to go in, we'll be right behind you.'

Reston turned back to Mayer. 'Do you think I could have your report by the weekend, Paul?'

'I don't see why not.'

Reston then gave Mayer his home phone number and suggested that their meeting place should be at his home in Bethesda. He also mentioned that the Comptroller of the Currency might insist upon being brought into the weekend get-together since he was co-responsible with the Fed and the FDIC for situations like this. Reston did not explain why the

Comptroller had not been invited to lunch. Mayer suspected that it was because of the eternal rivalry among the three bank regulators. In this instance obviously the Fed and the FDIC were going to present the Comptroller with a *fait accompli*.

Peter Krogh signed for the lunch. As they left, the Swiss Ambassador to the United States, who was just about to wind up his lunch with the man from the State Department, watched the foursome disappear into the elevator and then checked his watch. It was too late to get hold of anybody in Berne by phone; so he'd have it put on the telex. When the Chairman of the Fed and the Chairman of the FDIC had lunch with Dr Paul Mayer something of major significance was brewing in the world of international finance: probably trouble. More precisely, what was involved was probably big trouble for a big bank, a big American bank.

The Swiss normally don't like big trouble where their favourite commodity, money, is concerned, unless they can somehow come out winners. It was one of the prime functions of Switzerland's embassies around the world to try to ensure a winning status for the *Eidgenossenschaft* by providing their government in Berne with economic intelligence. What they were especially on the lookout for was any event that could affect the competitive stature of Switzerland as one of the world's pre-eminent money centers. They knew that Switzerland's prosperity depended upon that country's banks' ability to attract a constant supply of cheap money. If people around the world remained convinced that Switzerland was the safest haven on earth, they would continue to leave their money there at 3 percent, 1 percent and very often 0 percent interest rates, or less. For in especially turbulent times, the banks actually *charged* their depositors 1 percent or 2 percent for the privilege of having their money stored in Switzerland.

All this allowed the Swiss banks, in turn, to take the cheap, and often dirty, money they raked in from abroad and lend it at very low rates at home. Thus a Swiss citizen could get a mortgage at 4 percent while an American or Englishman paid an interest rate triple that much. More important, the Swiss banks provided massive low-interest loans to their Swiss industrial clients, such as Nestlé, the giant food company in Vevey, which, in turn, used such cheap money to buy Stouffer in Cleveland, Crosse & Blackwell in London, and the Carnation company in Los Angeles, much to the chagrin of the people who had been running these companies for decades, and suddenly found themselves on the street – courtesy, in the final analysis, of the Swiss National Bank. Or take Hoffman-La Roche, the pharmaceutical company in Basel which could finance massive R&D programs with the same type of long-term, low-interest loans, giving them an enormous cost advantage *vis-à-vis* their competitors in other countries who had to pay double or triple those rates to finance their businesses. So it was Roche who came up with the biggest selling drugs of the post-war era, Librium and Valium, and cleaned up financially for decades, especially in the American market, until the patents finally ran out in 1985.

So if the Swiss banks flourished so did Swiss industry and ultimately the entire country. The banks had had it very good for a very long time. Result: the Swiss citizenry enjoyed the highest standard of living of any people on earth. But of late, due to the challenge of America and its banks, it had become questionable as to how much longer the Swiss could live so well at the expense of the rest of the world.

The Swiss Ambassador concluded that if the scene at the Metropolitan Club meant big trouble for some big American bank, this could only be good news for Swiss banks, and thus also his people. This explained his subsequent behavior. When he returned to the embassy, he personally drafted the telex addressed to the Political Department, the Swiss equivalent of the State Department, in Berne, an exercise he normally considered beneath his dignity. Then, at dinner that evening, he sent back the usual bottle of Dôle, the Swiss red wine that is so heavy you can almost walk on it, and instead requested a '76 Château Mouton Rothschild. The occasion deserved celebration: the arrogant American bankers were in trouble yet again, and maybe this time they were finally headed for a big fall! If so, billions would soon be fleeing back to the safety that could only be provided by Swiss banks.

The Chairman of the Fed, who had his limo waiting, offered the Dean and Mayer a ride back to Georgetown. They accepted, and spent most of the trip discussing the Redskins, who had not only made the playoffs, but were expected to return to the Super Bowl in January when it would once again be played in Palo Alto. They dropped Mayer off at the corner of Dent and 35th Street and wished him luck.

At 8.00 that evening Mayer was on Pan Am headed for London. He had managed to get hold of George Pace, Bank of America's CEO, and they were set for dinner the next day at the Savoy Grill. Then he had excused himself from the formal dinner party that he had been scheduled to attend that evening at the German Embassy. Maria had pressed his 'smoking' for naught. But it was only when Mayer was halfway across the Atlantic ocean that he remembered the other matter that had been pending – the invitation from Sergio Dobrovsky to drop by and see him at the Center for Strategic and International Studies. He'd completely forgotten about it.

Chapter 2

Roberto Martinez, brother of José Martinez, Sr and uncle, therefore, of José Martinez, Jr, student at Georgetown University, took off from Simon Bolivar International at exactly the same time. He had almost missed the plane, since the road from Caracas down to Maiquetia had been a disaster as usual. It was twenty-eight kilometers of magnificent highway winding down the mountain and involved a trip which would take thirty minutes in most other countries. However, in Venezuela, which may have more bad drivers than any other country in the world, it routinely took an hour. It was not that there was anything special going on for it was still ten days before the first Mass of the Christmas season, the day when the citizens of Caracas turn out in droves to sing carols as, according to tradition, they speed through the streets and plazas on roller skates, creating total chaos out of the normal havoc which prevails on the Venezuelan byways.

Roberto Martinez was a powerful man in Venezuela. As the nation's oil minister, he personally controlled Petroleos de Venezuela. This was not just another oil company. It was the company which had a monopoly on the nation's production of petroleum and petroleum products, the sale of which supplied the government of Venezuela with the greater part of its income. The company had come into being when two decades earlier Venezuela had decided to nationalize the oil industry and bought out all the oil fields and refining facilities which Shell and Esso and British Petroleum had developed there, making Venezuela one of the world's great oil powers. Although Petroleos de Venezuela was completely state-owned, as it was a corporation, once a year its management went through the motions of holding a shareholders' meeting. What made the meeting different from those held by most other oil companies was that only one man attended, Roberto Martinez, since he, as the representative of the government which owned all the shares, controlled all the votes. Thus his word was literally law in Venezuela where oil was concerned. Since Roberto controlled the country's oil, while José, Sr controlled the nation's finances, it could be said – and in fact *was* said by many – that the two brothers Martinez controlled Venezuela; that the nation stood or fell with them.

The reason that Roberto Martinez was on KLM, headed for Zurich, was that Venezuela *was* falling, was slipping back into poverty. Why? Because the oil price was falling again. Why? Because, as anyone who was not afraid to speak the truth knew, the United States of America wanted it to fall and, in fact, had been forcing it to fall ever since the early 1980s by rigging demand, by encouraging non-OPEC supply, by forcing everybody to deal on the spot market in Rotterdam and thus totally undermining the oil cartel which Venezuela had co-founded in the first place. What carnage was wrought as a result, how many people starved to death in the mountains behind Caracas, or in the slums surrounding Mexico City, could not bother the Yankees less. They ruled the world, and as long as the Yankee dollar ruled supreme, as long as the American banks and Wall Street called the shots on a global basis, Americans would continue to do exactly as they pleased with total impunity.

Roberto Martinez ground his teeth at the very idea that America was getting away with it again. That facial action did not exactly endear him any further with the KLM stewardesses, who had already rolled their eyes at each other when Roberto Martinez had boarded the plane. The cloying odor of his cologne and the cream that glued down his black hair had given him away instantaneously: another of God's gifts to women. At least in his own Latin mind. From the moment he had taken his seat, he had given them the eye, from bottom to top and back to bottom, occasionally favoring one of them with a smile, sure in the knowledge that these Dutch women could hardly wait to get their hands on him. Just the anticipation of it would have made him one of the happiest men on the KLM flight, were it not that his thoughts kept returning to the fucking Yankees.

But then his mood improved. To be sure, if Venezuela – and the Martinez brothers – stood or fell with oil, then America stood or fell with the Almighty Dollar. Venezuela, through its child OPEC, had damn near wrecked the dollar in the 1970s, and gained unprecedented prosperity and power in the process. The Martinez brothers had been instrumental in this process. When the OPEC cartel had jacked the price of oil to $34 a barrel, inflation had taken hold of the United States, the dollar had fallen like a rock and America's power had fallen with it. Result: Venezuela, and the Martinez brothers, had demanded and had finally gotten respect in Washington.

To be sure, that 'millenium' had lasted less than ten years. And now the Venezuelans, and the Mexicans, and the Argentines, in fact all of Latin America with the notable exceptions of Cuba and Nicaragua, were back where they had started: once again forced to live on the American dole! Today, with oil at $16.50 a barrel and the dollar again strong world-wide, Venezuelans were once more treated as they always had been by the Americans: like dirt!

But if last time around Big Brother in El Norte had been brought to heel when it lost control of a single commodity, oil, this time around it could – and Roberto Martinez and his brother had sworn that it *would* – be brought to its knees through its losing control of a still more important single commodity – money!

That end would justify any means. In fact, the brothers had concluded just last night that even if it required them to seek out the help of Venezuela's most famous citizen – Carlos – so be it.

It was not Carlos, however, who met Roberto Martinez at the airport in Zurich, but rather someone who could hardly have been in greater contrast to the dean of the world's terrorists. It was Dr Ulrich Huber, Chairman of the Board of Switzerland's largest commercial bank, the Swiss National Bank, and thus Establishment personified. From its co-equal headquarters in Switzerland's three most important cities, Zurich, Basel, and Geneva, the Swiss National Bank commanded well over $100 billion in assets, and considered itself the leading steward of the glue which held the civilized world together – rich people's money. Its mission was to keep that money safe from the grasp of the world's rabble.

Rabble, from the Chairman of the Swiss National Bank's point of view, included terrorists like Carlos, of course, but also all tax collectors, Communists, Socialists, any male with long hair, and almost all Americans who, despite being capitalists, were so primitive in their behavior yet so superior – so arrogant – in their attitude that it was enough to make Dr Ulrich Huber sick every time he had to kowtow to them.

But maybe the need to kowtow would soon be over. That, at least, was the silent hope of both men as the Venezuelan oil minister and the Swiss banker shook hands in the early morning of December 7th, 1988 at Kloten airport. In fact, as they subsequently rode together in the direction of the Hotel Baur au Lac, it was the Venezuelan who suggested that, if they succeeded, the date might well go down twice as one of infamy – at least where the United States of America was concerned.

'We've heard something very interesting this morning,' Dr Ulrich Huber then said, ending the levity. 'From our government. It almost certainly relates to our activities.'

'By "interesting" I hope you mean "good",' replied the Venezuelan.

Paradoxically, they conversed in English, despite the fact that both regarded not only America but also England with utter contempt. The Venezuelan's dislike had very specific origins: it had been Britain which had been instrumental in pulling the rug from under OPEC by dumping its North Sea oil at bargain prices on the spot market in mid-decade. He, Roberto Martinez, had *personally* pointed out the folly of such action to Margaret Thatcher in the summer of 1985. He had stressed that it was in Britain's interest to cooperate with OPEC, and to cut back on North Sea output forthwith. Only by limiting supply *now* could the slide in the price of oil be stopped and ultimately reversed. The Arabs, the Africans, the Venezuelans were all doing their share: all had cut back output severely at great cost to their nations. Was it too much to ask that the British also act reasonably?

She had not even deigned to give him the courtesy of an answer. Instead she had dismissed him two minutes later . . . essentially thrown him back onto that damned Downing Street like a servant whose services were no longer required. The bitch! As a result, just months later, the oil price had plummeted from $31 a barrel to $10, and damn near bankrupted Venezuela in the process.

The Swiss banker took a more detached view of the people who populated that small island off the coast of Europe. He simply disliked the English on general principle: they were lazy, untidy, and poor. This dismissal of the British on such grounds did not amount to prejudice against Anglo-Saxons, however. He disliked the Portuguese for the same reasons. Also the Turks. And the Syrians. Etc.

Continuing in English, Dr Huber then said: 'Good news.

Yesterday our ambassador in Washington observed a very interesting meeting. It involved the Chairman of the Federal Reserve, the Chairman of the Federal Deposit Insurance Corporation, and Dr Paul Mayer.

'Our ambassador did not know the specific reason for this meeting, but he suspected it might mean that a big American bank is in trouble. He had no idea which one.'

The Venezuelan laughed out loud. 'But we know, don't we Ulrich?'

The Swiss banker winced. He did not like *anybody* calling him by his first name but for his wife of thirty-one years.

The Venezuelan didn't notice a thing. He just reached into his breast pocket, took out his cigar case, pulled out a Monte Cristo, cut it – leaving the droppings on the floor of the limo, adding to Dr Huber's discontent – and lit up, filling the Mercedes 600 with black fumes.

'So you see,' the banker continued, coughing slightly, 'we are doing our part. And you?'

'I talked yesterday with my counterpart in Mexico City. He had talked earlier with our friend in Brazil. The Argentines don't have to be talked to. They have been promoting the same idea for years. So you see,' he added, somewhat petulantly, 'I do what I promise.

'Now may I remind you, my dear Ulrich,' the Venezuelan continued, 'that "your part" also included making arrangements with our friends in the East.'

'Don't worry. We shall be seeing one of them over lunch at the bank,' Dr Huber replied, and then, putting the Venezuelan firmly in his place, added: 'We must all be very, very discreet about this. I must demand that you maintain absolute, and I mean absolute, silence about this, both now and in the future.'

He glared at the Venezuelan through the smoke. He knew that it was naïve to hope that a Latino could comprehend the meaning of the word discretion, but it was at least worth a try.

'Of course, of course,' replied Martinez, as if it were the very last thing in the world that either of them should waste one second worrying about. By this time they were approaching the Bahnhofstrasse, and were thus only about ten blocks from the hotel.

'Could you perhaps answer one further question, Ulrich? This Dr Mayer: what opinion do you have of him? Could he be dangerous?'

The Swiss banker looked at his watch. It was 8.15 a.m. and he was already forty-five minutes late for work. He would make it quick, and then get rid of Martinez for the next couple of hours.

'He could be very dangerous! The man simply cannot be trusted. You may not know this, but despite his claim of Swedish origins, Mayer is really a Swiss. Everything he knows he learnt here. His father came to Basel from Stockholm in the late 1930s with Per Jacobson. The two of them stayed in Switzerland for twenty years, and essentially ran the Bank for International Settlements – until Jacobson went to Washington and took over the IMF. The point is that Paul Mayer grew up here. Not only that but after he got his degree in economics at the University of Basel, he went to work for our bank in that same city. In fact, he and I started there at the same time. First we did economic analysis. Then we were both sent to New York to learn the ropes at our branch there. Mayer was later sent to London, where he ended up taking over our world-wide loan syndication operations. I came back to Switzerland.

'Mayer returned home a couple of years later and subsequently became the youngest general manager in the history of the National Bank of Switzerland in 1971. In fact, he became my boss. Of course, it was hardly all due to merit. His mother, you see, was a Wallenberg. Through the family ownership of the Enskilda Bank in Stockholm, the Wallenbergs have controlled the private sector of Sweden's economy for two generations. They have their hands in everything from shipping to airlines to mining, to the manufacture of office machines, sewing machines and even nuclear power plants, with operations all over the world. Thanks to his mother and the Wallenberg connection, young Paul Mayer could bring in big business. In the United States they would have called him a "rainmaker". The bank knew what they had and they paid him a huge salary. Not that money mattered to Paul Mayer. He knew that when his mother died, she would leave him a fortune, which she subsequently did. Anyway, to cut this story short, two years later he quit. That had never happened before. Nor since, I might add.

'He had been offered the post of Deputy Managing Director of the International Monetary Fund in Washington at the age of thirty-six . . . obviously a result of his *father's* connections. If he had stuck to his neutral heritage – after all, he did have a Swedish passport and he was brought up in Switzerland – and operated accordingly at the IMF nobody – and least of all I – would have ever criticized him in the slightest.

'But he didn't. When, ultimately, the top post at the IMF became available after Jacques de Larosière retired, the American government backed him for the job. The Americans should have no regrets about it. Like so many of the same ilk – Kissinger and Brzezinski are the best examples – Mayer is a prime example of an immigrant who became a super-American. First under de Larosière, then under Mayer, the International Monetary Fund became nothing less than the instrument of American foreign economic policy. They kept the Third World debt situation under control by imposing austerity programs on already destitute populations in Latin America in order to protect the American banks; Mayer did not say a word to his masters in the White House or at the Treasury when the American budget went completely out of control. He did not utter one word of warning when capital from all over the world began moving to the United States, attracted by the outrageously high interest rates there – *our* capital. He did not murmur a syllable of criticism when that money – *our* money – was then used to finance Reagan's immense deficits and to finance American industry, creating American prosperity while our continent sunk into a condition which the Anglo-Saxons cynically termed "Eurosclerosis". Why do you think there are now 31 million people unemployed in Europe today?

'Is Mayer dangerous? Even more so today than ever, in our judgement. He finally left the IMF last year – saying he had spent fifteen years there "in the service of the world", if I recall his words, and that it was time to move on. At the age of fifty-two! What arrogance! The first thing he did after "retiring" was to turn in his Swedish passport for an American one. And now he's teaching. But what he is really doing is conniving with Kissinger and Brzezinski and Schlesinger and a whole gang of former high officials of the American government, both Republicans and Democrats I might add, at a "research" institution in Washington. They operate under the guise of academics, using Georgetown University as their cover. But in fact they are anything but academics. They are in business, the business of collectively using their names, their connections, their personal power to influence world affairs. They work discreetly, employing the so-called "back channels". Let's face it, if Kissinger calls Gorbachev, Gorbachev answers. If Mayer calls the Governor of the Bank of England, or the finance minister of Mexico, they also answer and right away. Their aim is very clear: to maintain the *status quo* under which America continues to rule supreme. They are backed to the hilt financially by every big bank, every big oil company, every big defense contractor in the United States.

'That's why Dr Mayer is dangerous. Now he is one of them. If he finds out what we're up to, he and his friends will be the first ones to try to sabotage us.'

The limo had come to rest in front of the Baur au Lac. As the bellboys removed the Venezuelan's luggage, Dr Huber reminded Roberto Martinez that he would be picked up at 11.55

exactly, and hoped that he would be waiting in the lobby.

It had been a long night for Martinez and he knew that he should go to bed for a couple of hours. But the West-East trips are always the ones that are the most difficult to adjust to. On top of that, the Swiss banker's last words had left the Venezuelan somewhat disconcerted.

That Mayer fellow: Huber was no doubt right. Martinez remembered the first time he had met Mayer. He and his brother, representing the two ministries, oil and finance, where they worked, but which they did not yet control, had been summoned to the top floor of International Monetary Fund headquarters in Washington. The reason: to explain a late interest payment on the $2 billion that the Fund had advanced to Venezuela to tide them over an earlier period of financial stress – it had been back in 1977, Martinez recalled. They had been forced to cool their heels for half an hour in the Deputy Managing Director's office while he chaired some unimportant meeting in the adjacent executive boardroom. The Managing Director himself had obviously felt that Venezuela was not important enough to waste time on.

When Mayer finally emerged, one could hardly fail to be impressed. He was almost six and a half feet tall, which made him one foot taller than either Roberto Martinez or his brother. Mayer had been dressed in an impeccably tailored Italian suit, sported a red handkerchief in his breast pocket, and moved with the energy of a professional sportsman. Roberto Martinez even remembered the initial handshake. Mayer hadn't pressed his hand; he had crushed it, no doubt deliberately. And then, surprisingly, he had asked his guests if they would join him in a drink. After all, he had said, it was now 5.30 in Caracas.

Mayer had personally gone to the bar in the nether regions of his immense office, and returned with two very large glasses of Chivas and water. And two Monte Cristos! How could you help but like the man!

But like him or not, what Mayer had subsequently done had been unforgivable and an absolute insult to the persons of Roberto and José Martinez and the sovereignty of Venezuela. Instead of taking them at their word – that they would immediately invoke restraints on imports, and effect massive changes in fiscal and monetary policy at home and bring down inflation, provided the IMF gave them a period of grace on the interest payments – Mayer had sent a whole team of foreigners to Caracas within weeks, a pack of IMF economists. He said they were there simply to monitor Venezuela's progress; in fact, they were there to dictate! Cut back the fiscal deficit: reduce the increases in money supply, put a prohibitive tax on the importation of Scotch whisky! Or else they, meaning the IMF, meaning Mayer, would cut them off.

The son of a bitch!

It had worked. But not because of Mayer. Venezuela had gotten out of its financial jam already in 1979 but only because – thanks to OPEC – the oil price had gone from $20 a barrel to $34 and Venezuela was once again flush with dollars. They had not only paid the back interest; they had cut their debt to the IMF in half!

But then the oil price had collapsed to below $20 a barrel once again, at times *way* below, and now Venezuela was back where it had been before. Only now they owed the IMF, and the American banks which it protected, five times as much as back in 1977. And the interest rates in 1988 were higher. So the interest now payable was staggering. And it was already twelve months overdue. With oil at $16.50 a barrel, there was no way that Venezuela could pay it either now or after another twelve months or maybe even twelve years. Fidel Castro had foreseen this and suggested already back in mid-decade that the only 'solution' – the only alternative to revolution throughout Latin America – would be if the IMF could arrange a twenty-year moratorium on *all* payments – principal *and* interest.

But the American banks could never accept that. So their obedient servant, the IMF, had returned to Venezuela and was more firmly entrenched than ever in his nation. Now the IMF people did not even attempt to be diplomatic. 'Comply with our economic targets,' they had told the Venezuelan Cabinet last week, 'or you will not get one more dime from us, from the World Bank, or from any commercial bank in North America.'

Sure, Mayer was no longer running the show *directly*. But, as Roberto Martinez's brother had often told him, it was Mayer who had been instrumental in sending his boys down to Venezuela in the first place for the express purpose of running the country. The son-of-a-bitch Yankee! No, according to Huber he wasn't even a full-fledged Yankee, for God's sake! He was just another immigrant who had barely traded in his green card for citizenship!

How to keep Mayer's nose out of this?

Roberto Martinez reached for his wallet, and extracted a small piece of paper with a phone number in Germany, in Frankfurt-am-Main. He picked up the phone. But then a new idea crossed his mind. So instead of dialing the Frankfurt number he dialed one in Caracas – that of his brother's home. It was three o'clock in the morning in Caracas, and Roberto realized he had made a mistake when not his brother, but his brother's wife answered the phone. It seemed that José was not home yet. They both knew where he was: over at his mistress's apartment fucking his brains out. So when Roberto asked for José, Jr's phone number in Washington DC, it was only after having to put up with a ten-minute tirade about what animals the Martinez brothers were that he finally got it.

'Fat, stupid cow!' But he said it *after* he had hung up.

José, Jr answered the phone in a sleepy voice, but immediately became alert when his uncle explained what he wanted.

'When you find out, call me immediately, José, and if I'm

not here, leave a message with the hotel operator.' He gave the number of the Baur au Lac and hung up. Then he set his alarm clock for 11 a.m. and went to bed.

When Dr Ulrich Huber arrived at the Swiss National Bank, the first thing he did was summon one of the girls from his secretariat to go over the day's agenda with him. The victim, as usual, was Hanni Graber. And, as usual, she was wearing her hair in a *Zopf*, a Swiss-style pony tail, which looked ridiculous on a woman of fifty-one years in Ulrich Huber's opinion.

The first appointment of the day had been for 8.00 a.m. It was already 8.37.

'So where is Herr Weber?' Huber asked. 'He was supposed to be here.'

'He was here, Herr Doktor,' Hanni Graber explained. 'He waited for fifteen minutes, and then went back to his office.'

'So call him. And tell him to get back here. And Hanni, why don't you think about doing your hair differently. It looks silly the way it is.'

By the time Hannelore Graber had retreated to the secretariat she was in tears. And last night it had been so good! Maybe she would make a quick call and tell him that. Huber might not like the way she did her hair, but her boyfriend sure did. It was just too bad that he lived in Berne and could only come over to Zurich once a week. Well, she sighed, once a week was better than once a month. Yes, she was definitely going to phone him, even though he had repeatedly told her not to call him at the office. But first, she had to get hold of the bank's chief financial officer and give him the good news that Herr Doktor Huber had just arrived.

When Herr Weber appeared, minutes later, he was nervous, because he was the bearer of bad tidings.

'Guete Tag, Herr Weber. Hänt Si d'Zahlen barat?' Huber immediately asked.

'Jo, Herr Doktor,' was the reply.

'Und?'

'S'gseht nit guet us, Herr Doktor.'

And with that he handed over the figures giving his forecast of the end-of-year balance sheet and P&L statement of the Swiss National Bank. It was December 7th, and thus time to plan the bank's window-dressing operations, an exercise that all Swiss banks engaged in at that time of year.

What it involved was the temporary juggling of the key financial statistics reflecting the bank's status. The purpose of the 'adjustments' was to put the bank in the best possible light when the year-end figures ultimately appeared in the annual report. The aim: to impress upon the shareholders – and the depositing public – that their bank was not only safe and sound, but profitable and growing. In the United States if a banker pulled such stuff he would end up, not in Leavenworth perhaps, but for sure in Lompoc or a similar country club for at least a couple of years. In Switzerland, where the banking rules are loose, and where there is no governmental deposit insurance like that provided by the FDIC to calm depositors' nerves, it is considered stupid if not downright unpatriotic not to make the best appearance possible at year end. For as its banks go, so goes Switzerland.

As Huber immediately saw as he scanned the computer printout, the figures for December 31st, 1988 were going to be disastrous! The state of the bank, and thus of the Swiss Union, was not good.

Interest income had stayed steady. But the cost of money had risen enormously. They were not even going to break even on their lending operations in 1988. And their assets had declined precipitously. This was the second year in a row that this had happened. The bank's earning base was eroding at a pace unprecedented in its history and money was flooding out the door in what amounted to an invisible run on the Swiss National Bank. To make matters worse, the exodus of funds from the Swiss National Bank was not being caused by customers transferring their funds to his competitors in Zurich or Basel or Geneva and ending up with the Union Bank of Switzerland, or the Crédit Suisse because they offered better terms. No, they were leaving Switzerland altogether.

Headed where?

Where else: the United States! To Chase and Citibank and Wells Fargo and even Continental Illinois! The Americans were sucking in the whole world's money! Because they were offering 8 percent interest while the Swiss were offering 3 percent. Somebody had recently said that the resulting 5 percent differential was enough to pull in money from the moon. The problem was compounded by the fact that in 1988, in the new era of electronic transfers, it was so easy to move money quickly. At 10 a.m. it was in Zurich; at 10.01 a.m. in New York.

And to what end? Helmut Schmidt, the former Chancellor of West Germany and, in the minds of many, Europe's most able living economist, had put it very simply: 'The astounding recovery of Reagan's economy rests on other people's money.'

On Europe's money. On Switzerland's money!

Something had to be done and quickly, was the conclusion that Dr Ulrich Huber reached, for perhaps the hundredth time. The difference on December 7th, 1988 was that now, finally, something *was* going to be done.

Aeroflot Flight 76 from Moscow arrived at Kloten at 10 a.m. bearing, along with about twenty other passengers, one Vladimir Dolgikh. Dolgikh was a candidate member of the Politburo, meaning he was one step short of full membership in the thirteen-man body which rules the Soviet Union. His boss was Nikolai Ryzhkov whom Mikhail Gorbachev had made Prime Minister shortly after he had succeeded to power in 1985. Together, Ryzhkov and Dolgikh ran the economy of the second most powerful nation on earth. Despite the fact that he was the junior partner to Ryzhkov, Dolgikh was regarded as especially powerful since he had a dual role in the Soviet system of government: he was solely in charge of the Soviet Union's energy and mining/metalurgy programs at home, and was also regularly deployed abroad, especially in Eastern Europe, as an economic troubleshooter.

This mission involved a total overlap of his two functions and was one which brought Vladimir Dolgikh directly to the building on Zurich's Schützengasse which housed the Swiss branch of the Soviet Foreign Trade Bank. It was the center of Russia's financial operations on the European continent. There had been no official greeting at the airport; the car that transported Dolgikh into town was a completely unmarked black Citroen, the private vehicle used by the bank's manager. At the bank itself no fuss whatsoever was made over the visitor from Moscow. His presence, however, gave witness to the key position that Zurich played in Soviet financial affairs in regard to that nation's two principal sources of hard currency income. For the Swiss branch of the Soviet Union's Foreign Trade Bank handled all of the Soviet Union's gold sales; it also managed most of the income generated by Russia's other major export to the West: energy. Of the $35 billion a year earned in the West by the Soviet Union, these two exports alone accounted for over $30 billion.

Gold and oil: without the dollars they generated, whole sectors of the Russian economy would revert to the nineteenth century as the importation of everything from Canadian wheat to German machine tools to Finnish electronic components could no longer be financed. Thirty-five percent of Russia's investments in new machinery and equipment, acutely necessary if the Soviet Union were to grow at all, came from the West. If the dollars available from exports of energy and gold diminished further, such imports would have to be sharply reduced, and the Soviet Union would enter an era of *negative* growth.

This Gorbachev could not allow to happen. That is why he

had personally dispatched to Zurich the man in charge of Russia's oil and gold, Vladimir Dolgikh.

The men who ran the Foreign Trade Bank never got within ten kilometers of Gorbachev. They were nothing more than technicians. They provided the letters of credit that financed their country's foreign trade. They played the spot and futures markets in dollars and Swiss francs and yen and Deutschmarks just like their colleagues at Chase or the Swiss Bank Corporation or Barclays, trying to make more money with money. They planned and executed the sale of newly-mined Russian bullion in the Zurich gold market, and also played the gold futures game in New York and Chicago when they decided to lock in what looked like good gold prices. In this sense, they operated exactly like the Iowa farmer did with pork bellies and soybeans. Their motive was also the same as their capitalistic counterparts: profit.

But where the Soviet bank was concerned, it was to gain profit for Mother Russia, not any distant shareholders. There was another incentive for performance that was peculiar to the Russians who ran the Soviet bank in Switzerland: if they did not produce profits, they would be sent back home where they would face disgrace, or worse.

Fear of just that had been precipitated by the announcement by telex of the pending arrival of a candidate member of the Politburo. For everyone at Russia's Swiss banking operation remembered a fateful day back in November of 1984 when another man from the Kremlin, though hardly from the lofty level of the Politburo, had arrived, accompanied by six other Russians – from the KGB.

Prior to that day, the Russian financial presence in Switzerland had had a different form and a different name. The bank's name had been the Wozchod Handelsbank AG. And its form had not been that of a branch, but rather of a wholly-owned, though financially independent, subsidiary (thus the AG, or Inc.) of the Soviet State Bank, the Russian equivalent of the Federal Reserve.

The bank's chief trader and foreign exchange dealer, a Swiss employee looking out for the main chance, had become over-zealous in his attempts to maximize profits for his Soviet masters and had gotten involved in some heavy speculation. He had been betting, and betting heavily in the futures markets, that the dollar was going down – like a lot of other Swiss traders that year. In fact, the dollar soared to its highest level in twelve years. Result: the Swiss dealer lost $350 million of Russia's hard-won cash, but – or at least so goes the story – he did not bother to report it to his Soviet superiors. When the truth inevitably came out, the man from the Kremlin and six heavies from the KGB came to Zurich. On Aeroflot's return flight to Moscow later that day, the Soviet group of seven had grown to twenty. The other thirteen were the thirteen Russians who had been responsible for the overall management of the Wozchod Handelsbank AG, all of whom claimed that they had not known a thing: it was all the fault of that damn Swiss foreign exchange trader!

Nobody – neither the Russians nor the Swiss Bank Commission, which is the Swiss equivalent of the Comptroller of the Currency – bought their story. All agreed that such a heinous crime – after all, they had lost $350 million dollars and besmirched the reputations of both countries – deserved an appropriate punishment.

Two weeks later, thirteen volleys were heard in a forest in Siberia.

Four months later, on Friday, March 1st, 1985, the Swiss Bank Commission announced that the Wozchod bank had been closed permanently. The bank liquidation, Soviet-Swiss style, had been completed.

The chief trader got off scotfree, proving once again that it pays to be Swiss where money, especially other people's money and the loss thereof, is concerned. Provided the 'other people' are foreigners.

When the new branch operation of the Soviet Foreign Trade Bank, or the Vneshtorgbank as it is known in Moscow, rose out of the ashes of the old Wozchod, it was run by a very nervous new crew of Soviet technicians. Their nervousness was approaching the acute phase on that December 7th because they knew that 1988, like 1984, had proved to be another disastrous year. But in contrast to the earlier year which had produced such serious morale problems in Soviet banking circles, they also knew that *this* time it was not due to any fault of their own. After all, the Zurich branch of the Foreign Trade Bank of the Soviet Union didn't set the world gold price; even less so could it influence the price of crude oil in world markets. It was not because of them that the price of both gold and crude petroleum was in a state of semi-collapse. The fault lay exclusively with Sheikh Yamani. Back in 1986 he had decided to teach the other oil-producing nations of the world a lesson. If they would not practice discipline, if they would not adjust their output to market conditions in order to maintain price, then neither would Saudi Arabia. It had played 'swing man', to its detriment, for too long. So Yamani had doubled Saudi output to 4.5 million barrels a day in spite of an already existing oil glut. But instead of the price's dropping a few dollars, and proving Yamani's point, it had collapsed, plunging from $31 a barrel to $10 within weeks. That Russia's dollar income had collapsed with those prices was not their doing. Could they help it that while all this was happening on the income side, their dollar expenditures had been higher than ever before in Soviet history: who could have foreseen that they would have to buy that much wheat in 1988?

Maybe they could not have foreseen that, but the people at the Russian bank on the Schützengasse could foresee the net result of all these unfortunate trends: as of the end of 1988 the Soviet Union would be flat out of dollars.

Then what?

So something had to be done, and quickly. That was no doubt why a candidate member of the Politburo had come to Zurich in response to the vague invitation which had been extended just five days earlier by Dr Ulrich Huber of the Swiss National Bank. And that was why every single employee at the Foreign Trade Bank of the Soviet Union had been warned to keep his or her mouth absolutely shut about the whole matter. Which they would have done anyway. For they sensed that if Vladimir Dolgikh succeeded, maybe they could all stay in Zurich for another three or four years and enjoy all the Scotch they could drink, all the Swiss veal they could eat, and all the German pornographic films they cared to watch on their Japanese VCRs.

The dining-room of top management of the Swiss National Bank was no different than dining-rooms provided for the chairmen and presidents of banks in London, New York, or Frankfurt. They had all cost the lives of a lot of trees: oak where American and British banks were concerned, walnut when the Swiss and German élitist canteens were built.

The drift of conversation in that walnut-paneled dining-room in Zurich was also no different than anywhere else: it led up to just one thing, the making of money at the expense of somebody else. There were, however, a few idiosyncrasies of the Swiss gnomes that set them somewhat apart from the rest of the world's bankers. One was their directness. The Swiss did not feel it necessary to babble on about the weather and the Arabs and the Concorde like the British bankers did: nor to talk golf – did you ever play this course in Scotland? that one in Palm Springs? – like the Americans did. No, the Swiss got right down to it.

Thus, after having seated Roberto Martinez to his left and Vladimir Dolgikh to his right, Dr Ulrich Huber began his opening ploy immediately after the *hors-d'oeuvres* – consisting as it so often did in Zurich of *Bündnerfleisch* and *prosciutto* – had arrived. He spoke in simple language, leaving ample opportunity for the Russian to understand what he was saying.

This was not just because they would be using a language foreign to them all: it was principally because the Swiss regard Russians as being even more simple-minded than most foreigners.

'Mr Dolgikh, we both have liquidity problems.'

Pause.

'And the cause of our problems is the same: the fiscal and monetary policies of the United States during the past eight years.'

Pause.

'The Americans have kept their interest rates so high that everybody in the world is in dollars, in dollar bank deposits, in dollar bonds, in dollar stocks. In dollars.'

Pause.

'Where they are *not* is in Swiss francs, Swiss bank deposits, Swiss bonds, Swiss shares.'

Pause.

'They are also not in gold. For the same reason they are no longer in Swiss francs. Because of Ronald Reagan's policies that require the United States' government to continue to borrow huge sums of money, making dollars scarce and thus expensive. If the United States' government is ready and willing to pay 8 percent to anybody who will lend them money why should our clients – increasingly our *former* clients – keep their money in gold where they get nothing? Or in Swiss francs where they get 3 percent?'

Pause.

'So they continue to move their money out. Out of our banks and your gold.'

The Russian just ate his *Bündnerfleisch*.

'Our clients must be taught a lesson. That greed is not enough. The Americans must also be taught a lesson. That they can no longer thumb their noses at the rest of us. That they can no longer unilaterally set the world price of money, of gold, of oil.'

At this first mention of 'oil', the Russian's fork paused, leaving a slice of *prosciutto* dangling in the clean Swiss air.

The banker sensed that this was the moment for his clincher. 'My dear Dolgikh, if we succeed it may very well solve our liquidity problem, your liquidity problem, and that of our Venezuelan friend. We all stand to benefit. Equally.'

'Explain,' he then said, turning his attention to Roberto Martinez.

By the time the next course – *geschnelzeltes Kalbfleisch Zürcher Art* and *Rösti*, accompanied by a well-chilled St Saphorin wine – had come and gone, the Venezuelan was still talking. He finally shut up when the creme caramel and coffee arrived.

Vladimir Dolgikh still just sat there – and drank his coffee.

Ten minutes later the Russian left the Swiss National Bank and at five o'clock he boarded the Aeroflot return flight to Moscow. He had been tempted by that Venezuelan and his Swiss co-conspirator. Sorely tempted. But something bothered him. Was he being set up?

Just about the time that the Aeroflot flight was landing at Sheremetyevo airport in Moscow, José Martinez, Jr was getting out of bed in Georgetown. A glance at his diamond-studded Rolex told him that it was 2.00 in the afternoon, in other words the usual hour for rising.

Most Georgetown juniors lived off campus since there was never enough dormitory space on campus to go around. They lived in the basement apartments of ancient and very small Georgetown houses which, as late as the early 1950s, had been going for $20,000. Now they were going for ten or twenty times that much. Despite the price change, the basement apartments remained the hovels they always were; the only difference was that they now rented for $600 a month.

No basement apartments for José Martinez, Jr, however. He

had a two-bedroom, two-bath suite in one of the most exclusive residential buildings in town, the Georgetown Arms. The amenities included a year-round heated pool and maid service. It cost José Martinez, Sr $2,000 a month and José, Jr could not have cared less.

José, Jr decided that the place to begin his mission was the Tombs. All his buddies would be there. And one of them, no doubt, would know a way to get the information that his uncle wanted. That the old geezer had actually called him from Zurich and damn near begged him! Jeezuz, this ought to be worth a Jaguar, or even a Ferrari if he came through. For a change, then, José Martinez, Jr began his academic day fully motivated.

The Tombs is to Georgetown's students what Mory's is to Yale's or the Nassau Tavern to Princeton's: *the* hangout. It is located at 36th and Prospect, right across from where the School of Foreign Service used to be and *under* one of the better restaurants in the Washington DC area, The 1789. In contrast to most campus hangouts, the Tombs actually has excellent food, and serves not Budweiser or Coors but Heineken on draft.

At the large table way in the back sat, as usual, José, Jr's pals. Since it was now 2.30 in the afternoon, and since it was December 8th and thus mid-term exam time, most students were either at class or studying at the Lauinger Library. In the Latin tradition, however, the boys from Brazil and Argentina and Venezuela scorned such behavior until it became absolutely, irrevocably necessary. Then they hired the best tutors they could find, and squeaked through the exams.

You had to maintain a 2.0 grade point average or they kicked you out of Georgetown, even if you played basketball. The average of the point averages of the boys at the table in the back of the Tombs was 2.1, as they had once figured out . . . with great difficulty. In other words, just about perfect. So what if their transcripts looked terrible? Nobody would ever look at them anyway. Their parents, who had gotten them in in the first place, would make just as sure that they got out, even if they had to appeal to the Pope himself, Georgetown being a Jesuit school. They would also make sure that their kids got a proper job in one of the banks or trading companies which they controlled either at home or in New York or in Europe.

So why break your ass?

The first thing that José, Jr did upon arrival at the table in the rear was to order a round of Heineken drafts for all present.

'Anybody know anybody in Dean Krogh's office,' he then asked, and added, 'like, intimately?'

Everybody knew Jan. Intimately. She answered the phone at the School of Foreign Service and she was also preparing for a career abroad by learning both Spanish and Portuguese the easy way, i.e. in various and sundry beds within ten minutes' walking time of the campus.

'She working now?'

Shrugs all around.

There was a phone booth just beside the stairs which led down into the basement restaurant from 36th Street. José, Jr dialed 625–4216 and the phone answered: 'School of Foreign Service: the Dean's office.'

'Jan?'

'Yes.'

'José Martinez.'

'Gee, José, it's been a long time. But could you make it quick. The Dean is hanging around the office today.'

'How about dinner at my place tonight?'

'I'd rather go out. Italian.'

'OK. How about Tiberio's?'

Tiberio's was the most expensive Italian restaurant within a radius of 200 miles.

'I'll pick you up at 7.00,' José continued, without waiting for an answer.

Then: 'Hey, could you help me on one small thing?'

'Sure, and make that 7.30. I've got to stay here late.'

'No sweat. Now, could you track down Professor Paul Mayer for me?'

'What do you mean, "track down"?'

'Like where he lives and where he hangs out.'

'I'm not supposed to do that.'

'It's all right, believe me. My dad just wants to send him something.'

'Well, maybe. See you at 7.30.'

The bill at Tiberio's came to $195.

After Jan had gotten an advanced lesson in Spanish she came through with the other thing José, Jr wanted. It seemed that Professor Mayer lived at 3514 Dent Place. But he was not there right now. She had brought a message into the Dean's office that afternoon and, while waiting to see if he had a reply, had overheard Dean Krogh tell somebody on the telephone that Professor Mayer had gone to London for the rest of the week and could probably be reached at the Bank of America office there.

José, Jr rewarded her generously by teaching her the Venezuelan position, soon to become the rage throughout Georgetown, at least that part of Georgetown that was ten minutes' walking distance from the campus.

When he had finally gotten rid of Jan, José, Jr called the number in Zurich that his uncle had given him. He wasn't in. But, as José had been instructed to do, he passed on everything he had learned about Professor Mayer's whereabouts to the hotel operator and asked her to mark it urgent and leave it in his uncle's mailbox.

Chapter 3

After Roberto Martinez had returned to the Baur au Lac following the sumptuous lunch at the Swiss National Bank, he decided to take a nap. Aided by the two Kirschwassers he had had with coffee, the nap lasted until well into the evening of that December 7th, 1988. Since it was late by Swiss standards, and since a winter storm seemed to be brewing outside, the Venezuelan decided to stay in the hotel and dine alone in its Grill Room, the first time he had eaten by himself in many a year. His mood was not good, therefore, although it was lifted somewhat by the excellent bottle of white Burgundy, bottled under the Baur au Lac private label, that had accompanied the meal.

It was almost eleven o'clock when he checked his mailbox at the front desk for the final time and found his nephew's message. His mood lifted. He immediately went up to his room and picked up the phone. Now he would dial that number in Frankfurt.

He completed the dialing process, but then hung up abruptly before anyone answered. This was not smart, he told himself. The Swiss special police in charge of the surveillance of foreigners – the famous *Fremdenpolizei* – no doubt had the Baur au Lac wired from top to bottom. If not that, at least they would get a listing of every phone call that was made from the hotel on a daily basis. That Frankfurt number was the last thing he wanted them to get – from *him*. If the Swiss *Polizei* followed up, and unpleasantness resulted, and if the people in Frankfurt figured out how the authorities had gotten onto them, then he, Roberto Martinez, would no doubt end up very dead, very soon.

So should he really make the call at all?

He looked at the number again. It had been given to his brother – personally – by one of Carlos's cousins who lived in Caracas and who for years had basked in the notoriety of his famous terrorist relative. While not basking, he was a clerk in the Ministry of Finance, run, of course, by the other Martinez brother.

The Venezuelan oil minister suddenly put his overcoat back on. Why not do it like they did it in the movies?

He left the Baur au Lac and walked to the Bahnhofstrasse. It was 11.10 by now, and Zurich was dead. A look down toward the lake, and then up in the direction of the Paradeplatz was totally unobstructed by any living creature. The look also failed to detect any phone booths. And a wind was now coming off the lake, dropping the wind chill factor further and further below the freezing level. Snow was beginning to fall.

His situation was, Martinez thought bitterly, so different from how it had been in the good old days of just a few years ago. When an oil minister like him had come to Switzerland then, it had been with an entourage of a dozen, including press spokesmen and bodyguards. It was he and his colleagues from Riyadh and Kuwait and Teheran who had been the lords of energy, and who had thus been at the center of world attention. It was they – and he, Roberto Martinez, who had been among their leaders – who had put all the Swiss back onto bicycles when, for reason of energy conservation, Sunday motor traffic in Switzerland had been banned.

How different it was. No press crowding around, recording his every word, filming his every gesture. No entourage. Not even a bodyguard to find a goddamn pay phone. Or, failing that, a goddamn taxi which could take him to a pay phone before he froze to death.

Now it was the *Swiss* who were denying *him* transportation!

Roberto Martinez was again ready to give up the idea when – and it was perhaps an omen – a taxi finally appeared, a large well-heated taxi driven by an English-speaking driver by the name of Uri who suggested a bar in the old city where he knew there was a pay phone.

Ten minutes later, after telling Uri to wait outside the place which was called Zum Ochsen, he was sitting at the bar sipping a Swiss beer which had come in a large brown bottle bearing the label of the Feldschloesschen Brauerei. It tasted like warm molasses. After what he considered to be a decent interval, he asked where the phone was, and was directed to the corridor leading to the men's room.

A woman answered in Frankfurt. She spoke flawless English. She knew who Martinez was. She told him to go to the Zurich train station, to the row of phone booths situated inside and immediately to the left as one entered the Bahnhof from the Bahnhofstrasse. The booth he wanted to be at was the last one in row of ten; its number was (01) 797–4422. Could he make it there in half an hour?

He could.

She hung up. Just like in the movies.

Roberto Martinez was so pleased with himself that he ordered a Scotch, drank it down, then ordered a second which he drank more slowly while periodically checking his watch. After a quarter of an hour had passed, he put his overcoat back on and walked out of the door of the Zum Ochsen into the frigid Swiss night where his faithful driver, Uri, was still waiting, motor and heater running.

At midnight the Zurich train station was deserted, as were the city's streets. All ten phone booths were, therefore, empty. When the call came in, the ringing sounded so shrill in the silence of the cold hollowness of the Bahnhof that, for the second time that evening, Martinez was tempted to cut and run.

Instead he picked up the phone to stop the noise. After he identified himself, the voice – now it was a man's voice – told him in Spanish to be on the 3rd floor of the art museum in Basel at noon the next day. Where the Holbeins were.

Then Frankfurt hung up a second time, just as abruptly as the first.

Uri got his Latin American passenger back to the Baur au Lac Hotel within five minutes. He also charged him 200 francs.

The man at the front desk told Martinez that there was a train leaving for Basel at 10.48 the next morning, arriving at 11.56, and that the art museum was perhaps a seven-minute ride, maximum, from the train station.

Was he going there to see the Picassos?

No, the Venezuelan answered, the Holbeins.

The concierge nodded his approval. Apparently all Latinos were not barbarians.

Ten minutes later Roberto Martinez, comforted by the thought that even *sans* entourage he was still able to operate as effectively as ever, was asleep under the duvet provided by one of the world's finest hotels.

In a room in a building two blocks from the Frankfurt train station, which was as seedy a location as that town could offer, the man and woman to whom the Venezuelan had spoken were in bed, though not yet asleep. They were arguing. About the risk of his taking the early train to Switzerland to meet with the Venezuelan. She said that crossing the frontier, taking a chance on being recognized by the border guards or the customs people, was insanity. It was simply not worth it.

He said it was. He needed the money.

'Just look at this dump,' he said. 'That Carlos is down to this!'

He fell silent for a while.

Then: 'They keep spreading rumors that I'm dead. If I can't pull this one off, maybe I'll be better off dead.'

'Don't talk so silly,' she said, and then asked, 'Why doesn't Gaddafi help you out?'

'Maybe because I'm not an Arab. Maybe because I'm getting old. Who can figure that man out anyway? He's crazy. But at least he hasn't taken away my villa. Although he doesn't have it fixed up any more either. In a few more years it will look like this place. Unless I get some money and can fix it up myself.'

'How much money is the Venezuelan talking about?'

'Five million dollars.'

That impressed her.

'If it works out, we can move into the Frankfurterhof when I get back.'

She giggled.

'But it is not just the money,' Carlos said. 'We need a new direction, and the Venezuelan might provide it.'

Why a new direction?

Because, Carlos explained to her, the old one was getting them nowhere. It had become obvious to him that for years now they had been going after it in the wrong way. 'We're failing, and I'm simply getting too old to be able to afford to fail much longer.'

Carlos was now sixty-one. For years, now, he had lived most of his days in that increasingly decrepit villa on the outskirts of Tripoli, forgotten by the world. The failure he referred to was that of the 'new' brand of Euroterrorism that had evolved in the late 1970s. It had been his idea, his last big idea, and he had personally gone to Frankfurt from Libya in the spring of 1977 to convince the Red Army Faction that it should be their mission.

There was no way that European society, in this case West German society, could be moved away from endorsing private ownership of the means of production while its government was still under the control of the powers which ran NATO. Destroy Germany's allegiance to NATO, and the bonds which held West Germany captive to capitalism would be broken, and the door opened to full accommodation with the East. If Germany went, so would the rest of the alliance.

Destruction of that alliance, in turn, could only be brought about by breaking the will of the leaders within Germany who stood behind NATO – who stood behind it because they benefited most from it. This meant not just the generals, but the barons of German industry who supplied the generals with the weapons, and the bankers in Frankfurt and Düsseldorf who supplied the armaments industry with the money.

One could also not overlook the judges. For it was they who protected the capitalistic predators as they destroyed the environment, killing the German forests. It was they who presided over a legal system which was specifically designed to protect property more than human dignity, a system which had already managed almost to ruin the German soul by creating a *Konsumgesellschaft* on the Rhine where the people of Deutschland were taught that fullfilment lay in the ability to buy refrigerators, to ride in a Mercedes, to vacation in Spain rather than in the contemplation of Goethe's words, of Bach's music, and of Marx's ideas.

The military/industrial/financial/legal complex which had wrought all this was the target. They would start in Germany. They would establish the pattern there. But soon all of Europe would be added to the agenda. Then no banker or industrialist or general, from the Atlantic to the Elbe, would be safe. All would be fair game. In fact, if the Red Army Faction succeeded in Germany, Carlos had told them, then he would personally ensure that the same methodology would be applied also in France, in Italy, in Belgium . . . wherever necessary.

The new approach had begun a few months later, in the summer of 1977.

The first target was Germany's leading banker, Jürgen Ponto, head of the Dresdner Bank. Why Ponto? Because the German banks, principally the two biggest, the Deutsche and the Dresdner, not only lent money to the military/industrial complex of that country, they were also the principal shareholders in the corporations which were at the heart of the system. Get at the big banks and you shook and eventually destroyed that system's very foundation.

Ponto had come to greet his goddaughter at his front door and was gunned down – slaughtered, would be the better description – seconds later by the guns of the Red Army Faction. The banker, lying in a pool of blood in front of his own doorstep, was a picture that was imprinted on the mind of every German through media coverage that was unprecedented in post-war Germany. It was terrorist theater at its best. Carlos, in another room in another safe house outside of Frankfurt, had watched it all.

The next victim had been Hans-Martin Schleyer, President of the Federal Association of German Employers, the most powerful and influential grouping of 'capitalists' in West Germany. Again, the Red Army Faction was going for the heart, not the limbs.

Becoming more theatrical, they started out with a big bang, and milked the 'event' for all it was worth. First they kidnapped Schleyer, dragging him from his limousine after killing his two bodyguards in cold blood in broad daylight. Great stuff for television. Then they periodically sent pictures to the media showing him to be alive, reading yesterday's newspaper stories about himself. Finally, tiring of the game, they murdered him and dumped his body where they knew it would be readily found.

Moving on, the next year they killed one of Berlin's leading judges – one who had put some of their Red Army Faction colleagues behind bars – and put the entire German legal system on notice that no one in Germany's decadent society was off limits.

The year after that they got even closer to the heart of the matter. They tried to blow up the general who commanded NATO, General Alexander Haig, as he was being driven to the alliance's headquarters in Brussels.

But this time they failed. Their timing was off by five seconds.

It was not, in fact, until 1985 that the Euroterrorists finally managed to murder a general. The victim, General René Audran, was France's arms salesman – the man who supplied Saudi Arabia with Mirage aircraft, and Argentina and Iraq with Exocet missiles on behalf of France's Department of Defense. They cut him up with a machine gun in front of his house in the Paris suburb of La-Celle-Saint-Cloud. And this time they made sure that the world knew that the terrorist malaise was being spread in a deliberate, coordinated manner; that this assassination had been the result of a joint venture involving the German Red Army Faction, the French Action Directe and the Belgian Cellules Communistes Combattantes.

A few weeks later, in a suburb outside Munich, members of the same grouping entered the house of Dr Ernst Zimmermann just as he was about to leave for the office. They tied him up, laid him out on his marital bed, and then 'executed' him with a shot to the head while his wife, Ingrid, looked on. His crime? He was Chairman of the Board of the Motoren-und-Turbinen-Union, the leading West German aerospace company. Zimmermann, or at least his company, supplied the engines for the German 'Leopard' tank and the NATO fighter-bomber, the 'Tornado'. So he had to go.

And so forth.

The Wall Street Journal summed up the situation in Europe in 1988 by stating that 'Every big shot in industry and finance is afraid of being shot to pieces.' And continued: 'That, of course, is what terrorism is all about: causing fear in the minds of the enemy.'

But somehow, though the fear was present, it was reflected more in the private lives of the big shots, forcing them to cut back on the conspicuous consumption so dear to their pushy wives: no more balls, opera openings, racing meets. But where their public allegiance to NATO and the West was concerned, it remained totally intact.

Not only was the *new* tactic of striking terror in the hearts of the men who ran Mercedes Benz or the Swiss Bank Corporation or Royal Dutch leading nowhere. The *old* tactic of intimidation of the politicians in Europe was likewise proving increasingly ineffective.

Thus, despite the menacing presence of the Red Army in Germany, the Christian Democrats under Helmut Kohl still ran the country just as effectively as they had done earlier under Adenauer and Erhardt. If anything, the identification of terrorism in West Germany with the far left helped the Conservatives remain in power since the CDU/CSU was regarded by most Germans as a more effective counterforce to terror in the streets than the Social Democrats, not to speak of the Greens.

Margaret Thatcher and her Conservative government still ran Britain in spite of the attempt of the Irish terrorists to blow her and her entire Cabinet up in that hotel in Brighton where they had all gathered for their party's annual convention. Despite decades of terrorism coming from both the left and the right, despite the kidnapping and murder of dozens of Italy's élite by the Red Brigade, including former Prime Minister Aldo Moro, the democratic process had not only survived but during the second half of the 1980s was flourishing as seldom before. And in every election since 1976, the Communist Party's vote had been falling.

And where was the power of Arafat and the PLO in 1988? They had provoked the ultra-Conservatives in Israel once too often, so Begin had simply gone after them in Lebanon and driven them, literally, into the sea. Their attempt to get at the Saudi régime by inciting revolution in Mecca had been a total failure. In the end, Arafat had become a political leper, even in the Arab world.

So from the Pyrénées to the Elbe, from Dublin to Tel Aviv, terrorism in its traditional mode had proven a failure.

Carlos knew it.

And in these final days of 1988 he also knew why. They had been going after the wrong targets!

They had thought that they could 'win' by undermining the state of Israel through terrorist attacks from Lebanese bases, that they could finish off the rule of the upper class in England once and for all by killing Mountbatten on his yacht, by incinerating the Prime Minister of the United Kingdom and all of her Cabinet in Brighton, that they could drive West Germany into the arms of East Germany by kidnapping and murdering the bankers of Düsseldorf and the industrialists of Munich.

What Carlos now realized was that all of this had involved acts of terrorist theater that were missing the point.

That point was that the real enemy was not the gangsters running Israel, nor throwbacks to the nineteenth century in control of Britain, nor the reactionary primitives making up the Royal Family of Saudi Arabia, nor the totally corrupt capitalistic clique in power in West Germany.

No. The enemy – the West – stood or fell with one nation and one nation only: the United States. The rest – the Israelis, the British, the Germans, the Saudis – simply did what the Americans told them to do.

And the one country which, amazingly, had remained essentially immune from terrorism was the United States. Sure, 280 American marines had been massacred by terrorists as they slept in their barracks in Beirut. Sure, when the Shi'ites had kidnapped that TWA jet they had held fifty Americans captive in Lebanon. But in the United States proper? Terrorism on American soil?

Nothing.

In fact, since the time the Los Angeles Police Department had decided to incinerate the Symbionese Liberation Army on live television, organized terrorism had virtually disappeared from the American scene. A lot of would-be terrorists had probably concluded: Why fool around in a country where the cops act like mad dogs?

Yet, Carlos had concluded, if you wanted to destroy the enemy you go for his heart. The heart was composed of the fifty states of the United States of America.

But how?

How to create a climate of fear in the United States, and thus undermine America's ability to govern itself . . . and, by extension, its ability to govern the rest of its half of the world?

One way was simply to transfer the old methods to the new continent. The massacre of the marines in Beirut had proven that the Americans were highly vulnerable to psychological effects of terrorism. Within weeks of the massacre, the United States' government had been forced to pull *completely* out of the Middle East by the pressure of American public opinion. After thirty years of dominating the politics of the region, the suicide mission of one single driver of a truck loaded with explosive and aimed at an American marines barracks situated a few hundred meters from the Eastern shore of the Mediterranean had driven the Americans out. When the TWA jet was later hijacked to Beirut, and the American hostages arrogantly displayed on live American television day after day, the American public became even more convinced that the Middle East was a place that the United States' government should stay as far removed from as possible.

Could a series of similar acts, in America itself, cause yet another massive American retreat – this time from Europe? Would not the spilling of sufficient blood of American bankers, industrialists, judges, politicians convince the American public that, as earlier with the Middle East, so now with Europe: the price for further involvement was simply too high? That the time had come to pull back to 'aircraft-carrier' America. Or better, to 'starship America'.

For, after all, the Strategic Defence Initiative had been going forward now for four years and would soon be bearing fruit. Star Wars' hardware would soon be deployed. Then who needed NATO? Why should Americans be the targets of crazed European Commie terrorist bastards just because the United States continued to support an obsolete alliance?

But that alone would hardly do it. And Carlos knew it.

It would help though. In fact, it would probably help a lot. And it would restore Carlos to the front pages of every newspaper on earth.

But it alone would not suffice. Something totally new was needed. Something on a much larger scale.

Something on a totally different plane.

Enter his cousin back in Caracas. He had told Carlos in that long phone call to Libya just three nights before that the Martinez brothers, who had ruled Venezuela, were mad as hell. They were the key members of that class, and especially the clique within that class, which had always run the country. All of them now hated the North Americans as never before. Because the IMF and the American bankers had essentially usurped their power. The Martinez brothers were now, finally, ready to do something about it. Their support within Venezuela would be near 100 percent and would range from the president of the country right down to the heads of the labor unions. He, Carlos's cousin, had been told that they had an idea for a 'joint venture' with their fellow Venezuelan, Carlos, and wanted to talk to him about it.

It sounded as if it could be exactly what was needed. In any case, it was what he, Carlos, needed. Some action! His host, who now completely ignored him, would love it. Not that he would say a word to Gaddafi. The man was crazy and might do something, or say something, that might wreck the whole thing.

Was he surprised that a man of the stature of Roberto Martinez, oil minister, and his brother José, finance minister, would want to have anything whatsoever to do with him, Carlos, terrorist? Not at all. They were, as his cousin had pointed out, fellow Venezuelans after all. And they all knew that the liberator of Latin America, a revolutionary, a fellow-terrorist if one was honest about it, had been absolutely right when, over a century and a half ago, he had warned them *all* about who their *common* enemy was.

'The United States,' Simon Bolivar had said, 'seems destined to impose misery upon the Americas in the name of freedom.'

Among those freedoms seemed to be the liberty to impose massive debt upon the Americas, to impose usurious interest rates on that debt, and then to demand repayment on schedule in the name of free enterprise no matter what the cost might be in terms of human misery.

No. That went too far. That simply could no longer be tolerated. Some *drastic* counterforce had to be organized. And all Venezuelans, ultimately all Latin Americans, had to be part of that counterforce.

Thus in the closing weeks of 1988 they – the oil minister, the finance minister, and the revolutionary – had a common cause if there ever was one.

So three hours later Carlos left his bed and his still sleeping companion and walked through the pre-dawn dark of Frankfurt.

Half an hour after that he was on the Rheingold Express heading for the southern frontier of Germany and the city of Basel which lay just beyond it.

Chapter 4

The first moment of truth on that Thursday, December 8th, 1988 arrived for Carlos when the Rheingold Express stopped at the Badischer Bahnhof. That train station is a German territorial enclave surrounded by the Swiss city of Basel. The privileges that went with that status had been taken advantage of to the hilt by the Nazis in the 1930s when they used to hold Hitlerjugend meetings for Swiss boys there.

The Nazis had come and gone, but the Badischer Bahnhof had remained an enclave. All trains coming from the north stopped there for a few minutes, but usually only a few passengers got out. Among those who remained on board, some started to get nervous. This stemmed from their foreknowledge of the fact that it was at the Badischer Bahnhof that the Swiss immigration and customs authorities boarded the train.

As always, so also on that day they stayed on the Rheingold Express for the next ten minutes as it moved through the city of Basel toward its ultimate destination on the other side of the Rhine river, the main Swiss Hauptbahnhof. As the train moved slowly, so did the Swiss border authorities, as they deliberately, suspiciously checked the credentials of each and every passenger. They seldom opened luggage. But they often referred to the thick books they carried with them, reference books containing the numbers of passports to be on the lookout for, containing pictures, either photos or sketches, of the men and women that Interpol or the Swiss Police and Justice Department wanted badly.

An international arrest warrant had been out for Carlos ever since the time he had organized the kidnapping of the OPEC ministers in Vienna. The sketch Interpol had of Carlos dated back to the same time. It was, therefore, thirteen years old; in other words, useless.

The passport list was equally useless since the Mexican passport that Carlos carried was hardly included. It was totally legitimate and, in fact, had been provided to him by the police chief of Mexico City. The policeman – now in a Mexico City jail – had needed some help with the drugs trade that he was so deeply involved with. The need for assistance arose from the fact that two of his customers in Europe had double-crossed him. He had wanted them killed. Since he was a very busy man, having to fulfill his duties as a law enforcement officer at the same time he was meeting the responsibilities involved in directing a very large international trade in drugs, the police chief needed outside help for that project. Carlos had taken care of it for him very quickly. In return, the Venezuelan terrorist had received a lot of pesos – fifty of which being still as good and as solid as a dollar back then – and a stack of fresh Mexican passports.

But, even knowing all this, it still required enormous self control for Carlos to maintain his cool when the Swiss *gendarme* in his green uniform issued the command: '*Pässe, bitte.*'

The passport listed his occupation as 'pharmaceuticals'. Basel was the headquarters of three of the world's largest drug companies: Hoffmann La-Roche, Ciba-Geigy, and Sandoz. So it made sense. Carlos got his Mexican passport back, and the Swiss border police moved on.

Five minutes later Carlos was on Swiss territory, still a free man.

*

Train #476 of the Schweizerische Bundesbahn left Zurich at 10.48 a.m. precisely, bearing a lot of Swiss businessmen and one Venezuelan oil minister. Roberto Martinez was travelling first class, of course. He had immediately spotted the red-upholstered smoking section in the third car of the eleven-car train and minutes after the train had begun to move was already well into his second Monte Cristo of the day, which he began to puff on with increasing fury the further he got into the December 8th edition of the *Herald Tribune*.

On page one the lead story dealt with the confirmation of the ceasefire between Iran and Iraq. It was estimated that with peace apparently now restored, in 1989 both nations would probably be pumping oil at pre-war levels – meaning 6 million barrels a day for Iran and 4 million for Iraq. On page two, President Reagan was quoted as saying that his last budget proposal would probably call for the smallest deficit of the decade. But it would still raise the national debt to around $2.7 trillion. The editorial on page six noted that when Reagan had taken office eight years ago, the national debt had been under $1 trillion and raised the question: If this had happened during eight years of conservative Republican rule what would now happen under the liberal Democrats?

Specifically, what would happen to Gramm-Rudman? That was the act passed by Congress in 1985 that had been hailed by some as the means for achieving the fiscal salvation of the United States; by others, as a programmed train wreck. What it legislated was this: if the Congress failed to cut the budgetary deficit to a specified level each year, and ultimately to zero in 1991, then *automatic* across-the-board cuts in the government's expenditures would go into effect to meet those targets. These cuts would have to be made regardless of the consequences for defense or many social services; even the budgets of the FBI and the IRS were not immune. Thus the 'programmed train wreck'.

So far that wreck had not occurred. Because under President

Reagan, the economy had kept growing and growing, producing ever-rising tax revenues. The result: The Gramm-Rudman targets had been met every year without causing any major economic dislocations. Those dire cuts in government services had never been required.

Now, the *Herald Tribune* said, with the economy starting to sink, Gramm-Rudman would be automatically suspended. The authors of the bill had wisely foreseen this necessity. But, the editorial asked, with the Democrats about to reassume power, is it not probable that Gramm-Rudman will be repealed altogether? Would it not have to be repealed in order to give the new man in the White House sufficient fiscal lattitude to deal with the rising unemployment that now seemed inevitable in 1989 and beyond? And, when the Democrats start *really* to prime the pump, would the United States' Treasury not once again have to start to borrow on a massive scale?

Would the $2.7 trillion then become $4 or $6 trillion? Would the rest of the world once again be forced to finance half of the ever larger American debt? And if not, then what?

The results of the news were reflected on the financial page. The 'good' news of peace between Iran and Iraq had driven the crude oil price down another 50 cents. There was even speculation that a new oil glut would develop, one of such proportions that it could eventually drive the price down into single digits, to $9 a barrel or less. That would mean lower inflation, and lower long-term interest rates down the line. But the 'bad' news of the United States being doomed to sink further and further into debt, had sent short-term interest rates up in New York and the dollar down in Europe. This had the financial columnist of the *Herald Tribune* puzzled. Usually, in fact almost always, when American interest rates rose so did the dollar. Why were they suddenly moving in opposite directions?

The Venezuelan loved it. He knew! And soon – maybe very, very soon – they would know too. What was it that Reagan said when he was elected the second time? 'You ain't seen nothing yet!'

Martinez folded the paper, and looked out the window at the Swiss landscape flying by. No mountains here. Just rolling hills, lightly covered with snow, then a small village, five minutes later another one. Everything immaculate. Peaceful, tranquil, rich, safe Switzerland. Maybe he should just buy a place here and quit. Why take risks at his age? Why not just forget the Americans. Forget the oil price. Forget . . . Carlos.

Another village. The sign said 'Aarau'. Yet another, 'Rheinfelden', zipped by.

No. Dammit. It was simply too tempting. Because the more he thought about it, the more he was becoming convinced that it actually might work. It might wind up as the biggest financial happening of all time.

Jeezuz! He could just imagine the headlines in the *Herald Tribune*. Three inches high and in *black*.

THE PANIC OF '89!

It was worth taking a risk. Even a huge risk. Even the risk of being seen in public with Carlos. Because, later, if somebody put two and two together it would be too late. For *them*.

The Künstmuseum is the oldest public art museum in the world. The universality and excellence of the art on display there reflect a city-state culture which was, and is, unique in Europe for its level of bourgeois – *bürgerliche* – yet aristocratic sophistication. Were that a description of a city in any other country but Switzerland, it would obviously involve a contradiction in terms.

But not where the city of Basel is concerned. It is, perhaps, the last remaining bastion of classical humanism in a world where 'mass' culture – a *true* contradiction in terms – is now irrevocably dominant. The credit for the establishment of such an admirable state of affairs in Basel is given, for the most part, to the Huguenots, who had been driven out of France because of their Protestant beliefs in the late sixteenth and early seventeenth centuries. Many of them had emigrated to Basel and had brought with them a work ethic that allowed them rapidly to create wealth in their adopted city. The wealth they kept to themselves in the sense that their ethic did not include any imperative demanding that they hand some of it over to the poor. Their French Protestant ethic did demand, however, that they use their wealth to educate their fellow citizens in their new homeland, in spite of the fact that most of them were of primitive Swiss peasant stock. They felt obligated to enrich them culturally, to bring them the Renaissance in the hope that Basel could become to Central Europe what Florence was to northern Italy.

So, to a remarkable degree, their wealth was used by them and their descendants to promote the arts in every form, from theater and ballet to paintings and sculpture.

Thus the *public* art museum, the world's first.

But a closer look at the city-state's history immediately tells one that the origins of Basel's unique claim to cultural richness are to be found not in the seventeenth century and the Huguenots, but rather in the late fifteenth and early sixteenth centuries: in the Church, and in the invention of printing. For it was in 1431 that the Pope, then back in Rome after the long exile, had invoked the Council of Basel, where all the universe met for eighteen long years, attempting in vain to stem the tide of corruption that was beginning to undermine the very foundations of the One True Church. Out of that Council arose the university in 1456, endowed by the Papacy. The university, in turn, attracted the printing industry, and one of its pioneer master craftsmen, Froebenius. Here in Basel, then, it was all coming together already at the end of the fifteenth century.

The city-state, as a result, soon became a magnet for some of the greatest minds of Europe. In the early decades of the sixteenth century Erasmus of Rotterdam, Paracelsus and Hans Holbein all came to Basel.

Thus the Holbein collection in the world's first public art museum in Basel.

And in the room which held Holbein's greatest works stood, on that December day in 1988, a Venezuelan oil minister who was completely, totally, oblivious of all of the above. But that did not mean that he stood there untouched and unmoved. For the Holbein painting which dominates that room, in fact that museum, is a huge canvas of Christ Crucified. It is so powerful that it had actually evoked emotion, visible in the form of a tear, from the eyes of Roberto Martinez, a man as thoroughly anchored in our secular world as anyone else on earth. Or almost anyone.

For by arrangement there was another man in that same room whose credentials made even a Latin American oil minister appear saintly by comparison. He was a short, dark, aging man, and as he moved to take his place beside Roberto Martinez he bowed his head in respect of the scene before him. He had arranged that they meet there for a reason that had absolutely nothing to do with the Papacy, the university, the printing industry, Holbein or the Huguenots. His reason was that he knew that museums have traditionally served as excellent meeting places for sophisticated thugs such as spies and terrorists.

'*Buenos días, compadre*,' he said.

'*Buenos . . .*'

The terrorist's hand silenced him. 'We speak English!' he commanded.

'Magnificent, isn't it?' Carlos, nodding in the direction of the immense canvas in front of them, then continued, 'It fills one with awe.'

He was lucky that the museum was lightning proofed.

Carlos, alias the Mexican pharmaceutical man, then shuffled off to the next room which housed Dürer's portrait of Luther and Holbein's of Erasmus. A guard watched him from a distance. He was trained to spot people who seemed out of place. The foreigner, in his shabby suit and worn shoes, certainly fit that description. But he also appeared harmless. The guard moved on, and the terrorist and the oil minister continued their clandestine conversation.

'You are Señor Martinez?' Carlos asked.

'I am, of course.'

'I know a coffee house on the Rhine. It has the best patisserie in Switzerland. We can walk there and converse on the way.'

Carlos knew Basel because it was in that city that one of his professional colleagues, the Turk, Oral Çelik, accomplice of yet another member of the international terrorist brotherhood, Mehemet Ali Agça, the man who shot the Pope, had set up a heroin ring. Both Agça and Çelik had belonged to the Grey Wolves, the dominant terrorist organization in Turkey. When Çelik, who had purchased the Browning 9-mm pistol that Agça had used on the Pope, escaped, the Grey Wolves put him under their protection. They had set him up in the drugs business by supplying him with heroin in Istanbul. They had also introduced Çelik to Carlos's organization, which had not only arranged that his face be altered by plastic surgery in a clinic outside Frankfurt, but had also helped him set up a distribution center in Basel to serve the market north of the Alps. Çelik's main job then was to move the heroin from the Bosporus to the Rhine, through Greece, Yugoslavia and Italy. He moved a lot of it over the years. Carlos showed up occasionally in Basel to collect his share of the proceeds.

The walk took them along the Rittergasse, past the Cathedral, and down the Rheinsprung. Their conversation included the mention of $5 million and of three names: the President of the world's second largest bank, Bank of America, the Chairman of the Federal Reserve Board of the United States of America, the world's key central bank, and . . . Paul Mayer.

The coffee house was called Spielmann's. The patisserie fully lived up to its billing. The conversation had reverted to 'the good old days' in Caracas. When the bill arrived, Carlos paid.

Outside Spielmann's was a public phone booth. Carlos, not one to use credit cards or to go through an operator, had enough Swiss coins to make a three-minute call to London. The call took less time than that.

'My man will be on it immediately,' he said to Martinez after emerging from the telephone booth. Then: 'I will expect $5 million to be available here in Basel tomorrow before the banks close. They should be cabled to this name and this account number at the Swiss National Bank.'

The terrorist handed the oil minister a small slip of paper. And then waited.

'Perhaps you could arrange that right now,' he said, pointing at the still empty phone booth.

Roberto Martinez, who had no qualms about using his credit card, was fortunate. His brother was at home. He said he would attend to it the minute the banks opened in Caracas the next morning. This would mean that the funds would be in Basel between 2.00 and 3.00 p.m. the next day.

'And how are things going otherwise?' José Martinez, Sr asked from Caracas.

'Excellently. Perfectly.' replied his brother, in Switzerland.

'And the Russians?'

'They are taken care of. Now, José, it's up to you.'

'I am leaving for Mexico City tomorrow morning.'

'What about the man from Brazil?'

'He's already in.'

'Good. I think we'd better hang up. You never know,' said Roberto Martinez, and then proceeded to do just that.

He stepped out of the phone booth and gave Carlos the good news. The two Venezuelans, the oil minister and the terrorist, then shook hands and disappeared into the daytime crowd of innocent Swiss *Hausfrauen* making their daily rounds of the butcher, the baker, and the watchmaker in downtown Basel, all, naturally, oblivious of the fact that trouble had just been created in their midst.

Before it was over, it would affect them all, just as it would the entire world. But some would be affected more than others. Much more.

Among these chosen few would be Dr Paul Mayer.

Chapter 5

Paul Mayer had enjoyed breakfast in his rooms at the Savoy on that December 8th, 1988. It was the first time he had eaten kippers in years. As he ate, he reflected on what had happened over dinner the previous evening. On the whole, with one exception, it had gone well. Very well.

George Pace had arrived at the Grill Room all smiles, overjoyed to be with his old friend Paul Mayer once again, and, on top of that, to be with him in London, a city which both knew well and loved a great deal. Both were old enough to like martinis, and, while they had two, most of their talk was of the good old days in the 1960s and 70s when the big banks of the world were fat, and when the men who ran them were proud in their calling and secure in their future.

But then, after they had ordered dinner, the head of Bank of America asked the question that, temporarily, changed the atmosphere. When he, Pace, had telephoned Mayer on Monday, it had been to ask his help. But he had hardly expected Mayer to just drop everything and hop on a Pan Am for Heathrow. What had prompted such precipitous action?

Mayer told him about his lunch at the Metropolitan Club.

Pace listened, and the longer he did so the more his expression changed.

'Done?' he finally asked.

'Yes, I guess so,' Mayer replied.

'Look, first I want to tell you that I appreciate your candor, Paul. You've always been a straight shooter, and you've proven it once again this evening. But you have also put me in a bind.'

'Why?'

'I'll be just as straight with you. When I called you at the beginning of the week it was to ask you to come on board at B of A. We hadn't exactly worked out the title, and perhaps one is not really necessary. By "we" I mean the full Board of Directors which has already cleared this. In essence what we are talking about is your becoming a special advisor to the Office of the Chairman. In other words, me. It would be you and me against the bastards out there.'

'I'm flattered, George. Immensely flattered.'

'But are you still a free man?' asked Pace.

'No I'm not. The Fed has, in essence, pre-empted you, George. I'm now committed to taking an "objective" look at you, and then reporting back to the Federal Reserve and the FDIC.'

'In one way that's regrettable,' Pace said.

'Yes. But that arrangement will hardly be forever. And then, provided that everybody agrees that it involves no conflict of interest, there is no reason that we could not discuss your very generous offer again.'

'Generous? I didn't even mention compensation, Paul.'

'I think you know that money is not of paramount importance to me, George. I meant generous in regard to the position of trust you offered,' Mayer replied. 'But let's go on from where we stand now. I'm supposed to take a quick, cold and calculated look at the current status of your bank. Are you willing to cooperate?'

'Absolutely. One hundred percent.'

'Terrific. I can tell you right off that I'm sure that Bob Reston will be absolutely delighted. So will the FDIC. The boys over at the Office of the Comptroller of the Currency might be something else. They're probably ready right now to send in a couple hundred auditors next week. But I'm sure that the Fed can calm down the OCC. And keep them away from the bank for as long as necessary. Provided, of course, we can stop the rumors. Which brings up the big question. What about them?'

'You mean that we are going to have to take the hit of the century next year?'

'Exactly.'

The roast beef and Yorkshire pudding and a '79 Pommard began to arrive just then. And, as they ate, George Pace spoke. 'First we are going to have to take a hit but it's nothing like the $2 billion that those idiots are talking about.'

'Where?'

'All in the good old US of A.'

'How much?'

'A billion, max.'

'What would that do to your capital base?'

'Bring it below the 6 percent minimum by about half a billion dollars.'

'Which means . . .'

'That we are going to have to go outside again and raise that half billion.'

'Which means?'

'Trouble. Because it would tend to confirm what the rumors are saying. And maybe start to affect our deposit base, or in any case, our cost of money in a big way. And something else.'

Pace paused.

'This is between us girls, Paul,' he then said, 'but we've been hearing distant rumbles of somebody taking a shot at us.'

'Takeover.'

'Right.'

'Who could afford it?'

'Look, $6 or $7 billion might do it. Eight max.'

'Who's got that?'

'General Motors, maybe. Another banking group, maybe. An oil company, maybe.'

'What about the Fed? Would they allow that?'

'What about them? Look, nothing's sacred. Look at what's happened to the TV networks. They were always regarded as untouchables. Not just because the stations they owned had to be licensed, but somehow they were always thought of as being bearers of the public trust, and as such, above the financial fray. Well, that didn't prevent a yahoo like Ted Turner making a bid for CBS.'

'Banks are different.'

'Oh yeah? Who says?'

Then the Chairman of B of A changed the direction of the conversation. 'Look, Paul, that's not my immediate concern. There's somebody lurking out there, and we've got to find out who. And then, if necessary, build up our defense. But our problem right now is those goddamn rumors that are making our big depositors nervous.'

'What can I do to help?'

'Squelch them. Right away.'

'How?'

'Get the message out that, yeah, we're going to take a billion dollar hit, but that it's already being taken care of. Now that you're working for the Fed, if it comes from you they'll believe it.'

'Can I talk numbers?'

'Absolutely. We've got it broken down to the last nickel.'

'Where's the biggest trouble?'

'Real estate, agriculture, and those goddamn energy-related loans. That oil price is starting to head south again and as a result one customer a week is going belly up in Houston or Beaumont or Denver, taking a few millions of our money down with them every time.'

'It's all domestic.'

'Yes.'

'What about Mexico and Brazil and Venezuela and Argentina. What's your exposure?'

'A shade over 6 percent of our assets. Or 100 percent of our capital base if you want to be nasty about it. But so what? Nothing's going to happen there that would require any writeoffs. Look, I hardly need to tell you that Latin America's bust. But as long as nobody south of the border goes bust in a *public* way, there will be no trouble as far as we are concerned. So that billion doesn't include any further writeoffs on sovereign loans.'

'All right. I just wanted to know exactly what we're talking about. In any case, I totally agree with your logic and so will everybody else.'

At the end of the evening it had been decided that Pace would bring all the key data related to the status of the bank over to the Savoy in the morning. Mayer would go over the numbers with him. And then, when they had their story straight, Mayer would begin his European rounds before returning to Washington where he would give the Fed the good news.

Paul Mayer had barely finished both his breakfast and his reflections on the previous evening when George Pace arrived. The head of Bank of America had, as promised, brought along the full computer printouts on his bank's classified loan situation and the writeoffs they would require. The 'problem' was, as he had suggested, just over a billion dollars.

'May I show this to the people in Washington?' Mayer asked, after he had scanned the numbers for a good quarter of an hour.

'Absolutely.'

'All right. But first, as we agreed last night, I'll get the word out in Europe. I'll start here in the City. In fact, if you don't mind George, I think I'd better get on the phone and line up a few appointments for this afternoon. I'll do Frankfurt and Zurich after that, and then back to Washington. Sound right to you?'

'Precisely what I had hoped for,' the head of B of A replied. He then got up, and, as he was about to leave, added: 'I would appreciate it if you would keep in very close touch, Paul. Especially if things appear to be starting to slip out of control.'

'Don't worry,' Mayer answered. 'I will, and they won't.'

'I've got another idea. I think you should come out to San Francisco and talk to my Board. We're meeting again at the beginning of next week. Then you could tell them face to face that the Fed is behind me. They need to know that, Paul, and the sooner the better. Some of them are starting to get a little shaky.' Pace continued: 'I know it will be getting very close to Christmas, but . . .'

'Not to worry, I've no family, as you know. But it will be up to Bob Reston. I'll put it to him as soon as I get back to Washington. I'm sure he'll agree.'

'If he does, why don't you stay with Annie and me in Belvedere?'

Then the phone rang. Mayer picked it up, and, after listening to a few words, waved the phone toward George Pace. After no more than thirty seconds, Pace mumbled a few words of thanks and hung up.

'That was my secretary in San Francisco,' he explained to Mayer. 'It seems that *The Wall Street Journal* wants to talk to me. Urgently. They know I'm in London in spite of the fact that the bank people here have apparently been stonewalling. As a result, the reporter involved is getting mad as hell.'

'That's precisely what we don't need,' Mayer said.

'I'm getting used to things we don't need, Paul,' answered his friend from B of A.

George Pace was only forty-eight years old. He was a chunkily-built man, and had, in fact, played halfback for the

Stanford football team when they had still been known as the Stanford Indians. He was known around San Francisco as an ever-cheerful man who invariably added a lot of fun and life to any group he was a part of. But the quality that usually came first to an observer's mind when he entered a room was strength. Now, on this dreary December morning in London, even that quality was beginning visibly to disintegrate. Pace moved over to the bed at the far side of Mayer's small suite and slumped on its edge, his color gray, his shoulders tensed. He looked like a fifty-eight-year-old who was a prime candidate for the cardiac ward.

'You know, Paul,' he then continued, in a brittle voice, 'they asked me to take over the bank two years ago. I was on top of the world. The executive suite, the limo, the G-III, the Pacific Union Club. I loved it. Annie loved it. The kids loved it. It's not that I had any illusions. As you know, this bank was in deep trouble in the early 1980s. My predecessor came in and did a helluva job. He solved many of the problems and I thought I could finish the job. Now I'm not so sure.'

He ran a hand across his eyes.

'Let me take care of the *Journal*,' Mayer said quickly. 'After all, that's what I'm supposed to be here for now. To help. Right?'

'Let me call that reporter,' Mayer continued.

Pace nodded.

'What's his name?' Mayer then asked.

'It's not a him,' Pace replied. 'It's a her. And her name's Sally Brown.'

'I know the name. She phoned me a couple of times when I was still with the IMF. Is she here in London?'

'Apparently.'

Mayer went over to the desk and fished out the phone book from the drawer. It was dog-eared and dirty, somewhat symbolic of the general state of affairs in the country where he was currently a guest. *The Wall Street Journal* was listed at an address near Fleet Street. The number was 353-0671.

He got Ms Brown immediately, and introduced himself, explaining that he was calling from the Savoy Hotel.

'*The* Paul Mayer?' she asked.

'Yes. If you recall, we've spoken with each other a number of times in the past.'

'Of course I remember. But you're no longer with the IMF are you?'

'No.'

She waited.

'Well, I understand you are trying to get hold of George Pace of Bank of America.'

'That's right.'

'Why, may I ask?'

'I'd rather tell that to Mr Pace himself.'

'I can understand that, but I can assure you that he has empowered me to answer whatever questions you might have on his behalf. But off the record.'

A long pause ensued. Ms Brown obviously didn't go for that 'off-the-record' business. 'I didn't know you were associated with Bank of America.'

'I'm not. I'm here on behalf of the Federal Reserve. And in that capacity I have been visiting with George Pace. You are not the only one, Ms Brown, who is currently interested in what's happening at Bank of America.'

'All right. Could you come over here to talk?'

'About what, specifically?'

'There are rumors all over the place about the bank's bad loans, a possible takeover. You must know more than I do.'

'Maybe. Let's meet . . .' Mayer thought quickly, searching for a place as unobtrusive as possible, 'at the bar of the Carlton Tower. You know, on Cadogan Place. Say at noon?'

She agreed immediately.

After he had hung up, Mayer glanced at the face of B of A's Chairman. His color had returned.

'This could be a big break, George,' Mayer now said. 'If I can convince her that you've got things under control, and *she* gets the right word out, it will spare me making the rounds here in Europe.'

'I sure hope so. By the way, what does she look like?'

'Ms Brown?'

'Yes.'

'I've got no idea. We've never met.'

'Then who knows, Paul, maybe we'll both get lucky today.'

Chapter 6

The Carlton Tower Hotel has had its ups and downs over the years, but the Rib Room and its bar have remained intact and popular nevertheless. A lot of American businessmen have always stayed there, and, as usual, the bar at noon was full of them. Paul Mayer, who had arrived slightly early in his Brooks Brothers' suit and vest, blended in perfectly.

Within a few minutes, first one, then a second unescorted lady entered the bar area. Neither was very attractive, and neither turned out to be Sally Brown, much to Mayer's relief. After George Pace's remarks, for some juvenile reason he had high, and probably totally unrealistic, hopes that Sally Brown might turn out to be more than some type of *Blaustrumpf* who got her kicks out of staying late at the office, churning out vicious articles designed to skewer yet another victim.

The moment he saw her he knew that she was Sally Brown, and also that a bluestocking she was not. She was maybe five feet six, had tawny blonde hair, a tanned complexion, and was exquisitely dressed in a beige Anne Klein suit which managed to reflect good taste while at the same time advertising the fact that her legs weren't bad either.

When Paul Mayer rose to his full six feet four to greet her – because she had come directly to his table without a moment's hesitation – the eyes of every guy in the bar were drawn to them. 'To be able to spend a few days in London with that!'

was the obvious collective thought that prompted most of them to order another bourbon and water as a poor substitute.

'Mr Mayer, I presume,' she said with a businesslike smile, followed by an even more businesslike handshake.

'Ms Brown,' he answered. 'We finally meet. Would you join me for a drink?'

'No,' she replied as she sat down, her hand indicating that she needed no help from Mayer. Then, as she watched him lower his tall frame into a chair, she changed her mind.

'Why not? A Manhattan. I haven't had one since I've been over here.'

'Nor have I,' Mayer replied, 'although I only got here yesterday.'

She smiled the same automatic smile, and kept watching him as he ordered.

'You're younger than I thought,' she then said. 'And I suspect you might even have a sense of humor.'

'What did you expect?'

'I don't know exactly,' she replied. 'I recall thinking of you as being a little on the heavy side. Professorial. Teutonic. Very International Monetary Fund, if you know what I mean. But now that we've met . . .'

Then, as if catching herself, she reached for her notebook in the small briefcase that she had placed on the table.

Now it was Mayer who was watching her. She reminded him of Leslie Stahl on PBS. They shared the same blondness, the same slenderness where it paid to be slender, the same softness of voice; yet there was also a glint in her eyes that warned of toughness.

'Shall we get going?' she asked, her tone cooler, the glint in her blue eyes more pronounced.

'By all means.' She's probably thirty-one or thirty-two, Mayer speculated, and a bit young for me. That's probably why she came up with that Teutonic thing.

'You've heard the rumors?' she then asked.

'Yes. We hear they're coming out of Zurich.'

'Zurich and Frankfurt. And Tokyo.'

The 'Tokyo' caused Mayer to wince ever so slightly.

'Who in Frankfurt, Zurich and Tokyo?'

'Sorry,' she answered.

'OK,' Mayer continued, 'if it's a no go on the "who", then let's move on to the "what".'

'Three items. B of A is going to have to take a $2 billion hit on domestic loans. You are going to have to cough up on a couple of those standby letters of credit that you've kept hidden from the trusting public for so long. And . . .'

'Hold on. What's that second item again?'

'That $118 billion dollars worth of contingent liabilities that does not appear on B or A's balance sheet. We hear that half a billion are coming home to roost.'

Paul Mayer looked very skeptical, and Sally Brown could see it. He knew full well that every large bank in the United States engaged in the practice of issuing loan guarantees and that none of these activities was reflected on the balance sheet. They varied from insuring that the city of San José would pay off on the municipal bonds it issued to the public, to guaranteeing interest payments arising out of interest-rate swaps, to future foreign exchange purchase and sale commitments, to just simple loan commitments. None of these items was 'at risk' in the normal sense. So it made eminent sense to leave them 'below the line' in Mayer's judgement: in his very International Monetary Fund judgement, as she would probably put it, he thought.

'I'll have to check that one out,' he said, 'but it sounds like a red herring. Maybe something has cropped up in that area, but in no way could it involve anything even approaching half a billion dollars. What else?'

'Venezuela.'

'What about Venezuela?'

'That it is both unable and unwilling to pay any further

interest on its foreign debt. Because of the oil price going further south every week.'

'That's completely untrue. And I'm surprised that you would fall for an old chestnut like that. First it was Argentina, then it was Brazil, then Mexico, then the Philippines, now Venezuela. Has any of them ever defaulted yet? Hell no. So forget that one too. Anything else?'

'One more. That some of the Board of B of A have had enough of George Pace. They feel he's running the bank into the ground. It is further said that these same people are actively seeking out a merger partner who will bring in a lot of new capital – which the bank will need after all these writeoffs – and a new head guy who will make sure that all this doesn't happen again.'

'Who told you that?'

'Come on, Mr Mayer. Or do you prefer Dr Mayer?'

'Neither. Paul will do. It's less Teutonic.'

She seemed to be thinking about that, and then decided to relent a bit. 'OK, Paul it is. If I'm Sally.'

'It's a deal.'

Mayer then reached to the floor for his briefcase, and pulled out the computer printouts that George Pace had given him a few hours earlier.

'Let's start with the classified loans. Here they are, fresh out of the IBM.'

She took the papers from his hands, and started rapidly to scan their contents.

'Are you actually *authorized* to give this to me?' The astonishment was apparent in both her words and her expression.

'To show; not to give.'

'Fair enough.'

She kept turning the pages.

'This isn't going to hurt B of A, you know,' she commented after coming to the last page. 'Everybody thinks that the number is twice as large.'

'We know. Now you know. And soon, I trust, the rest of those curious people out there will know.'

'What about my second item?'

'What was it again?'

'Those contingent liabilities that have gone sour.'

'I frankly don't know, but I doubt that there's any trouble there of any substantial proportions. And if there were, it would no doubt affect every money center bank in the United States.'

'Why?'

'Because everybody does it, and on a large scale.'

'How large?'

'OK. Let's take the fifteen largest banks in the United States. They have, give or take a few tens of billions, combined assets of around a trillion dollars. OK? How much, collectively, would you guess they have in such off-the-balance-sheet commitments?'

'I give up.'

'Also a trillion. In fact, right now I'd say the number's closer to $1.2 trillion.'

'That's frightening.'

Mayer shrugged.

'Why do they do this?' she then asked.

'To make money. To be more precise, to make money *now*. They collect the fees for these guarantees on the front end.'

'Even though they might remain in effect for years?'

'For years and years,' Mayer said. 'Their added attraction is that since they are not included on the balance sheet they don't count in calculating a bank's minimum capital requirements. If they were, the banks would have to increase their capital by many billions. Capital, as you know, is expensive.'

Ms Brown seemed to be following all this, so Mayer decided to go on. 'There's one final attraction. Usually these guarantees are in the form of standby letters of credit. The courts have ruled that if a bank fails, even though they are not on the balance sheet, the FDIC is obligated to make good on them.'

'Why?'

Mayer shrugged again.

'I mean that question,' Sally Brown then said. 'Why?'

'Because without FDIC backing of these off-the-balance-sheet guarantees, depositors, at least sophisticated depositors, might get nervous. Unfortunately, especially during the past six or seven years, we have seen hundreds of bank failures in the United States. But fortunately, with the exception of some small thrift institutions in Ohio and Maryland which were backed only by state-sponsored guarantees, no banks have been faced with runs such as we used to see regularly throughout the nineteenth century all the way up to 1933. Because since 1933, when the FDIC was created, to panic is to demonstrate ignorance. The FDIC stands behind all banks' obligations, on or off the balance sheet.'

Sally Brown thought that one over for a moment. 'Now Paul,' she said, testing the use of his first name for the first time, 'you can tell that to the Rotary Club in Petaluma, but you're not kidding anybody over here in Europe. Including me.'

'Who's trying to kid you?'

'You are. And to make my point, let's walk through this one together. OK?' She didn't wait for a response. 'First, tell me: Are European deposits with Bank of America backed by the FDIC. Yes or no?'

'No. None of the overseas deposits with *any* of the money center banks in the United States is covered by the FDIC. That's why none of these banks pays any insurance premiums on them.'

'Why?'

'Because overseas deposits are always institutional in nature. They come from European banks, corporations, pension funds, in other words, institutions. By definition, then, they are all very sizeable. A million dollars is not an "official" minimum, but it represents the normal unit where Eurodollar deposits are concerned. That means they are all well above the

$100,000 mark where FDIC insurance stops, and stops no matter where the deposits come from, Europe or Santa Rosa, California.'

'Got it. Next question: What percentage of the total deposits of B of A come from overseas, meaning, I guess, Europe and Japan for the most part?'

'I can't give you those figures, since I don't know them.'

'Fair enough. Let's just generalize then. Let's take the ten largest banks in the United States – B of A, Chase, Citibank, Security Pacific – you know the list. Taken collectively, what percentage of their total deposits come from abroad?'

'Half.'

Now it was the second time for Sally Brown to appear openly astonished. 'It's *that* high?'

'Yes.'

'And you admit it?'

'It's a fact.'

'Who is aware of this?'

'The Fed, the FDIC, the Comptroller of the Currency to name a few. Other than that, well, let's put it this way: I'd say that about 99.9 percent of Americans *aren't* aware of it.'

'All right,' the lady from *The Wall Street Journal* continued, 'now let's play "what if?" '

'OK,' although now Mayer's eyes reflected a heightened sense of wariness.

'What if you *really* wanted to do in an American bank, one of the really big ones?'

'Like B of A,' Mayer added, dryly.

'You got it,' she answered.

'What would *you* do?' he countered.

'Spook the European depositors!' she said.

'By spreading rumors about $2 billion hits.'

'Right.'

'But in the end rumors must have substance if what you are speculating about would really start to happen.'

'Granted. So let's now say that the rumors about the $2

billion hit turn out to be wrong. That the loan loss provision required will *only* amount to $1 billion. Now what if, on top of rumors of that now $1 billion hit on domestic loans, it was also rumored that Venezuela, and then Mexico, and then Brazil had decided that they were no longer willing to pay interest on their debt. Not because of any big conspiracy but simply due to the fact that the prices of everything they export, from bananas to oil, were falling out of bed, with the result that their dollar incomes were simply not sufficient for them to service their debts. Meaning that they would have to borrow yet more money from the American banks in order to keep up their payments. And why? Merely to enable the Yankee banks to maintain the fiction that all those Third World loans on their books are good. So what if Venezuela concluded that that was the banks' problem, not theirs, and decided to default, officially and openly. That could trigger a process south of the border where one financial domino after the other could start toppling.'

'Follow me?' she then asked.

'Perfectly,' he answered.

'So what would happen?' she asked.

'Our government would step in, and that would be that. No run, no panic.'

'Oh, really? Would you keep your money in B of A if that happened – if you were a totally uninsured depositor here in Europe? If you were not only uninsured but also without the clout necessary to talk the powers that be in Washington into including you under the FDIC umbrella even though, legally, they didn't have to?'

Paul Mayer didn't answer right away. Then: 'I gave you the party line. If you want my personal opinion, if I were in that position I'd get out. As illogical as it would be, my feeling would be: Why run the risk of even one in a million that the US government will leave us foreigners out in the cold? I'd get out and bring my money home – whether home was London, Tokyo, Hong Kong or Zurich.'

'From what you've told me, if everyone over here reacted the same way you could see *half* of B of A's deposits pulled out. Sixty billion dollars!'

'That's right.'

'Paul Mayer,' the reporter then said, 'you're really something! I've never met anybody yet in the financial establishment in the United States who would have given that answer.'

'Fine. But remember, we're off the record. And before we go any further with your "what if?" game, let me ask *you* a question.'

'Fair enough.'

'Why would Venezuela or Brazil or Mexico do that? It would be suicidal. For they know full well that if we go, they go. Even Castro knows that.'

'Maybe. Maybe not,' she answered. 'Let me now tell *you* something. Off the record.'

'I'm listening.'

'Have you ever heard of a certain Señor Martinez from Caracas?'

'Sure. But there are two of them: José, and I forget his brother's name.'

'Roberto.'

'Right. He's their oil minister. And?'

'He's been making the rounds in Zurich.'

'Where these rumors started.'

'To be honest, they started before Señor Martinez arrived. But they've intensified since.'

'Thank you for that.'

'You're welcome. Next little bit of information – again off the record: A certain Comrade Dolgikh, member of the Soviet Politburo, or at least almost a member, was in Zurich the same day as Señor Martinez and, in fact, had lunch with him at a bank there the day before yesterday.'

'And?'

'Well, is all this coincidental?'

For the first time Paul Mayer laughed, and it was a pleasant laugh.

'Now Sally Brown, I'm afraid you're letting yourself get carried away. We're talking about banks and bankers and loans and balance sheets. This is not material for Le Carré or Freddy Forsyth, as much as I admire them both. Forget the Venezuelans and the Russians and probably even the Swiss. I think, in fact I'm afraid, that what has been happening during the past week or so has a very simple explanation, and I also think you are on to it. Somebody is working on a takeover scheme, or at least a merger scheme in cahoots with somebody on the B of A Board. And what they are trying to do is soften the price of B of A stock by starting these rumors – as *they* start accumulating the stock.'

Sally Brown appeared chastised.

'Do you know who it might be?' Mayer then added.

'Let me think about that,' she answered.

'Over lunch?' he asked. 'The roast beef here is terrific.'

'I'd love to. But first, where's the Ladies?'

He watched her leave as did everybody else in the bar. He paid the bar bill and then went over to the maître d' to arrange for a table. He wanted one on the terrace at the rear, where, he calculated, they could sit side by side and overlook the entire Rib Room. When Sally Brown reappeared, the maître d', who remembered Mayer and the £5 note he always slipped him, personally arranged their seating. Sally was a bit surprised by the side-by-side arrangement, but didn't fight it.

'Nice,' she commented, as she settled into the red upholstery. 'I've never been here before.'

'Well, its mostly American businessmen and Middle Eastern types who stay here.'

As if on cue, the maître d' showed up again, this time leading a stunning and richly-endowed woman of olive complexion, probably one of those very wealthy Iranian expatriates, Mayer figured, from the hautiness of her bearing and the ultra-expensive stylishness of her dress. The guy that she was with, a head shorter and a bit on the greasy side, was so outclassed it was pathetic. It turned out that they got the table to the right of Mayer's. Her perfume momentarily filled the air as the exotic pair joined the two Americans on the red upholstered banquette on the terrace.

'I see what you mean,' Sally Brown said to Mayer in a whisper. 'Would you rather change tables?'

'No way. I hear they all get fat when they're over thirty.'

'In that case, shorty next door has lucked out. She's over thirty, but she looks absolutely gorgeous. Although I must say she is a *bit* on the *saftig* side.'

'I prefer present company, if I may say so.'

'You may. As often as you like, Paul Mayer.' Then she added: 'Let's have another Manhattan.'

'You read my mind,' Mayer responded, and proceeded to wave at a waiter.

'You see, that's the advantage you have with us American girl reporters,' she then said. 'We may not be *saftig* but at least we know how to drink. We all learn it in college.'

'Which one in your case?'

'Duke.'

'It figures,' Mayer answered.

'Why?'

'Because you have, as you Americans say, a touch of class. Southern class.'

'Thank you again, dear sir. But why that "you Americans"? Are you not an American?'

'I am now. But I grew up in Switzerland. There "class" is defined differently. One is taught to be stiff, reticent, cautious at all times. You're not supposed to expect to have much fun in life, as I strongly suspect you do.'

'Poor baby!'

Mayer was starting to struggle.

'Aren't you having fun now?' she asked.

'Of course.' Mayer seemed surprised to hear himself give that answer.

The new round of Manhattans had arrived. At the table next door they got a pitcher of iced tea.

'Here's to the two-Manhattan lunch, Paul,' Sally Brown now said, and clinked her glass against his.

The waiter arrived to take their order. Both took roast beef. Mayer also ordered a bottle of light Burgundy wine to go with it.

'What the hell,' Sally said, 'we might as well destroy the rest of the afternoon. But before we do, could I return to semi-business for a few minutes?'

'Sure.'

'How do you fit in with George Pace of B of A?'

He told her. At length. And while he spoke, neither of the two Middle Eastern types at the table next to them exchanged a word. The Iranian woman did drop her napkin, twice, and each time she recovered it, she showed a good part of her very ample bosom. She also seemed to shift her position on the banquette ever closer to Paul Mayer. He sensed the nearness and could not help but glance at the bosom. If it had not been for the equal attraction of the American beauty on his left he would have been tempted to examine the lady from Iran even more carefully. Sally Brown obviously noticed what was happening.

'I think there's a little lust in the heart of the lady-next-door. And guess who seems to be the target of her Middle Eastern desire?'

'If you were with a greasy spoon like that, you might be dropping your napkin all over the place too,' he answered.

'Touché.'

'Now tell me,' he continued, 'who is rumored to be on the make for B of A? Karl Miller?'

This was the third time that afternoon that Sally Brown's delicate jaw dropped.

'How the hell did you know that?'

'I didn't.'

'Sneaky!'

'Now that you've told *me*,' Mayer continued, 'who told *you*?'

'You know I can't tell you that,' she answered. Then: 'All right, I will tell you. After I started to chase down the rumors about B of A that were beginning to circulate around Europe, I asked some of our people at the *Journal* in New York to nose around a bit. They came up with the Miller thing.'

'How reliable are they normally?'

'Well,' she began to answer, 'let me put it this way: I'm always pretty skeptical. Half the people on Wall Street are always trying to plant rumors with us, for obvious reasons.'

'Bank of America is big even for Miller. Too big, in my opinion. It would take at least $6 billion. Maybe $7 billion. Where's he going to get that kind of money?'

'New York also has an answer for that.'

'Who?'

' "They" say Miller's enlisted the help of Drexel Burnham Lambert – the junk bond house.'

Mayer's look of dismay upon hearing Sally Brown's last words told all.

'Can you imagine the reaction that might provoke in Europe?' he said. 'America's second largest bank being taken over by a notorious asset stripper, a corporate raider, and all that being financed through the issue of $6 billion worth of junk bonds. Jeezuz!'

'Not good,' she said. 'Which brings us full circle.'

'What's that mean?'

'Back to our little conversation a while ago about how to spook the European depositors.'

Mayer chose not to comment on that.

'If I were you I'd check it out,' she continued, adding an afterthought, 'and then let me know.'

'How?'

'Call Drexel Burnham.'

'I don't know anybody there. The IMF did not deal in junk bonds.'

'Maybe not, but B of A must do a lot of business with them all the time. Have your pal George Pace call them.'

'Good idea. Thanks.'

'You're welcome.'

When the check came, she grabbed it. A small struggle ensued, involving Paul Mayer touching her in earnest for the first time. But he lost.

'You must let me reciprocate some time soon,' he said rather lamely as the waiter walked off with her Platinum card.

'With pleasure.' And this time it was she who reached over to touch his arm.

When they emerged from the hotel, the drizzle that had been coming down all morning had stopped, and there was even a hint of the sun coming through. The doorman, in his Beefeater costume, signaled for a cab.

'May I drop you off?' Mayer asked. 'We're going in the same general direction. I'm staying at the Savoy.'

'I've got to go to Harrods first. I want to get some steaks at their fabulous meat department.'

'I'll walk you. It's only five or six blocks.'

She hesitated. And then agreed.

The taxi that had pulled up had not done so in vain. The two Middle Eastern types had emerged just behind Paul Mayer and Sally Brown. One of them, the woman, took the taxi. The man tipped the doorman, and stayed behind, looking at his watch as if wondering how to kill a little time before the next appointment. As his lunch partner's taxi disappeared around the corner, he appeared to have decided to take a short stroll through Knightsbridge. He stayed about half a block behind the American pair.

*

When Mayer got back to the Savoy after dropping Sally Brown off at the *Journal*'s London office, he immediately called Bank of America's main office in London and got through to George Pace after a very short delay. After reporting the essence of his conversation over lunch, he repeated Sally Brown's suggestion. She had been right. B of A did a lot of business with Drexel Burnham and George Pace knew the head of the firm reasonably well. Pace said he would call him first thing the next morning.

'I'd do it now if I were you,' Mayer said.

'Why?'

'Then I can get back to the lady at the *Journal* this afternoon – before she files her story. If it's bad news I would rather *we* tell her about it.'

'It's 8.00 in the evening in New York,' Pace said. Then: 'You are right as usual, Paul. I'll track him down. Stay put for the next hour.'

Pace called him back forty-five minutes later.

'I got him at home in Greenwich. He gave me his absolute assurance that Drexel Burnham are not involved with Miller or anybody else in financing a takeover bid for the bank.'

'Do you believe it?'

'Yes.'

'One other thing. Have you got any problems with your standby letters of credit?'

'Fifty million.'

'That's all?'

'That's all.'

'I believe it.'

When Paul Mayer called Sally Brown she believed it too.

'Which leaves us with the rumors, but no known source of them,' she then said.

'No source, and, as I hope I was able to demonstrate, also no substance,' Mayer replied.

'I agree.'

'Will your story reflect that?'

'It will. If they print it.'

'If they do print it, when will that be?'

'Tomorrow morning.'

'Thanks. Enjoy the steaks.'

He had not been invited to share them, which bugged him more than a little bit.

Mayer decided to gamble on the story appearing in the *Journal*. If it did, London's *Financial Times* would pick up on it, and the net effect would be exactly that calming of the European waters both he and George Pace had been seeking to achieve. So there was no use in making the rounds of the European banks. To do so would amount to 'protesting too much', as the British put it. He'd get a morning flight to Washington and report back to Bob Reston over the weekend as had been originally planned. He had the computer printouts necessary to calm those waters also. The net result would be that he had accomplished his initial mission for the Federal Reserve in record time.

But Mayer was still left with two nagging questions: Who was circulating the rumors? And why?

He came closer, much closer than he could even suspect, to the 'who' the following morning.

Mayer was one of the last passengers to board the Washington-bound Pan Am 747 the next morning. He had been assigned seat 6a in the first-class section. When he was settled in, the first thing he did was frantically to page through the European edition of *The Wall Street Journal* which he had picked up on the run at the airport kiosk.

It was there on page three, second column at the top.

It was perfect! He read it a second, then a third time to make sure. It was still perfect. Sally Brown had come through!

Thus the 747 had already left the dock, headed for Number 2

runway at Heathrow, before Mayer even took notice of the last passenger to board the plane, a woman who had been seated next to him in 6b and had remained buried behind the morning's edition of the *Herald Tribune* ever since.

She was a beautiful and well-endowed woman of dusky Middle Eastern complexion.

PART II

Chapter 7

By the time Paul Mayer was over the Atlantic, it was well past noon in Moscow and Vladimir Dolgikh was at his favourite lunch venue and already into his second vodka.

The Yama Café, which is just up Pushkinskaya Street from the Bolshoi, and thus only about five blocks from Dolgikh's Ministry of Industry and Commerce, does not just have propinquity going for it. In a city known for its grim bars, where one is forced to stand at small, chest-high, grimy tables ankle deep in breadcrumbs and spilt liquids, and its equally grim restaurants, smelling eternally of cabbage, where one is served gray, tasteless food by sullen waiters in stained aprons, the Yama stands out like an oasis in the Gobi desert.

It is situated in the basement of an ancient house which had been the headquarters of the French Marshal Murat when Napoleon's troops had occupied Moscow in 1812. When you descend the steps from Pushkinskaya Street you find yourself among a series of small, intimate, interconnected rooms, exquisitely restored. Westerners who stumble onto the Yama after spending weeks fruitlessly searching for a decent place to eat and drink invariably spend the rest of the day or night there. It is as if they have miraculously found haven in a Moscow equivalent of that London pub or that Paris brasserie they now sorely regret having left behind. To the Eastern European of some cultivation, the Yama resembles those ancient cellar cafés that you find in the old Baltic cities of Riga and Vilnius or further south on the Danube in Budapest.

Vladimir Dolgikh lunched there three times a week. It was a place where he could either mull over things past in alcoholic solitude, or plot things future with his cronies from the Ministry. As a candidate member of the Politburo, he could and did demand both privacy and privilege at the Yama. The table at the very rear was always held for him; his bottle of Stolichnaya was always in the freezer, was always full, and was always free. But in addition to being accorded privilege, Dolgikh was also accorded respect. For unlike so many of his counterparts who were among the power élite who ruled the Soviet Union, Dolgikh never showed up in a limousine, and he was never in the company of anybody from the KGB.

On top of that, Dolgikh was a likeable man. He was short, stocky, and his hair seemed out of control most of the time. He dressed in a rather scruffy manner, and told bad, often dirty jokes in a loud voice after he had downed a few shots. Once a month – always on a Friday afternoon – he met there with a very pleasant-looking, though somewhat plump, girl. One of the other regulars at the Yama claimed that she was in the typing pool at the Kremlin. It was assumed that after drinks Dolgikh took her to his dacha and screwed her blind. No one at the Yama thought ill of him for that. Quite the contrary. It showed that he was a *Mensch*.

On this Friday, December 9th, 1988, Dolgikh was not feeling very much like a *Mensch*. He was alone and he was also worried. His thought processes were rapidly switching back and forth between mulling and planning.

The mulling related to the written report he had submitted to his boss, Nikolai Ryzhkov, immediately following his return to Moscow from Zurich. Ryzhkov, Prime Minister, crony of General Secretary Gorbachev, and economic czar of the Soviet Union did not abide either fools or mistakes. Would Dolgikh's report mark him as a fool? Had he correctly interpreted what the finance minister of Venezuela was proposing to do? If so, should it be taken seriously? If the answer to that last question was yes, it raised yet another: why had they – the Venezuelan and the Swiss banker – insisted on telling the Soviets?

The planning related to what he would recommend to Ryzhkov at the two o'clock meeting that his boss had requested. If just the Venezuelan had been involved, coming up with a recommendation would have been easy. Ignore him. He's just another nut from Latin America. But the truth was that if just the Venezuelan had been involved, Ryzhkov, and *his* boss, Gorbachev, would hardly have sent him to Zurich in the first place.

It was the involvement of the Swiss, especially the Swiss National Bank, that had tipped the scale. For it was that same Zurich bank which had put together a syndicated Swiss franc loan for the Soviet Union in 1984, the first major financing the Russians had gotten from Switzerland since the revolution. In the four subsequent years, the Swiss National had developed into one of their lead banks in the West, providing directly or indirectly well over $5 billion. A good portion of that financing had been used to purchase oil-drilling equipment, equipment which was essential if the Soviet Union was to be able to continue to develop sorely-needed new energy sources.

When the invitation had come in to their Ministry from the Swiss National Bank, it had stated that matters would be discussed which involved both oil and gold. The Swiss knew that when oil and gold were involved, so were key national interests of the Soviet Union. For it was oil and gold, but especially oil exports to the West, which made the Soviet Union creditworthy. The Swiss had not said it *that* bluntly, but the definite implication had been there. For the Swiss National Bank, like all Swiss banks, demanded collateral. Where sovereign loans were concerned, the good faith and credit of the nation involved were not enough. What they wanted to see was whether a nation had sufficient hard currency earnings to pay back any loan they might provide, to pay back such loans in full, on time, with interest, and in Swiss francs. If something started to happen to the value of that collateral, no more money. It was a vicious circle: if something happened to the oil income of the Soviet Union, no new hard currency credits; if no new credits, then no new drilling equipment; if no new drilling equipment, then no new oil fields, meaning that as the older producing fields were depleted, as was rapidly becoming the case, the Soviet Union would earn less and less from its oil exports. And its standard of living would continue to stagnate . . . at best.

So Ryzhkov had sent Dolgikh to Zurich 'to go along with the Swiss'.

'It is not,' his boss had stated, 'because of any interest whatsoever in the Venezuelan or in anything the Venezuelan might possibly propose.'

Ryzhkov's opinion of Venezuelans had been made clear. 'They are greedy, unprincipled, conniving capitalist bastards who would betray anybody for a profit,' he had said.

Maybe. But could one afford still to ignore the Venezuelan after having heard what he had said in Zurich? If he *could* be taken seriously – one was back to that again – what he proposed to do would certainly affect the future price of both oil and gold in a major way. But more, much more than that was involved. If either one of the Venezuelan's alternative plans were implemented, it could – no, in Dolgikh's opinion, it inevitably *would* – change the global position of the Soviet Union:

— for the worse, if the Venezuelan's Plan 1 were implemented.

— for the better, and *much* for the better, if Venezuela, and then Mexico and then Brazil and then probably the rest of them, went for the alternative Plan 2.

He had said just that in his report to Nikolai Ryzhkov. What bothered Vladimir Dolgikh as he finished off his second vodka, however, was this: If all that the Venezuelan had said turned out to be nothing more than the babbling of a psychopath, would he, Dolgikh, have blown any future possibility of gaining full membership in the Politburo? Or worse?

He looked at his Rolex watch – the manager of Vneshtorgbank in Zurich who had chauffered him around had insisted he take it as a souvenir – and decided to have one more Stoli for the road.

At two o'clock to the second, Vladimir Dolgikh walked into the ante-room of the office of the Prime Minister, Nikolai Ryzhkov. As the man responsible for three key sectors of the Soviet economy, energy and mining and metalurgy, Dolgikh appeared at Ryzhkov's suite of offices in the gray building on the Novaya Plashed often. In spite of his position, however, he was often kept waiting . . . sometimes for hours.

Not on this Friday, December 9th, 1988.

In fact, he had barely arrived when Ryzhkov burst out of his office. He was a wiry man of fifty-five, a serious man who reminded many of a younger Andropov. He was an intellectually impatient man. He hated long-winded people and, as if to set an example, had a tendency to speak in short sentences.

'Keep your overcoat on, Vladimir,' he commanded, 'I have a car waiting. Mikhail Gorbachev is expecting us in his office at 2.15.'

Thank God for the two vodkas, was Dolgikh's initial thought. And thank God, also, that vodka is odorless. Mikhail Gorbachev was a fanatic in his disapproval of the use of alcohol. As Ryzhkov donned his coat with the help of an assistant, Dolgikh asked: 'Has he seen my report?'

'No. Let's go.'

Dolgikh, knowing his boss, decided to shut up.

There are two principal ways of getting into the Kremlin. One entrance is through the Troitskaya Gate, off Karl Marx

Prospekt, and it is for the tourists, and although there are armed Soviet military at the gate, they tend to stay in the background. The reason for their nonchalance is that this section of the Kremlin is reserved for tourists and is hermetically sealed off from the rest of the huge compound. When, after coming up a walk through immaculately tended gardens, a visitor enters the building complex itself and is asked to take off his shoes, the whole place takes on an unexpected old-world quaintness. For it is in stockinged feet, or in the thick brown felt slippers that are available, that one pads through the rooms which house the Czarist treasures of old. One is amidst old men, young mothers, children, rich Germans, Soviet peasants in their Sunday clothes, all of whom are also in stockinged feet or wearing the same thick brown felt slippers. To that feeling of quaintness is soon added a realization of the historical and cultural richness of this capital of the Russian people as one walks through the rooms which once housed the court of Catherine the Great. One cannot help but be impressed by the babble of languages that surrounds one, including not only the many dialects of the Asian provinces which number among the 'Socialist states' of the Soviet 'Union', but also Chinese and Spanish and English and Zulu. The Kremlin, in 1988, was a Mecca to a remarkably large percentage of the peoples of the world.

But not because of its quaintness or its cultural past. The source of the magnetism that attracts such a diverse multitude to the heart of Moscow lies in the power, the absolute power, that is resident in the other part of the Kremlin, sealed off, and accessible only through the Spasskaya Gate which faces Red Square. At this entrance, the Soviet military is out in force and very visible. There is no foot traffic here; just military vehicles and black limousines like the one that bore Nikolai Ryzhkov and Vladimir Dolgikh on that winter afternoon in December of 1988. The snow flurries had started again, but neither man noticed them. Both were deep in thought as they arrived at the Kremlin gate.

The guards, in thick gray coats with the blue insignia of the Kremlin élite, obviously had instructions from on high: their Chaika limo was waved through before it had even come to a full stop.

The 'working section' of the Kremlin is a strange mixture of the ancient and the modern. The Congress Hall, all glass and steel, stands in stark contrast and right next to one of the oldest and certainly one of the most ornate buildings in the walled compound, the one containing Gorbachev's offices. Lenin and Stalin, Khrushchev and Brezhnev, Andropov and Chernenkov had all ruled the Soviet Union from the same suite of rooms on the third floor.

The late twentieth-century style of Gorbachev – which many have said more resembles that of a Wall Street attorney than a Slavic potentate – stood in equally stark contrast to the seventeenth-century artifacts which graced the ante-room to his personal office. The two visitors were greeted by one of his assistants and immediately ushered into the inner sanctum. The room was lined with blue silk wall coverings. On the wall behind the Chairman's desk hung portraits of Marx and Lenin. Gorbachev, impeccably dressed in a blue pinstripe suit, diagonally striped tie and white shirt, came out from behind it and shook hands first with Ryzhkov, then with Dolgikh. He motioned for them to join him at a coffee table in the middle of the huge room.

'Comrade Ryzhkov has told me about your trip to Zurich, Vladimir,' he said to Dolgikh. 'Please summarize what happened there . . . in as few words as possible, please.'

His two visitors listened with enormous intensity since Gorbachev had the habit of speaking in a deep, soft, near whisper.

'I will try, Mikhail.'

On the surface there has always been an easy informality among the Politburo members, and all, including the current *primus inter pares* Chairman Gorbachev, use the first name with each other.

Dolgikh removed a sheaf of notes from his briefcase.

'Leave the notes be,' Gorbachev commanded. The whisper had suddenly disappeared and had been replaced by a sharp, cutting tone.

Dolgikh put them back.

'On Tuesday of this week,' he began, 'I met with the oil minister of Venezuela. We met in the offices of the Swiss National Bank in Zurich. The invitation for the meeting had come from the head of that bank, Dr Ulrich Huber.

'The Venezuelan's name is Roberto Martinez. He explained that the financial situation of Venezuela has become impossible. Their foreign income is based almost solely on their export of oil. Without that income, they can no longer pay for the imports which their population needs, and demands. On top of that, they now owe $45 billion to the Americans, and the Americans demand that they pay the interest on that debt before anything else.'

'I'm aware of all this,' Gorbachev said. 'Get to the substance.'

'The substance is: They now propose to do something about it.'

' "It" being what?' Gorbachev asked. 'The oil price or the debt to the Americans?'

'Both,' answered Dolgikh.

'Go on,' said Gorbachev.

'Where oil is concerned, they and Mexico, in consort, propose to do one of two things: *Either* produce to absolutely full capacity to get the fullest possible income quickly, regardless of what happens to the oil price —'

'Meaning the end of OPEC,' interjected Ryzhkov, 'and probably meaning a price as low as $6 to $8 a barrel as compared to the $16.50 we are still getting now.'

'Or,' continued Dolgikh, 'they would seek to blackmail the United States into establishing a floor price for petroleum at a minimum of $20 a barrel and keep production where it is.'

'How could the United States do that?'

'By contracting for hundreds of millions of barrels for their strategic reserve at that $20 price. The legal framework for that reserve has been in place for many years, and it is only half full according to the Venezuelan. So only executive action, by the President, would be required for the United States to resume buying oil on a very large scale.'

Gorbachev thought that one over. 'Would it work?' he then asked.

'Probably. The Americans have taken similar actions in the past. Their government at times has accumulated huge stockpiles of silver or zinc or copper to support the price and placate domestic producers. And it worked. For instance, by buying in two billion ounces of silver the United States' government kept the silver price at $1.29 an ounce for decades, in spite of a world-wide glut of the metal.'

'They said such stockpiling is necessary in case of a national emergency, to placate the voters,' added Ryzhkov.

Gorbachev looked skeptical.

'That might have worked in the 1950s for silver, but we're talking 1989 and oil. The United States cannot single-handedly mop up all the oil everybody in the rest of the world decides to dump on the market.'

'Of course not,' Dolgikh answered, hurriedly. 'It would mean that the Americans would have to lean on their allies – especially the Saudis, Britain and Norway – to reduce their output. And it would require that OPEC would finally have to enforce the output quotas of its own members.'

'And what about us?' Gorbachev asked.

'Clearly that is what part of the meeting in Zurich was about,' answered Dolgikh, the man responsible for the administration of the vast energy resources of the Soviet Union. 'They would want us to cut back on our exports too.'

'Did anybody mention a number?' Gorbachev asked.

'Not specifically. But a general figure of a global 20 percent cutback was mentioned more than once – if an American price-support program was to work.'

'For how long?'

'Again, there were no specifics. If you want my opinion, it would have to be for a long time. Two years at a minimum.'

'That would mean a loss of $20 billion income.'

'At the very least. It would also greatly reduce our credit rating,' Ryzhkov added.

'It would be an economic disaster,' Gorbachev concluded.

The room fell silent.

'What's the alternative?' he then asked.

'The Latin American oil producers would go crazy. They'd pump as much as they can, as fast as they can, and dump it on the spot market.'

'And what would happen to the price?'

'It could be cut in half. Sheikh Yamani tried exactly the same thing back in 1986. He doubled Saudi Arabia's output and the price of oil fell from over $30 a barrel to $10. If the Latin Americans repeated his folly, and halved the price from its present level, we would be down to single digits.'

'And what would that cost us?'

'In the long run? Forty billion dollars, maybe sixty.'

Gorbachev got up from the sofa.

'Goddamn Latin bastards! Castro costs us $3 billion a year. Now these maniacs are going to cost us twenty times that much!'

'They'll cost the United States much more,' said Ryzhkov.

'It depends,' countered Gorbachev, contradicting his fellow Politburo member. 'If they go the "volume" route, Venezuela and Mexico could easily force the world oil price down to $9 a barrel, as you said earlier, Nikolai, and the United States would save tens of billions of dollars on its imports. They would gain, and everybody else would lose.'

He was right. Or almost right.

'The Germans and the Swiss and the French and the

Japanese – they would also win, Mikhail,' said Dolgikh. 'They must buy *all* their oil. It would be the sellers in the Middle East and Africa and – us – who would lose.'

'But *only* under the so-called Plan 1 of the Venezuelans,' said Ryzhkov. '*That* is what I meant, Mikhail.'

Mikhail Gorbachev now began pacing the room.

'So what about their Plan 2 – to go the "price" route?' he asked. 'Is it feasible?'

'It is at best questionable,' answered Dolgikh. 'The so-called Plan 1 can be implemented unilaterally by the Venezuelans and Mexicans. They just have to turn on fully the oil spiggots which they alone control. The other plan, the "price" solution, depends solely on the United States. More specifically, on whether they can be blackmailed into setting that $20 floor.'

'What kind of blackmail?'

'They would threaten to bring down the American banking system unless a deal could be worked out.'

'How?'

'By mobilizing Latin America into open, official default on their loans.'

'Why would Brazil go along with that? Or Argentina? Or Chile? They want to be able to import cheap oil as much as does the United States.'

'They would want to extract their own concessions from the United States.'

'Such as?'

'Exactly what Fidel Castro proposed more than once. A *total* moratorium on all Latin American payments on their debts, including both principal and interest, for twenty years. What they would save on interest would more than make up for a somewhat higher price they would have to pay for oil.'

'And Venezuela and Mexico would make out on *both* interest *and* oil,' added Ryzhkov.

Gorbachev shook his head.

'That's nonsense. Castro knows that as well as I do. In fact, I told him so three years ago. He didn't listen to me and instead organized a conference of Latin American debtor nations in Havana. Nobody came. You know why? Because you simply cannot get people to push the Americans around like that. Why? Because they've got the governments of every nation in Latin America by the financial balls. If they default, the next day the Americans – the government, the banks, the corporations – would cut off their credit and would seize every one of their assets they could get their hands on. That would mean economic disaster. So they'd never risk it because none of them could *afford* to risk it.'

'The Swiss banker does not agree with you, Mikhail,' said Dolgikh.

His two superiors looked at him in surprise. Gorbachev even stopped pacing.

'Really,' he said. 'Now *that's* interesting! Explain.'

Dolgikh did.

When the limousine bearing Vladimir Dolgikh and Nikolai Ryzhkov passed through the Spasskaya Gate to the Kremlin for the second time on that Friday afternoon in December, this time outward-bound, the time was four o'clock in Moscow, and thus it had already been dark for a full hour. Dolgikh, flush with success, did something he had never done before. He suggested to his boss that, in view of the late hour, they might drop by the Yama Café for a drop or two of Stolichnaya instead of going back to the office. To his surprise, Ryzhkov immediately agreed.

What Dolgikh had overlooked was that it was the second Friday of the month, meaning that, as usual, the girl from the Kremlin typing pool was at the Yama waiting for him. When he came down the stairs from Pushkinskaya Street and spotted her at the bar, he was faced with yet another critical decision in a week of seemingly never-ending crises. Should he ignore her, and pass up a fuck in the forest? Or should he risk introducing her to Ryzhkov, who was known as a very strait-laced type?

He opted for dallying at the dacha.

As so often that week, risk-taking paid off. His boss took an immediate liking to Svetlana. And soon the three of them were wedged together behind the table at the very back of the Yama Café, where the only light now came from a single red candle. Dolgikh's cold and free bottle of Stolichnaya, of the 120–proof variety, had been at the table waiting for them. Since, as a result of earlier use that day, it was not full to begin with, the three Russians went through it almost immediately. When Dolgikh went up to the bar to order a second, Svetlana took the opportunity to excuse herself also, and headed for the Ladies.

The reason for her move was that a few minutes earlier Comrade Ryzhkov's right hand had been firmly implanted on her somewhat thick left thigh and, immediately thereafter, had begun steadily to inch its way north. Uncertain as to what privileges should be afforded a *full* member of the Politburo, she decided that a consultation with Dolgikh regarding protocol had become acutely necessary.

So as they both walked toward the front of the Yama Café, she explained what was happening in a hurried whisper. Before Dolgikh had time to reply, Svetlana went on to mention that she had a girl friend in the Kremlin typing pool who was probably still at work, but who was also probably available to join the party and thus make it a more wholesome foursome. Dolgikh leapt at the idea. As sweet and willing as Svetlana was, a little variety could hardly hurt. He told her to make the phone call. It worked. So the two of them ran up the stairs to Pushkinskaya Street where he put her into the waiting limo and gave the driver instructions.

When Dolgikh returned to the table at the back of the Yama Café with a new bottle of Stoli, but *sans* Svetlana, he immediately explained what he had arranged. Dolgikh concluded with the suggestion that they might consider moving on to his dacha after the girls returned. His boss actually clapped his hands with pleasure.

You never know about the quiet ones, was Dolgikh's silent comment, and I thought he was all business.

As if reading Dolgikh's mind, Nikolai Ryzhkov leaned over and said: 'Before they return, Vladimir, I should mention one thing which I think is pertinent: a few days ago I also discussed the Zurich matter with Viktor Chebrikov.'

That sent a chill through Dolgikh. Viktor Chebrikov was the head of the KGB.

'He called me this morning,' Ryzhkov continued. 'Apparently your Venezuelan also met with the terrorist, Carlos, in Switzerland. We don't know what the connection is, but Chebrikov is sure there is one. He also is sure that before this affair is over, somebody is bound to end up dead.'

'But why didn't you mention this to Comrade Gorbachev?'

'I didn't think it was necessary.'

When Ryzhkov saw the worried look on Dolgikh's face, he immediately put an arm around him. 'Not to worry, Vladimir. Viktor Chebrikov knows how to take care of things like this.'

A red light went on in Dolgikh's head. Events had moved into the danger zone, into the area of mixed loyalties. The problem had never been resolved in the Soviet Union. One line of loyalty went straight up through party lines to the General Secretary. The other, and *never* in a straight line, led through a labyrinth of intrigue to the head of the KGB. He knew that those loyal to Viktor Chebrikov were only one vote short of a majority in the Politburo. Perhaps they, the hardliners, were in the process of mounting a challenge to Gorbachev's leadership. Perhaps the man beside him, the Prime Minister, might in the end exercise the swing vote. And if they lost, maybe his neck, Dolgikh's neck, would be in a sling by virtue of guilt by association.

Dolgikh was neither party nor KGB. He was a bureaucrat,

pure and simple. He still had only a four-room apartment, and no limousine had ever been assigned to him. After being sent to Zurich, he had thought that maybe he was finally getting close to the brass ring and all the privileges he still lacked. But if it meant getting involved in an internecine struggle, it was definitely not worth the risk.

Dolgikh had heard from a friend in the Foreign Ministry that a minor diplomatic post abroad would be opening up in January: Ambassador to Ceylon. His wife would like the warm weather, and he was sure there would be servants. He wouldn't say a word about it to Ryzhkov. But tomorrow morning, he would put in his bid.

Chapter 8

By this time Paul Mayer was just an hour out of Dulles airport on the Pan Am 747, and was basking in a happy glow as he thought back on what was turning out to be a hell of a week. It looked as if, with the help of *The Wall Street Journal*, he had been able to turn around the Bank of America situation before it had even approached the crisis stage.

It also appeared as if he had lucked it out as seldom before on an airplane. His seatmate was all that he had remembered and more: the flowing black hair, her dusky complexion, and the fullness of the contours that were so apparent beneath her white blouse.

So he did something that he had seldom done before on a plane: he tried to start a conversation with a stranger. 'Please excuse me,' he said to her, 'but weren't we seated at adjoining tables at lunch yesterday?'

She turned fully toward him but seemed not quite sure what to do.

'It was in the Rib Room of the Carlton Tower,' Mayer added quickly.

From his embarrassed expression it was apparent that he already regretted having said a word. But then, as if out of sympathy for the awkward man next to her, the lady in the white blouse and black skirt finally said something.

'Yes, I do remember.' Her English was of the boarding school variety; her accent no doubt Levantine, he thought.

Then she added: 'You were with a very beautiful woman.'

The implication was made that the woman must have been his wife. The further implication, Mayer sensed, was that, as a married man, he should know better than to try to chat up a woman on a plane.

So Mayer fell silent. At fifty-two he was still not very adept at dealing with the opposite sex. He had been married once, at the age of thirty, to a German girl. He had met her at the university in Switzerland, and they had both received their doctorates in economics the same year. She was tall and bony, but her intellect, her skill at conversation, her intensity, her energy, more than compensated for that. At least that is what they had all said. In fact, everyone in the university circle in Basel had also said that they were a perfect match. So they married. It took him two years to discover that she was more interested in her intellectual pursuits than in him. She had no interest in children, and barely any in sex. Worst of all, she was totally incapable of ever being happy. So they had parted. She had gone back to Germany to teach economics at Tübingen. He had remained in Switzerland, where he had been so busy working himself up the organizational ladder at the Swiss National Bank that he never became involved in any serious fashion with another woman. By the time he had moved on to the International Monetary Fund in Washington, Paul Mayer had essentially reverted to reasonably content bachelorhood. But hardly celibacy. In fact, his thoughts had moved in quite the opposite direction: at 40,000 feet above the Atlantic ocean there were definite stirrings of lust in his heart. And loins. So he plunged on.

'That woman I was with . . . she's a reporter with *The Wall Street Journal*. I just met her, actually. This has just been a quick trip over and back.'

The dusky woman at his right, apparently noticing that his awkwardness was real, seemed to decide that he was not a latter-day lounge lizard after all.

'So you live in Washington?' she asked.

'Yes. I teach there. At Georgetown. And you?'

'San Francisco. Before that London. And before that, Teheran.'

'Ah, so you are Iranian.'

'Yes. I left there in 1979. My husband sent me to London.'

'And do you and your husband ever go back?'

'They killed my husband. He was on the staff of General Khatami. They killed both of them.'

'I'm sorry,' he said.

'I have been back, yes. My mother lives in Teheran. And my two brothers and my sister.'

A stewardess interrupted them, asking about drinks. To his surprise she ordered a gin and tonic. He went for a martini. When they arrived, he decided it was time to break the ice even further.

'My name's Paul Mayer,' he said.

'And my name is Azar. Azar Shahani.' She raised her glass to his, and smiled for the first time.

'Azar,' he repeated.

'It means "fire". It's a common name in Iran. In our tradition, fire is a symbol of purity.'

Now it was her turn to show embarrassment.

'That does not sound right in English, does it?' she added.

He grinned. 'And Shahani?'

'It means "Kinglike".'

Which explained her clothes, her manners, her impeccable English.

'I'm afraid that neither "Paul" nor "Mayer" can compete with names like that.'

'But your name sounds familiar,' she said. 'Why?'

'Perhaps because of my former position.'

'Which was?'

'I headed the International Monetary Fund for a number of years.'

'Of course. But then you must know Iran.'

'Not well, but yes, I've been there a number of times. And I got to know your former Ambassador to the United States, Ardeshir Zahedi, very well. A very charming man. I was apparently on the 'A' invitation list for his famous dinner parties. If I was in Washington I usually went, since I admit I love both caviar and champagne and Zahedi always had lots of both.'

She looked at him very carefully. 'My husband and I were at one of those parties in 1977. When the Shah visited the United States. It was in May. But I am sure you were not there then. I would have remembered.'

He liked that, but said nothing.

'But you are no longer a banker?' she continued.

'No. Now I teach.'

'But why?'

'Why the change?'

'Yes. You must have been a very powerful man.'

'I was. But then I had enough of that world.'

'But don't you miss all the trappings?' she asked, then adding, 'I'm sure everybody asks you the same question. I'm sorry.'

'Don't be. They all do, and I always answer: Not yet. After all, I've only been at the university for one semester now.'

Then he reflected for a minute. 'But now that you've brought it up again, I think I will have to change that answer. Yes I do miss the limousines, the suites, the invitations, and especially, and I hate to admit it, the planes that are always at one's disposal. So I'm in the process of putting one oar back into those waters. Which, by the way, will bring me to San Francisco very soon.'

If she noted the implications of that last sentence, she certainly didn't give on. Perhaps it was because the stewardess appeared at that moment with the dinner menus.

The conversation between the two never lagged from that point on. After they landed at Dulles, it seemed natural that they also sit beside each other on the bus that took them from the plane to the terminal. As they waited at the baggage carousel she told him that she would only be in Washington for a day and would then be returning to San Francisco.

So she *had* taken note.

'Perhaps we could have dinner there next week?' Mayer asked.

'I'd love to,' she responded.

'Which are your favorite restaurants in San Francisco?'

'Trader Vic's. Stars. L' Etoile.' She'd obviously been asked that question before.

'In that order?'

'Not at all. I like all three very much.'

'Trader Vic's, then. I will arrange it.' He paused, because it seemed like an awkward thing to do, but he had no choice. 'Would you mind if I asked you for your telephone number?' He actually turned a bit red.

'You are a very nice man,' she said, and reached over to touch his hand.

Now he really looked uncomfortable.

She extracted a business card from her purse and handed it to him. It read: Azar Shahani, Boutique, 121 Main Street, Tiburon, California.

'That's my little store in Marin County,' she said. 'I specialize in French and German fashions. I was thinking of opening up a store in London too. That's why I took this trip. But now I'm not sure.'

She then took out a pen, and, after retrieving her card, wrote a phone number on the back. 'That's my home number. I live in Belvedere, which is the island right next to Tiburon.'

'I know it,' he said, and added, 'Thank you, Azar.'

'You're welcome, Paul.'

And then the baggage started coming in. Her bag was first, and a few minutes later she disappeared.

A BMW was waiting outside for her. It contained three men:

one was Iranian, one was a Palestinian, and one was German, the driver. All were in their early thirties. When the Palestinian opened the boot, he had difficulty finding room for her suitcase. The reason was that it was a small boot and it already contained an Uzi submachine gun.

She took her place in the front of the BMW and, as the car pulled away, the driver, the German, a blond, chunky, brutal-looking man, looked at her and spoke.

'How did it go?'

'He remembered seeing me before,' she answered.

'So you blew it.'

'Quite the opposite,' she replied, and there was ice in her voice. 'I don't "blow" things.'

They had to stop at a booth to pay the airport parking toll.

'Now do you want to know what happened or not?' she continued when the BMW started moving again.

The German gave her a look that could have come out of the barrel of the Uzi in the boot. But he remained silent.

'In fact, it went perfectly. I sat beside him all the way from London. As I said, he remembered me. We had sat at adjoining tables in a restaurant in London yesterday. He thought it was pure coincidence. The man has no idea whatsoever that we've been on him ever since he checked into the Savoy.'

One of the night clerks at the Savoy was also an Iranian.

'The net result,' she continued, 'is that during the past eight hours I got most of his life's story – past, present and future. He'll be meeting the Chairman of Bank of America, George Pace, at the bank's headquarters in San Francisco next week. We will be seeing each other for dinner.'

'He must have taken a liking to you,' the German said. 'Perhaps love at first sight, huh?'

She didn't even look at him.

Then, from the small dark Arab in the back seat: 'Who was in charge over there?'

'Ahmed.' The way she said the name made it obvious what she thought about the swarthy Libyan who had taken her to lunch at the Carlton Tower, and then tailed Paul Mayer during the rest of the day.

'How did you manage to sit beside him on the plane?'

'When Mayer changed his airline reservation, he did so through the travel desk at the Savoy, with Ahmed watching. Your man at the front desk there – I never met him – got the details, and after that it was easy.'

'It was very fortunate that you were in London, Azar,' said the other man in the back seat, the Iranian.

'For you people, yes.'

The car once again fell silent.

'So tell us precisely what happened,' the German then demanded, 'and talk into this tape recorder while you do.'

He reached over to pull a small Sony out of the glove compartment and gave it to her. She didn't seem to know quite what to do with it.

'Push the red button, *Schätzchen*, and get started,' he said.

Still without looking at him, she began. She spoke in a monotone voice for forty minutes. Just as she finished, they pulled up in front of the Four Seasons Hotel on the edge of Georgetown. She handed the German his tape recorder, he turned it off, and stuck it in his coat pocket.

'You're booked here for the night, and on a 9 a.m. United flight to San Francisco tomorrow,' the German said.

'What am I supposed to do next?'

'We'll let you know,' he replied. 'Now get out.'

It was he who waved off the doorman before retrieving Azar Shahani's suitcase from the boot. The German was then handed a briefcase from the back seat of the BMW. He placed it beside Azar's suitcase and without any further words left her standing there, got behind the wheel of the BMW, and pulled out into the Georgetown rush-hour traffic.

Ten minutes later, after tipping the bellhop and locking the door of her room, she opened the briefcase. It contained her airplane ticket to San Francisco. And $20,000 in hundred dollar bills.

What a nightmare this was turning out to be! If only she had not gone back to Iran in 1981. But it had been the only way to find out if, and how, she could get her mother out. They were onto her the moment she had stepped off the plane in Teheran. And they had their proposal ready: be our eyes and ears, help us if we need help, and, in time, your mother will get an exit permit. The *mullahs* knew how to do it. They knew how sacred family is to all Iranians. So they had known that she would do anything, literally anything, for her mother.

After holding her for two days, and after insisting that she take off her Western clothes and put on a black *chador* and cover her face, they had finally let her go home, to her real home in North Teheran. A month later they had also let her leave Iran. But they had never let go of her.

Early that evening the phone rang at the luxurious Georgetown digs of José Martinez, Jr. He was there, waiting, in a totally exhausted state. For it had been a tough day by young Martinez's standards.

Even before the crack of dawn, his uncle had called him, this time from Madrid. He had delivered a very cryptic two sentence message: First, José, Jr was to be at his phone at 7.00 that evening without fail.

Second, he was then to do what he would be told to do at that time, also without fail.

That sort of ordering around really got him pissed off. So much so, in fact, that he couldn't get back to sleep. Which, as it turned out, had had its plus side. His mid-term in International Finance had been scheduled for two o'clock that afternoon, and, since he couldn't sleep anyway, contrary to usual practice, he had spent the entire morning boning up. This had subsequently turned out to be a brilliant move. Professor Mayer had not turned up for the exam, and, instead, his TA had been in charge. That meant that cheating was out since the little prick really took his job seriously. But thanks to his uncle's phone call, José, Jr was sure he had done well despite such a serious handicap.

However, the strain of taking an exam on his own had totally drained him, so after finally handing in his blue book to the little prick he had left the warm confines of the Intercultural Center, and, facing the biting December wind which had begun blowing off the Potomac, had staggered across campus, bound for the Tombs. By the time he had reached that safe haven, his Latin blood had begun to coagulate. It took a couple of straight shots of Bourbon, with beer chasers, to revive him.

Soon his pals, the boys from Brazil and Mexico and Venezuela, began to straggle in and join him at the large round table in the rear of the Tombs. They all came from the same mid-term exam. They were all depressed, having been victimized by that little prick of a TA who had maintained a relentless vigil. In the end, they had had no choice but to hand in their nearly blank blue books. A month later the grades would be sent to their fathers in São Paulo, Mexico City and Caracas and, once more, their allowances would be cut, and they would sink into poverty and despair.

It was, they agreed, a hostile fucking Yankee world out there.

So collectively they geared up for a night of sorrow-drowning and commiseration. It came as a shock, therefore, when, of all people, José Martinez, Jr looked at his watch at 6.45 and announced that he was leaving. He had been acting suspiciously anyway. When, earlier, he had gone to the bar to order another round, someone had suggested that it was because he had studied for the exam and probably passed it. But this was dismissed as malicious slander.

In any case, José Martinez, Jr was at home when, at 7.01 p.m., his phone rang. When he picked it up a voice asked: 'Is that José Martinez?' The man used the hard pronunciation of the 'J', the dumb fuck.

Overlooking this, José, Jr answered 'Yes' in what he thought was a bored and sophisticated fashion.

'Did your uncle speak to you?'

'He did.'

'So you know what you are supposed to do.'

He wasn't asking, he was telling, which started to get José, Jr steamed up once again.

'I'm supposed to do what you ask me to do,' he replied, adding 'sir' a couple of seconds later to let the guy know what he thought of him.

The dumb fuck at the other end didn't notice a thing.

'You know where Professor Paul Mayer lives?'

'I do.'

'Where?'

'On Dent Place in Georgetown.'

'What?'

'Dent Place. D–E–N–T.' He spelled it out in a loud voice. 'Got it?'

'Where's that?'

Jeezuz!

'In Georgetown like I already said.'

'Where in Georgetown?'

Now the voice at the other end had become menacing.

'Between Wisconsin Avenue and the Georgetown University campus. More or less.'

'I want you to show me.'

'Whatever you say.'

'Where can we meet in, say, thirty minutes.'

José came up with a brilliant idea.

'The Tombs?'

Which produced silence at the other end.

'Tombs? You mean a graveyard?'

José giggled. What a dumb, dumb fuck!

'No. It's a restaurant. It's only about six or seven blocks from where Professor Mayer lives. Where are you?'

'Assume I'm at Du Pont Circle.'

'From there it's real easy.'

Martinez, Jr, then explained exactly where the Tombs was, and how to get there. He said that he would be waiting at the bar, smoking a cigar. Then he put his overcoat on, and plunged back out into the bitter cold.

The boys were still at the Tombs, and the noise level at their table in the back reflected their much improved spirits. When they spotted José, a collective cheer rose from their midst.

'Sit down!' they yelled, as he approached their *Stammtisch*.

'I can't,' he replied. 'I'm here on business.'

That brought the house down.

'I'm not kidding you,' José assured them, and added when the noise died down a bit, 'in fact, I might need some help from you guys.' He had no idea why or how, but what the hell: they would eat it up!

And they did. For collectively they smelled money, which they all knew they would desperately need once their grades reached home. It happened every year.

'What kind of business?' asked one of the boys from Brazil.

'Surveillance,' José answered.

That shut them all up.

Taking advantage of the awe which he had just created among his compatriots from south of many borders, José Martinez, Jr headed toward the bar of the Tombs, and took a stool at the far end against the wall. He ordered a Margarita, and lit up a small Cuban cigar. He was ready.

At eight o'clock this great big blond guy wearing a fur coat, for God's sake, walked into the Tombs as if he had just bought the place. He was in his early thirties, he had a scar on his left cheek, and he looked like one mean son of a bitch!

José, Jr instinctively knew that this was his man. So he waved his Cuban cigar at him. The guy noticed immediately and came over.

'I believe we just talked on the phone,' the big blond guy with the scar said.

'Yes we did, sir,' and this time he meant the 'sir' bit.

'Do you have a car?'

'Yes, sir, I do.'

'Here?'

'No, sir. It's in the garage at the place where I live.'

'Get it.'

'Now?'

'Now!'

José Martinez got up and left without a further word. The big guy who had been talking to him took off his fur coat, sat down on the bar stool José had just vacated, and, rather brusquely, ordered a double brandy. The bartender came back with it in record time.

The Latin crowd at the rear of the Tombs, watching every move, loved it. 'That fucking Martinez wasn't shitting us,' one of them whispered, and all nodded in agreement.

Fifteen minutes later José, Jr returned. The moment the big blond guy at the bar saw him coming down the stairs into the Tombs, he tossed some bills on the bar, put on his fur coat, went up to José, and, grabbing his arm, turned him back in the direction from which he had come. Together they disappeared back up the stairs.

Ten minutes later, José Martinez, Jr, of Caracas, Venezuela, and Joachim Schmidt of Frankfurt, West Germany were parked on the corner of Dent Place and 35th Street in the young student's red Mazda. From their vantage point they had a clear and full view of the narrow house that bore the number 3514.

'That's his house,' Martinez said, pointing at it once he had turned off the ignition.

'Good,' said the man from the Red Army Faction. 'Now find out if he's there.'

'How?'

'Go look.'

José, Jr got out of the Mazda and strolled up the street. The lights were on at 3514, both downstairs and upstairs. He turned back toward 35th Street. There was a phone booth at the intersection, so José approached it, entered it, picked up the phone, and, faking a conversation, just stood there talking to himself and watching.

He stood there for ten minutes, then fifteen, then twenty. A number of people walked by in both directions. Nobody took any notice of him whatsoever since students in phone booths in Georgetown at all hours of the day and night could not have been more commonplace. Then he got a break. A delivery van from the French deli on Wisconsin Avenue pulled up in front of 3514 Dent Place. The driver, carrying his package of goodies, mounted the step at that address and pushed the buzzer. But it was a girl in a maid's uniform, not Mayer, who opened the door. She took the package, obviously gave the delivery man some money, and that was that.

'Dammit,' said José, Jr.

But he stuck it out, getting colder by the minute. And who should appear five minutes later, lugging a stack of blue books? The little prick! The hawkeyed TA who had destroyed the holiday season for half a dozen Latino students of higher learning who were now drowning their sorrows just seven blocks away. Again the maid opened the door. But now, as José, Jr watched, Professor Mayer appeared and soon the little prick was handing over their pathetic answers to the five essay questions which had been put to him and his fellow students of International Finance by the financial genius who lived at 3514 Dent Place.

The Professor and his assistant chatted for two or three minutes on the step in front of 3514 Dent Place and then Mayer dismissed the little prick. The door once again closed. The little prick disappeared down P Street. José, Jr hung up the phone and returned to his parked car.

'Professor Mayer's there. I just saw him,' he told the German, who sat huddled in the cold darkness.

'Who was the second guy?'

José explained.

'Good boy. Now here is my number in Washington,' the German said. He handed a small slip of paper to the young Venezuelan. 'When Mayer moves, you follow him. When he gets wherever he's going, you call and tell me where he is. Whoever meets him, anywhere, get the license plate number of his car. That applies to whoever comes here too. Got it?'

'Sure.'

'Burn that phone number after you're sure you remember it.'

'Yes, sir. But one thing. You don't expect me to stay here all night, do you?'

The German thought it over. 'No. If he's still here at ten o'clock, and if nobody else visits him, go home and come back at eight o'clock tomorrow morning. One more thing: have you got a Polaroid?'

'No, sir.'

'Well, get one right away tomorrow morning. And lots of film. Whoever you see with Mayer, try to get a picture of him. Or her.'

'How'm I going to get a camera at eight o'clock in the morning?'

'Have somebody get it for you.'

'What's he going to use for money?'

'Don't worry. I've got something for you.'

He handed Martinez an envelope. 'For expenses. Keep in touch.'

Then the big blond man with the scar and the deep voice left the car and started walking toward Wisconsin Avenue. José, Jr watched him in the Mazda's rear-view mirror until he had disappeared into the December darkness.

José, Jr then turned on the dash lights and opened the envelope. It contained fifty $100 bills.

Ten minutes later a cab pulled up in front of 3514 Dent Place and the maid, now in civilian clothes, came out and took it. Ten minutes after that the lights in Professor Paul Mayer's house went out.

'Fuck it,' said José Martinez, Jr, using his favourite English word yet again. He turned on the ignition, turned up the car's heater to full blast, and took off. The camera store on Wisconsin Avenue was still open. He bought the best Polaroid camera they had to offer, plus half a dozen film packs.

As he drove back toward his apartment, José started thinking about Professor Mayer. Sure, the guy was often way off base in his thinking, but there could be no doubt about him otherwise: Mayer was a class act. That's why he, José Martinez, Jr, had tried so hard to get into his seminar. He'd been surprised when Mayer had accepted him. After all, his grade point average wasn't *that* hot. And since then, despite his inclusion of what even *he* had to admit were some off-the-wall theories on the role the United States *should* be playing in Latin America, Mayer had never given him a grade lower than a B+. Then there was something else about him: everybody knew that Mayer was not only powerful, but also rich as Croesus. Yet he never showed it. Definitely a class act.

Then he thought of his uncle: a sleaze if there ever was one. What was most sickening about him was his Latin lover act. Everybody in Caracas knew that Uncle Roberto chased after every loose skirt in town, the younger the better, and everybody looked the other way because of his being such a big man. José, Jr's mother couldn't stand him.

When José, Jr got back to his apartment, he went straight to bed, and was asleep before his Rolex watch even showed 10.00. But before he had dozed off, his thoughts had continued, now coming closer to the point. What the hell was actually going on here? Why would anybody of the caliber of that fucking Nazi, scar and all, be watching Professor Paul Mayer. And why would his uncle, though admittedly a sleaze-bag, be stooping *so* low as to fool around with a guy like *that*.

And why was he, José Martinez, Jr, going along with all this crap?

Chapter 9

Paul Mayer slept in the next morning. He had learned long ago that sleep was the only cure for the effects of jet lag. But at ten o'clock he was awoken by the rustlings of Maria, downstairs. Then, as he knew would happen, ten minutes later the door to his bedroom was opened ever so slowly and ever so carefully.

'Come in, Maria,' he said.

She did, beaming from ear to ear, and bearing a breakfast tray loaded with everything from waffles to poached eggs.

As she poured his coffee she said, 'Oh, Professor Mayer, it is so nice that you could sleep so long. You looked so tired last night.'

'I feel just fine this morning, Maria. Thank you for your concern. Now tell me, could you possibly come in tomorrow? I know it's Sunday, but . . .?'

'Of course I could.'

'I was just thinking about putting on a lunch. Around one o'clock. There would be four of us. Could you manage that?'

'I would love to.'

She obviously adored the man.

'But first I must see if I can arrange it.'

She left his bedroom reluctantly as he picked up the phone and dialed the home number of the Chairman of the Federal Reserve.

'Bob?'

'Yes,'

'Paul Mayer.'

'So you're back. How'd it go?'

'Very well.'

'I gathered that from yesterday's *Journal*. Did you have anything to do with that?'

'Yes.'

'I thought so. How much of it is true?'

'All of it. That's why I'm calling. I want to lay out the details. I've got all the numbers with me. We had originally planned on meeting at your place this weekend but I'd like to change that, if you agree. How about coming over here instead? For lunch. Tomorrow.'

'Sure. I should warn you about one thing, though.'

Mayer listened.

'Our mutual friend, the Comptroller of the Currency, wants to be there.'

'Figures.'

'Do you want to call him or should I?'

'Why don't you do it, Bob.'

'All right.'

'What about the FDIC?'

'They'll want to be there too. I'll also take care of that. What time?'

'How about 1.00. Do you still remember how to find my place?'

'You're on Dent Place. Dent and 35th. Right?'

'Right. The number's 3514.'

'We'll all be there at 1.00, unless I phone in the meantime.'

'Great.'

Maria, who had been outside the bedroom door listening to the entire conversation, knocked a half minute later.

'Come in,' he said.

'So are they coming?'

'Yes. At 1.00.'

'I shall take care of everything, Professor Mayer. You don't have to worry about one thing.'

'I know.'

'Now, would you like me to bring some hot coffee?'

'Yes. And my briefcase, please.'

When she returned with both she presented them to Mayer with a lingering look that sent a strong tremor through Mayer's body as he lay there below the blankets. After all, upon examination she was in most respects a younger version of the Iranian woman: her complexion was olive, her bosom was ample and, as usual, half visible, and her hair was dark and flowing to her shoulders. And the weather outside was cold and his bed warm and half empty.

He pulled himself together with an enormous effort. 'That will be all, Maria,' he said, and then added, 'for the moment.'

She seemed to sense what was going on in the poor man's mind. As she left she gave him a smile that made him wonder how long he could hold out.

His briefcase contained the copies of the B of A printouts. Mayer knew that after he had presented them to his luncheon guests the next day, the heat would be off Bank of America where the regulatory authorities were concerned. But the numbers would not help resolve what Mayer considered to be the deeper and more important question: who had tried to start a run on the world's second largest bank in the first place? And why?

He took out a note pad and wrote down a series of items:

Takeover – Drexel Burnham.
Swiss National Bank?
Roberto Martinez??
Dolgikh???

All four items had been raised during his conversation with Sally Brown at the Carlton Tower. George Pace had checked out the takeover thing with Drexel Burnham and knocked that one down at least. If what they had told him was correct – that no takeover attempt was underway – then nobody in the United States seemed to be motivated to undermine the reputation of the bank in order to push down the share price. Which prompted Mayer to turn to his IBM PC.

He hit a few keys and up popped the Friday close on Bank of America's stock. Fifteen-and-a-half. It was down three-quarters on the week on the rumors, but, as the computer screen indicated, the volume had been only slightly above normal – 550,000 shares a day, on average. If somebody had been out to gain control of Bank of America, the process of accumulation would have already started, and the volume of trading in the bank's shares on the New York Stock Exchange would have reflected this. It didn't. So that confirmed it. Drexel Burnham had been telling the truth.

That meant that, for a change, the investment bankers on Wall Street were innocent. Which left the other three potential villains: the Swiss, the Venezuelans, and the Russians. Were they in any way involved? If so, should he mention them at lunch the next day? Or would that just re-muddy the waters?

He then added a fifth item: George Pace's request that he come out to San Francisco to attend Bank of America's next Board meeting. He must clear it with Reston. And he'd better also mention Pace's job offer, even though he had turned it down, at least for the time being. Full disclosure could hardly hurt. He didn't want to become known around town later on as a second Bert Lance.

Then he remembered, faintly, that there was somebody else he had meant to call after returning from London. But for once, regrettably, Mayer's memory let him down. So he started to read. Four days of newspapers and magazines and journals had been stacked up on the end table beside his bed. He spent the next eight hours going through them. He didn't like a lot of what he saw. As darkness took over, he finally got up, and went downstairs. A couple of sandwiches and a beer were waiting for him in the fridge. Maria, who had left early to do the shopping for Sunday lunch, had it all ready.

He took his supper into the living-room, picked out a movie from the book shelf, put in in the VCR, and watched Clint Eastwood massacre approximately twenty-one people on the streets of San Francisco as he ate. At 9.30 the lights in 3514 Dent Place went out.

José Martinez, Jr, who by this time had nothing to show for the day except six Polaroid pictures of Professor Mayer's maid, took off in his red Mazda one minute later. He went back to his apartment, called the number that the Nazi type had given him, and delivered his report to the answering machine. Then he called the girl who ran the switchboard in Dean Krogh's office and invited her over. When she arrived he picked out a movie from his book shelf, and together they watched *Debbie does Dallas* yet again. At times he attempted to simulate in life the art that the miracle of home electronics was bringing to the giant TV screen at the foot of his bed. Since Georgetown did not have a football team, and thus any cheerleaders, this was the closest José, Jr ever got to active participation in America's national sport.

The doorbell at 3514 Dent Place rang at 12.30 on that Sunday, December 11th, 1988. Paul Mayer looked at his watch in surprise.

When he opened the door it was the Chairman of the Federal Reserve Board, Robert Reston, who stood there. His visitor had an apologetic look on his face. 'I hope I'm not inconveniencing you by showing up early,' he said, 'but I'd like to have a few words with you before the others arrive.'

'Come on in,' Mayer said.

Before the door closed, José Martinez, Jr had gotten off a perfect shot of the two of them in profile.

'Glad you've got the fire going,' Reston said as he took off his overcoat and handed it to Maria who had appeared out of nowhere.

'Thank you,' he said to her, and then, turning back to Paul Mayer, added, 'It's damn nippy out there.'

'How about a warmer-upper? If I recall correctly, it's Dewars.'

'You're right as usual, Paul.'

'I think I'll join you,' Mayer said. 'After all it's Sunday.'

There was a small wet bar in Mayer's living-room, and Maria had everything ready to go.

'Well, what brought you here early?' Mayer then asked as he handed his guest his whisky.

The Chairman of the Federal Reserve was a Californian and still seemed somewhat out of place in the Georgetown setting. In spite of it being December, he sported a deep tan. And, instead of wearing a tie, he had on a sportshirt and sweater. He looked more like a middle-aged tennis pro than the head of the world's most powerful financial institution, the central bank of the United States of America. A lot of people had expressed their doubts when Paul Volcker had decided to leave the Fed and when Reagan had appointed Robert Reston as his successor. Even though he had been head of the largest bank in Los Angeles for ten years, the Eastern establishment still figured him as a lightweight whose major qualification for the job was his Californian origins. Most of them had changed their minds very quickly.

'We got the preliminary flash estimates on fourth quarter GNP and unemployment late Friday afternoon,' Reston replied. 'I'm afraid the shit's about to hit the fan, Paul.'

'How much is unemployment up?'

'A full percentage point. That's the biggest jump I can remember. And GNP for the first quarter, 1989, is probably going to be down two percentage points. Which guarantees that we are sinking and sinking very rapidly into recession.'

'What's that going to mean for Treasury receipts?'

'They are going to start plummeting.'

'Have you revised your estimate of the budgetary deficit?'

'When we factor in what's going to have to happen to the expenditure side, with unemployment and welfare benefits soaring as fast as tax receipts will be sinking . . . our guess is it will be back up to $250 billion in '89.'

'So it's finally catching up with us.' Mayer said.

'It's catching up like a runaway freight train,' Reston said, 'and when the people out there realize that it's going to be a big one, some of them are going to start doing their homework. The last big recession, as you know, Paul, was in 1981–82. When it started, our budgetary deficit was $46 billion. When it ended it was $210 billion. In other words, the recession led to a quadrupling of the deficit. In the last big recession before that, in 1973–75, the deficit went from $2.6 billion to $99 billion. If history repeats itself we could end up with a deficit just this side of half a trillion dollars.'

'You surely don't buy that do you?' Mayer asked.

'Of course not. But that's what the doom and gloomers are going to be coming out with once these numbers start to circulate. And they're going to start to circulate early next month, you can be sure of it. Our place has leaks just like every other one here in Washington. But even if the financial community accepts our figure of $250 billion, it's going to be devastating. That kind of deficit is going to push the national debt over the $3 trillion mark much earlier than anybody expected. Which means that interest payments alone are going to be around a quarter of a trillion dollars next year, almost equal to all the revenue we take in from income tax. Scary!'

'Yeah,' said Mayer.

Reston then added, 'Let's face it, Paul, the fucking thing's slipping out of control. And to compound the problem, we've got a lame duck administration between now and the end of January. Everybody in the White House and at the Treasury are packing as fast as they can. They want to be *gone* before the shit really hits. They want to be out of sight and out of mind. Which means that the only people left in this town who will be running the store, or holding the bag, are going to be us guys at the Federal Reserve.'

'How's Congress going to react?'

'They'll go bananas. They'll blame everything on Japan and Canada and Hong Kong and Brazil. Within a week after they reconvene Congress will pass some protectionistic bills that will make your hair stand straight up, Paul. It will be the Smoot-Hawley tariff time all over again. But nobody wants to hear that stuff any more. I've testified before those dumb bastards at least a dozen times this year, telling them again and again that it was American protectionism which started the world-wide beggar-my-neighbour binge in the 1930s which turned a deep recession into the deepest depression in history. They won't listen to me anymore. They're listening to their constituents. And they want blood. Japanese blood.'

'And the new President will go along with them.'

'Sure. He's a Democrat. He ran against the Japanese as much as he did against the Republicans. He told everybody that unless something changes drastically we are going to go from being a debtor nation which already owes the rest of the world over half a trillion dollars to a destitute one which would not even qualify for an American Express card. Remember that line? He must have used it a hundred times during the campaign. And the American people ate it up.'

'And then what?'

'If Congress puts a 20 percent surcharge on imports at the same time we are going into recession, our demand for everything from bauxite to bananas is going to collapse.'

'And there goes Brazil.'

'And Argentina. And the Philippines. And . . .

He stopped and then added: 'Well, you know the story.'

'What are your people now saying about oil?' Mayer asked.

'Are you sure you want to hear? If this recession is both long and deep – like the one we had at the beginning of the Reagan administration, or worse – demand for energy will plummet. So they're talking $7 a barrel. Back in 1986, when the price dropped temporarily to $10, Yamani warned that this could happen next and everybody thought he was calling wolf. In '89 the wolf is going to be a real one.'

'The Saudis will survive even at that price.'

'But Mexico and Venezuela and Indonesia and Nigeria won't. Nor will half the banks in Texas.'

'What's the Fed going to do?'

'To be honest, I really don't know. We are going to face an impossible situation next year. The White House is going to expect us to finance a big part of that $250 billion deficit. The Treasury is going to want us to help fund a bailout of Latin America. At the same time Congress will demand that we put a lot more liquidity into the system in order to bring interest rates down so that the economy will start moving again. Can you imagine the international consequences, Paul? We would have to create money and credit at a rate we haven't seen since the Civil War!

'How long do you think the foreigners are going to keep their money in our banks and our government paper when they get wind of that! Especially if Congress gets its way and dollar interest rates start sinking, at least temporarily, and even *that* incentive to keep their money in New York instead of Frankfurt or Tokyo disappears. Then on top of the budget crisis and the Third World debt crisis we would have a systemic bank liquidity crisis and a dollar crisis. So we are between a rock and a hard place like never before. If we force interest rates down to promote domestic economic growth, the foreigners pull their money out. If we push interest rates up to entice them to stay, the economy sinks even deeper and unemployment soars ever higher.'

'I can see now why Volcker quit while he was ahead,' Mayer said.

'Some people have said the same thing about you, Paul.'

Mayer shrugged and then replied: 'Not guilty. I've always had this feeling that it was all eminently postponeable, if that's a word. That we could continue to borrow here in order to patch up there; that somehow we could continue to grow enough so that our output kept pace with our budget deficits and our trade deficits and our national debt and our international debt. My hope was that *all* the numbers would keep growing. Then the ratios would stay the same. And everybody would remain tranquilized. That, I guess, was what Reaganomics was all about.'

'But if these early estimates of what's happening to the economy prove right, the music's stopped.'

'And some people are going to jump off the merry-go-round.'

'And as they jump they'll be dumping everything from jumbo CDs to Treasury bills.'

'Which means that the Fed is going to have to be there buying when everybody else is selling. Otherwise panic time.'

'Exactly.'

Bob Reston looked at his watch. 'Look, the others will be here in a few minutes. Let me tell you why I came early. We, and by "we" I mean the Board of Governors of the Federal Reserve, would appreciate it if you would accept a more permanent position as our consultant. We appreciated your going over to London on such short notice, and, apparently, calming the waters considerably. We are going to need that same type of help, but on a much broader scale if these things we've been discussing really start to come down on us in the weeks and months ahead. You know the players all around the world, Paul.'

'I appreciate the offer, and I accept,' Mayer responded.

'Terrific,' said Reston, adding, 'and now that you're on board I must tell you that, at least initially, there was not unanimity about my choosing you. Two members thought that we should try to bring back Paul Volcker as a consultant. Which is about all that I would need at this juncture, as you certainly must appreciate, Paul. If Volcker walked back into our Boardroom, he'd take over as he always does, and I probably would have no choice but to resign. Anyway, the point's moot since I talked them out of it. Which leads me to one other point, Paul, compensation. We're government, and as generous as we would like to be . . .'

Mayer cut in. 'I appreciate the sentiment, Bob, but as you know, I don't need the money. Just put me down for the symbolic one dollar a year.'

'You're sure?'

'Positive. Now *I've* got one other thing. George Pace wants me to go out to San Francisco tomorrow and sit in on his Board meeting the next day. He thought it would help if the Fed would demonstrate, through my presence, that it is prepared to see the bank, and especially Pace, through the current troubles.'

'Great idea. Do it.'

'Pace also suggested that, at some future date, he might ask me to advise Bank of America directly. I said that I'd think about it, provided there was no appearance of conflict of interest where you and your board are concerned.'

'I see no problem. After all, what helps Bank of America can only help the whole banking system. Look, let's work out the current problems first, and then, if you still want to trade in your dollar-a-year position with us for a more lucrative one with Bank of America, I'm sure our whole Board will give you its blessing.

It was then that the doorbell at 3514 Dent Place rang again. And as José Martinez, Jr's Polaroid duly recorded the event, both the Comptroller of the Currency and the Chairman of the Federal Deposit Insurance Corporation entered the home of Professor Paul Mayer a few seconds later. Within five minutes the young Venezuelan had matched up the pictures with the license plates of the cars which the three visitors had parked. It being close to one o'clock on Sunday, a lot of open places had been left on the streets of Georgetown by the natives who had either driven their cars to church or had headed for their favorite restaurant for Sunday brunch. So José's surveillance task had been easy.

'Now all that's left for that Nazi to find out is who owns the cars,' he reasoned as he climbed back into his red Mazda. And José also thought that it might not be that easy since two of the plates were from Maryland and one from Virginia.

The next morning a young Iranian who worked for the Maryland Department of Motor Vehicles made the connections within an hour. Like tens of thousands of other Iranian students who had been stranded in the United States after the Shah had fled Iran, he blamed all of his subsequent difficulties not on Khomeini, but rather on the stupid Americans who had allowed the whole fiasco to develop. He had gone from a student visa to a visitor's visa to a green card and finally to American citizenship. What other choice did he have? He couldn't go home. At least not yet. The citizenship papers had at least allowed him to get a job at the state DMV. But though that kept him alive for the present, he knew that if he would ever have a future again it could only be back in Iran.

So when 'they' had called, asking for this slight favor, 'they' got what they wanted within an hour. His desk computer could call up any license plate number in Maryland and identify the owner; a call to a colleague over in Virginia produced the same result within minutes where the car registered in that state was concerned.

If the gentlemen inside 3514 Dent Place had been aware of the machinations which had just been set in motion in the streets of

Georgetown, their mood might have been a little less relaxed. Not that it turned out to be so relaxed as it was.

'Why don't we sit right down for lunch,' Paul Mayer had said, 'and I will sum up what I know about the current status of Bank of America. While I'm talking, you might want to scan this.'

He handed out copies of the Bank of America computer printouts. 'I think,' he then said, 'that you will all be pleased by what you are about to hear and read.'

Two were, and one wasn't. The odd man out was the Comptroller of the Currency, Charles Thayer. He was a Bostonian attorney, totally humorless, a New Englander to the core who mistrusted everybody who lived on the West Coast, without exception. But he reserved his strongest feelings of antipathy for those who ran banks or savings and loans out there. In his mind, they ran their institutions like gambling casinos. As a result, on average, one bank and two S&Ls a month went belly up in the so-called Golden State alone, and every time it was the citizens of the rest of the country – including those in the Northeast – who were forced to foot the bill for their folly, through the agencies of the government of the United States of America.

He'd had enough of it. It was time to let those weirdos out there, with their gold chains and hot tubs, know that they, and the loose bank management policies they represented, would no longer be tolerated. They were undermining the faith of Americans in the entire *national* system.

As Maria served desert and coffee, he said just that.

'Look what happened to Crocker National Bank,' he said. 'It was one of the great banks of this country. They ran it down so far, so fast, that if Midland had not taken it over, who knows what would have happened. Thank God the British moved in. To their great regret later, of course. Midland ended up covering almost a billion dollars in hidden losses. A *billion*, gentlemen. They finally gave up and sold Crocker to Wells Fargo.

'At least in that instance, you,' and he pointed toward the head of the FDIC, 'were spared, for a change. But it cost you a pretty penny when the same thing happened with Seafirst up in Seattle, didn't it?'

'I wasn't around back then,' interjected the head of the FDIC, which deterred Charles Thayer not a bit.

'Maybe not, but you must be old enough to know that Seafirst was the biggest bank in the Northwest. It had Boeing, the lumber industry, the electric power industry at its doorstep . . . meaning that management had more than enough good people to loan money to within spitting distance of their headquarters in Seattle. So what did management do? They bought a billion dollars' worth of energy loans from an Oklahoma "banker" who drank beer out of his cowboy boots. They all went bad. And Seafirst came within a hair of going under.'

'What's the point, Charles,' Bob Reston asked.

'I'll get to the point, sir. Just hold your horses,' Thayer responded, sharply, and then continued: 'Look at what happened to Financial Corporation of America and their subsidiary, American Savings: the largest savings and loan operation in the world. The hot shot from LA who ran that place almost took it – and $31 billion of depositors' money – over the brink before we forced him out. He was financing thirty-year *fixed*-rate mortgages with ninety-days' deposits. In Boston we knew that that was a sure way to go broke a hundred years ago. Now they tell me that the newest game the banks and S&Ls are playing out there is to buy short-term Eurodollars in London at an exhorbitant price and then turn around and use the funds to buy junk bonds being peddled by takeover artists in New York. It's suicide!'

'We know,' Mayer said. 'But it's hardly just a West Coast problem. Continental Illinois is situated in Chicago, after all. And some of the biggest bank crises in this decade occurred in Ohio and Maryland.'

'I agree,' said the Chairman of the Federal Reserve Board, 'and remember, Charles, it has been your own auditors who have allowed all of those situations out there to develop in the first place.'

'No more,' answered the Comptroller. 'That was my predecessor who allowed that. But not me. And now I'll get to the point, Mr Reston. I won't tolerate any more such nonsense. I'm going to teach those fellows a few lessons.'

'What do you mean?' asked Reston.

'I'm going to send my own people out there to do the job this time.'

'What job?'

'A special audit of Bank of America.'

That stopped the conversation.

Then the head of the Federal Reserve Board, Robert Reston, spoke again. 'I think that such an audit at this time would be ill-advised, Charles. Especially if you intend to send out an audit team from the East Coast.'

Charles Thayer's back stiffened even more, if that was possible. 'I don't think I need to be told what or what not to do in regard to maintaining the health of this country's banking system. If that bank's in serious trouble, I want to know about it. Now!'

'That doesn't require a special audit, Charles,' Reston said. 'Paul's already given you all the key numbers, and he just explained them. B of A is going to have to write off a billion dollar loss. And Paul says they can handle it.'

Charles Thayer did not choose to respond. But his silence certainly said a lot: he didn't trust an ex-foreigner like Paul Mayer any more than he trusted the bankers-in-hot-tubs out West.

Robert Reston then took charge. 'Look,' he said, 'I just got the preliminary flash estimates on GNP and unemployment. Unemployment's going to be up a full percentage point in the fourth quarter and GNP is going to be down 2 percent. This is no time for anybody to start rocking boats. This country's going to get nervous enough as it is. And some of those people outside the country who have over a trillion dollars on short-term deposit with our banks could start to get really nervous if they feel the United States is headed for big economic difficulties in '89. They might start jumping to the conclusion that as the economy sinks, so may a few more banks here and there. And they might decide to get out. We can't afford that.'

He paused. 'Under the circumstances, I don't want anything to happen that could trigger a run on a bank the size of B of A. Like a special audit ordered by the Comptroller of the Currency. If necessary, I'll go to the White House with this. Tomorrow.'

Charles Thayer, who had just celebrated his sixty-fourth birthday, turned ashen white. Nobody talked to him that way!

'I totally agree with Bob.' This interjection came from the head of the FDIC.

'And so do I,' added the ex-foreigner, former head of the International Monetary Fund, Paul Mayer.

'So that's that,' said the Chairman of the Fed, and as he rose from the dining table he spoke the last official word. 'I want you to know, Charles, that at my request Paul Mayer will be going out to San Francisco tomorrow. He'll be working with the Chairman of B of A. We hope the two of them can quieten down any further rumors and start rebuilding the bank's deposit base. We have arranged for a standby facility of $5 billion which Paul will have available, on call, if it becomes necessary. It won't, I'm sure, if you cooperate, Charles.'

Paul Mayer then thought about the checklist which he had wanted to discuss, the list that contained the Swiss, the Venezuelans and the Russians. But by this time Charles Thayer had already, personally, retrieved his overcoat from the closet and was headed toward and then out of the door. He had not said one further word.

'Don't worry, Paul,' said Robert Reston as he and the head

of the FDIC followed the Comptroller out into the cold Georgetown street. 'You can tell George Pace when you see him next week that I'll handle the Comptroller. Then get back as soon as you can. I'm afraid that much bigger trouble than just this flap over Bank of America is brewing and we're going to need your help.'

Chapter 10

When the average American divides Latin America into good guys and bad guys the test is usually whether or not they are *perceived* to support the political and economic aims of the United States. Thus Cuba and Nicaragua and Argentina were usually included among the bad guys, while Brazil and Costa Rica and Venezuela were inevitably among the good guys.

Where Venezuela is concerned, this involves an error in judgement. Just think back to the 1970s. If there was anything that almost destroyed the economy of the United States during that decade, (if you leave out the presidency of Jimmy Carter), it was OPEC. And who co-founded OPEC and has always been one of its most ardent supporters?

Venezuela.

Or consider the 1980s. One of the greatest menaces to the security of the United States in this decade was perceived to be the foothold which Communism was gaining in the Western Hemisphere. The Sandinistas in Nicaragua were the focus of evil south of the border in the eyes of the Reagan White House and the Shultz State Department. So who was it that co-organized a meeting on the island of Contadora in January of 1983, the purpose of which was to extend Latin America's blessing to that violently anti-American régime?

Venezuela.

The grouping, which also included Mexico, Columbia and Panama inevitably became known as the Contadoran Four.

And so it was in the closing days of 1988 that, yet again, it was Venezuela which was there at the beginning. This time it had two other nations as its partners, Mexico and Brazil. So when the facts later came out, it was inevitable that they become known as the Madrid Three, even though it was five men from those three countries who were the 'founding fathers' of the conspiracy.

Why did they meet in Madrid? Because to have met in Mexico City, or Caracas or Rio would have been to invite the attention of the world, or at least of the Americans. However, for each of the five of them to go, separately, to Spain was in itself not unusual. All five of the men had 'vacation' homes, the euphemism for safe havens, in either Spain or Portugal – on the Costa del Sol or the Algarve. The intelligence agencies in and around Washington of course knew this and they also knew that all five had sizeable bank accounts in Madrid. So the fact that the oil and finance ministers of Mexico and Venezuela, plus the finance minister of Brazil all happened to be headed for Spain at the same time set off no alarm bells anywhere.

On top of that, Spain had the added advantage of being probably the most violently anti-American country in Western Europe. The vast majority of Spaniards, not just their government, were in full sympathy with the aspirations of the Spanish-speaking peoples who lived south of the Rio Grande. They fully understood their desire to keep the Yankees and their insidious influence north of that river. They themselves were trying to keep them west of the Atlantic and east of the Pyrénées. Thus for years, the Spaniards had been trying to get rid of the American naval bases on their soil and the nuclear submarines which they serviced.

So if there was one place on earth where Latin Americans could discuss matters that collectively concerned them and involved the United States in complete privacy, safety and – this being no minor consideration – in utter luxury, it was the Ritz Hotel in Madrid.

Later it was argued that it was really unfair to think of the 'Madrid Three' in terms of countries. For, it was said, and no doubt accurately, that it was the greed of extraordinarily venal *men*, not the noble nationalistic aspirations of the *countries* which they 'represented', which had brought them together in the Ritz Hotel in the first place. This argument was heard time and time again when their ambassadors were called into the Department of State only a month later to explain what was happening. Not that any of them apologized, even though they all thought, privately, that, perhaps, the Madrid Three had gone a bit too far.

The Madrid Three had *known* that they were going very far indeed. But they never worried about it for a single minute. Because since their actions were directed *solely* at the United States, they knew that nobody would object. Because the United States, by the end of 1988, had become the world's most hated country. It was precisely that violent dislike of America and Americans which would provide the 'working environment' which made it so easy for these venal men who had gathered in Madrid in December later to gain the cooperation of otherwise sensible men. And not just in Latin America where the United States had for generations been regarded as the world's last imperialist power. No, the same hatred was also endemic in Europe. Here the United States was seen as a bully nation led by primitive men who were forever threatening the extinction of mankind, obsessed, as they were, with retaining global power no matter what the cost might be . . . for others. If it came to a showdown with the Russians, many Europeans were convinced that the Americans would fight . . . to the last German and Frenchman and Britisher. Better *them* dead than *America* Red.

In Asia the United States was seen as a big cry baby. The Americans had, to a man, been for free trade as long as the rest of the world lay in ruins after World War II. Peoples everywhere were desperate for all those things which only America could supply. They bought them regardless of either price or quality. But when the productive facilities of the rest of the world were finally renewed, the Americans suddenly found that they were no longer able to compete with Japan and Hong Kong and Taiwan and South Korea in steel and automobiles and consumer electronics and textiles and even computers. When free trade no longer meant easy profits for Detroit or Silicon Valley – what did they do? Instead of working a little harder, they tried to force the government in Washington to close up their markets by establishing import quotas. And when it worked, they said to the foreigners: 'Too bad. We have to look after ourselves for a change.'

In the Middle East, the United States was seen as a nation which would never cease giving blind support to Israel. In black Africa, it was seen as a silent supporter of apartheid; in white South Africa it was seen as a nation of gullible wimps who would rather listen to Bishop Tutu than the Reverend Jerry Falwell.

So the Madrid Three knew that when they set their process in motion, the men in power from London to Frankfurt to Zurich, from Tokyo to Hong Kong to Riyadh would not be interested in any of their personal motives. Even if they were, and disapproved of them, at the very worst they would just stand by – remain 'sympathetic but disengaged'. For it was time, in their secret collective view, that Uncle Sam be brought down to size. What the Americans, collectively, needed could be summed up in one word: Come-uppance.

And if the Madrid Three succeeded, good luck to them.

And better *they* attempt it than Castro. Because nobody really liked Castro. He talked too much. And he had proven himself a loser. Twice Castro had tried to organize the same thing. Both times he had fallen flat on his bearded face. Why had he failed? Because he lacked clout.

Because Castro didn't owe the United States a nickel! By contrast, the Madrid Three – Brazil, Mexico and Venezuela –

had clout galore. Collectively, by December of 1988, they owed the United States and its banks a grand total of a third of a trillion dollars!

The exercise of *that* clout could send Uncle Sam reeling to the mat.

It would. Within thirty days.

Why the urgency? After all, the men who had come to Madrid were just as aware of the gathering storm clouds as were the men who had just met in Georgetown. Why not wait until the crisis deepened, as they all knew it surely must in 1989? If America was vulnerable in December of '88, would it not be even more open to 'attack' from abroad in, say, June of '89?

The answers to all of these questions were 'yes'. But the leaders of the Madrid conspiracy, the Brothers Martinez, had a problem. They would no longer be in power in June of '89.

When, later, the whole matter was reconstructed – in an attempt to allocate blame, and lay the groundwork for revenge – it immediately became apparent that the entire process began to unfold on the first Sunday in December 1988 which fell on the fourth day of that month. Just two days later, as the record showed, Roberto Martinez, had taken that KLM flight to Europe, ending up ultimately in Switzerland where, within a matter of days, he had enlisted the help of the head of the National Bank of Switzerland, Dr Ulrich Huber; had laid out his plan to the Russian, Vladimir Dolgikh, candidate member of the Politburo; and paid an 'advance' of $5 million against future services to the terrorist, Carlos, a fellow Venezuelan now domiciled in Libya.

It was three days after that first Sunday in December 1988 that his brother, José Martinez, Sr, had flown to Mexico City to convince the oil and finance ministers of that country that they would be serving both Mexico's national interests and their personal financial interests if they agreed to come to Madrid. Not that it took much convincing. In Mexico, oil and corruption went hand in hand. For years, the men who were in the positions of power there had simply stolen the country blind: they managed to divert at least $4 billion of oil revenues into their private accounts in Swiss banks. So the recruitment proved easy. In the evening of that same day, December 7th, they had made a joint telephone call to the finance minister of Brazil at his private residence in São Paulo. To be sure, the Brazilian had been pre-sold, but he had only finally agreed to join the Venezuelans in Madrid after he had been assured by the Mexican finance minister himself that Mexico could be counted in. Irrevocably. Why all this dancing around? Why the need for these mutual reassurances?

The answer to that was clear: no Latin American country could stand up alone against the United States and win. The last one to try it had been Peru. During his first three days in office, the newly-elected young president of that country, by the name of Alan García, came up with two bright ideas. First, he decided to kick out the International Monetary Fund people who were in essence running his country's financial affairs. Then he announced that now that he had regained control of his country's financial destiny, he would only pay 10 percent of the nation's export earnings to service Peru's foreign debt. Which meant that he was in essence reneging. For when he took office, Peru's debt amounted to $14 billion, which was the equivalent of the *entire national income of Peru for one full year!* To put Peru's situation into perspective, if the United States had been in a similar position it would have had a foreign debt of $4 trillion! All this was hardly news to the foreign bankers who had loaned Peru the money in the first place. What was new and unfortunately also news was the fact that the president of the debtor nation which owed them that $14 billion had now gone public with the admission that there was no way whatsoever that Peru could *ever* pay it back. The Peruvian emperor had confessed that he wore no clothes!

The immediate result was that the American banks had to

set aside a 15 percent reserve against their Peruvian exposure. It was peanuts in the overall scheme of things, but it irked the hell out of them. The fucking Peruvians weren't playing by the rules! So they had to be drummed out of the club. Thus quietly, but without exception, the banks cut off any further credits to Peru, even those very short-term credits which the country desperately needed to finance its foreign trade.

Twelve months later, after the country had sunk into a state of economic chaos, Peru repented. To be sure, the Peruvians *still* did not have enough money to pay even a tenth of the interest they owed on their foreign debt. But they agreed – re-agreed would be a better word – to shut up about it.

The next day Peru got back its Visa card.

Thus the need for *collective* action. The banks might be able to bully Peru, which owed them a lousy 14 billion bucks, into submission. They might even have been able to do the same to a Venezuela which only owed them $50 billion. But they could hardly take on the Madrid Three, which collectively owed them a third of a *trillion* dollars.

But back to the question of why the urgency. Here the answer did not involve logic. It merely stemmed from the fact that every four years Venezuela holds a presidential election. The *years* coincide with the presidential elections in the United States. But the *dates* don't. The Venezuelan elections are held not on the first Tuesday in November, but rather on the first Sunday in December. Which brings us full circle – back to December 4th, 1988. For it was on that Sunday that the incumbent Venezuelan president and his party lost the election. This meant that according to the Venezuelan constitution the new president would assume office on February 10th, 1989 to be precise. On that same day the incumbent oil minister and finance minister of Venezuela would be out of a job. Which was bad enough. What was even worse was that the Martinez brothers had not really prepared themselves for this eventuality.

They had waited too long. For, unlike hundreds of their counterparts throughout Latin America, the Martinez brothers had not taken full advantage of the perquisites of their ministerial status in order to prepare for the day when they would be tossed out of office.

Not out of any moral qualms. For in the Latin mind, when an oil minister accepted a bribe here or a kickback there for services to be rendered to a foreign oil company or a domestic whisky importer, it hardly differed from what American corporate executives did when they voted themselves 'golden parachutes'. No American had ever gone to jail just because he had paid himself a huge separation bonus when it became apparent that some corporate raider was in the process of taking over his company. The only difference was that in Latin America the men in power took their separation bonuses *before* they got dumped. And while the American corporate executive screwed his shareholders, the ex-police chief of Mexico City, or the finance minister of Bolivia screwed their nation's taxpayers. In both cases, the cost trickled down and was widely distributed among the thousands of shareholders or millions of taxpayers and thus nobody really got hurt. Where there was a difference was in scale. The heads of some of America's largest corporations might have been bold enough to pay themselves a couple of million, or even a couple of tens of millions of dollars where some were concerned, when they were forced out of office as a result of a hostile takeover. The ex-police chief of Mexico City, on the other hand, managed to accumulate as much as a *billion* dollars in *pre*-separation compensation during his term in office.

The best way to get *really* rich is to take over an entire country and then loot the hell out of it before the people finally kick you out. It does not have to be a particularly wealthy country. Duvalier proved that in Haiti, so did Ferdinand and Imelda Marcos in the Philippines, where they may have set the world's record for this sort of thing.

It was *those* kinds of bucks the Martinez brothers were shooting for. Yet so far, between them, they had only stolen $3 million, and they kept it in banks in Madrid and Miami since the amount was too petty for the private bankers in Geneva to even bother about.

So it was now or never. And now it all had to happen before February 10th, 1989, while the Martinez brothers still held power. If they succeeded they would not only leave their government posts very rich, but they would no doubt also do so to the applause of a grateful Venezuelan people for having restored their national pride by re-establishing their country's financial independence. They would be seen as latter-day Bolivars!

On the other hand, if they failed to meet that deadline, their successors might be petty enough to dig up the details on the measly $3 million they had stolen so far, and try to send them to jail.

Thus, in the agenda which they presented to their co-conspirators from Brazil and Mexico in the Ritz Hotel on the following morning, time was of the essence.

All agreed that it was too late in the year of 1988 really to do anything. In Europe, the whole banking and financial community essentially shut down a couple of days before Christmas and stayed closed until several days after New Year. That would mean that they would have to wait until the second week in January 1989 to set events in motion.

Their first, coordinated, act would be collectively to go for the jugular of the world's second largest bank. It was agreed that all five of them would act in concert. And they also agreed that the initial 'happening' should take place in the United States before full network coverage. Should it be New York or San Francisco? The Brazilian finance minister made a strong case for staging it at the Plaza Hotel in New York. It was there, he reminded his Latin colleagues, that the finance ministers of the Group of Five – the United States, Japan, Germany,

France and Britain – had met in 1985 and announced that they would solve the problem of the overvaluation of the dollar by intervening in the world's foreign exchange markets by selling dollars. Subsequently, over the next couple of months, the dollar had indeed fallen by one-third in a very orderly process. The Brazilian suggested that if the Madrid Three met in the Plaza in '89, *their* announcement would no doubt be much more effective although the process it would set in motion would undoubtedly be much less orderly. He thought they could probably drop the dollar by half in a couple of hours, since, after the world heard what the Madrid Three were going to do, everybody would be trying to get their money out of the United States at the same time. This time the governments would no doubt try to stem the panic by *buying* up the dollars that were being dumped. But with a couple of trillion dollars floating around the world, that would be like trying to soak up the Pacific Ocean with a sponge.

Everybody liked what the Brazilian said, but though his case was a strong one, in the end they decided on San Francisco because, as the Venezuelans pointed out, their argument was with the American *banks*, not the American *dollar*, and it was in San Francisco that their banking victim, their *initial* victim, was headquartered.

At five minutes before 6.00 on that Monday, December 12th, full agreement was reached. Ten minutes later, the Cristal champagne and the Beluga caviar arrived.

Shortly after that, the Mexican finance minister said a few words. 'In our country it has often been said that Bank of America can't make Mexico disappear, but Mexico can make Bank of America disappear. We shall soon demonstrate how true this is. Let's drink to it.'

He paused and raised his glass. 'Bye-bye Bank of America,' he proclaimed.

They all laughed.

The next morning they all left Madrid in separate planes.

Chapter 11

About the same time that the five gentlemen from Latin America were leaving Madrid in their respective airliners, in San Francisco, which was nine hours behind Spain, and where, therefore, it was just after midnight, Paul Mayer was leaving Trader Vic's restaurant. His gait was a bit unsteady. Not that he was drunk, but one might have described him as slightly tipsy. After all, during the past three hours he had put away two Mai Tai's, most of a bottle of a Jordan 1976 Cabernet Sauvignon, and a Kirschwasser, no two Kirschwassers, with coffee.

'I have a suggestion,' he said to the lovely Iranian woman at his side as they emerged into the not-so-romantic alleyway outside the restaurant. 'Let's go up to L'Etoile for an after-dinner drink. I hear it is the best place in town for that.'

'It is. But on one condition,' she said.

'And that is, my dear?'

'That we have one drink, and then I drive you to your hotel.'

'That is a splendid idea. Let's go.'

The doorman at Trader Vic's had gone to retrieve her Mercedes as soon as he had spotted her emerging from the restaurant. Three minutes later they were already on top of Nob Hill where D.W., the doorman at the Huntington Hotel – which was right next door to L'Etoile – made her car re-disappear just as magically.

'They seem to know you here,' commented Mayer.

'In a business like mine, you have to mingle,' she replied, 'and in San Francisco these are two of the places where I see some of my clients, and they see me.'

After they had descended the stairs leading down to the bar-*cum*-restaurant, the owner himself, Claude Rouas, was there to greet her, and, after kissing her hand, led them to a softly-lit corner table in the bar. Almost immediately a bottle of champagne arrived, compliments of the patron, the waiter said.

'I'm impressed,' Mayer said, and it was difficult to tell if he was referring to her, or to the bar of the Etoile where the atmosphere was that of the 1920s, an impression which was reinforced by the fact that in the background a Gershwin tune was being played by a young man in a tuxedo.

'I assume this is the West Coast equivalent of the Carlyle Hotel and Bobby Short?' he asked.

'Exactly,' she replied.

She rotated her swizzle stick in the Dom Perignon.

'That was a lovely evening, Paul,' she said, 'in fact, the best I have had in years.'

Paul Mayer's brain might have been slightly fogged by the Mai Tai's but it certainly did not fail to pick up on those words.

'Then we must do it again tomorrow night.'

She did not pause even a second before replying.

'Agreed. But it will be at my place.'

'But that was not what I had in mind, Azar,' he quickly said.

'But I did,' she replied.

The urge that Paul Mayer had felt while sitting beside her on the Pan Am flight from London returned in full force.

'You see,' she said then in a low, husky voice, 'I have never really spent any time with a man since my husband was killed.'

Despite all the drinks, Paul Mayer's throat went a bit dry. Was she telling him what he thought she was telling him?

Ten minutes later she suggested that they leave since it was way past the time she usually went to bed. She always opened her boutique at ten in the morning and since Christmas was less than two weeks off, it was going to be a long day.

That scuttled the thought that had been rapidly building in Mayer's mind.

'But,' Azar then added, 'I never open before noon on Wednesdays, so tomorrow night . . .'

She dropped him at the Clift Hotel, and half an hour later after crossing the Golden Gate bridge and driving to the island at the end of the Tiburon peninsula, was turning on the lights in her house in Belvedere to the sound of her phone ringing.

'Yes?' she said, after picking it up.

'How did it go?'

It was the German.

'As I told you it would.'

'What did you find out?'

'Nothing. Yet.'

'What does that mean?' Now the voice was more aggressive.

'It means exactly what I said.'

'Don't get huffy with me, *Schätzchen*.'

'He's coming over here for dinner tomorrow night. He'll be at the bank the entire day.'

'He'll be at the bank tomorrow, will he? My principals will like that. Very much. It fits in perfectly with their schedule.'

She said nothing.

'The way things are developing, it may well be that I will have to come out to San Francisco next week,' he then said.

'I see.'

'Maybe you could reserve a few days for me. I'll need somebody to show me around town. And maybe you could show me a few other things while we're at it, huh?'

'That will be impossible. Next week will be the busiest of the year for my business. I promised to find out what I can from Mayer. Nothing more. I will not get further involved with either you or your friends.'

'Heard from your mother lately?' he then asked.

'No,' she answered.

'You will . . . after we see each other next week. Now get some sleep, *Schätzchen*. You are going to have a long night tomorrow. At least we are all planning on it.'

He hung up.

She just stood there, still holding the phone, and trembling. This was beginning to strike much too close to her new home.

The next morning, for the first time in years, she arrived late at her boutique. Her two assistants were already there, but neither seemed to notice that anything was wrong. She knew she had to keep it that way. Because later on, if something happened, there were going to be a lot of questions asked. And she did not want her life destroyed a second time.

Paul Mayer had had no trouble sleeping. And he awoke the next morning in the best of moods. The day that lay ahead promised to be a good one. When he stepped outside of the Clift Hotel into the crisp clear air and brilliant sunshine of a December morning in San Francisco, he decided to walk instead of taking the limo that was there waiting for him. It was only ten blocks, and it took him down Geary Street to Union Square with its palm trees and flowers, over to Post Street and Dunhill's, where he stopped to get a few cigars, Partagas Rounds, then past Gumps, where he paused to admire the store's marvelous Christmas decorations, through the Galleria in the Crocker building where he walked around a bookstore for five minutes, and finally to California Street and the headquarters of the world's second largest bank.

Mayer took the elevator to the 40th floor, and was greeted there like visiting royalty. George Pace immediately took him to the Boardroom, where all present rose deferentially when Mayer entered. He shook hands with each of them, noting that their average age exceeded his by at least ten years.

'Sit here beside me,' the bank's Chairman said, 'and tell me how you like your coffee.'

'Black,' Mayer replied, and it was George Pace himself who went to fetch it from the silver urn.

'First we would like to welcome you to Bank of America, Paul,' Pace then said. 'I have informed the Board of your appointment as special advisor to the Board of Governors of the Federal Reserve, Paul. I have also told them about your activities on our behalf in Europe last week. We appreciate them.'

He paused. 'Normally we would *not* appreciate having an "outsider" attending our Board meetings, especially one who represents a regulatory agency. But I have told my fellow Board members of our past association, and have assured them that you are here not just as an advisor but also as a friend of Bank of America.'

'That sums it up exactly,' Paul Mayer responded.

A collective grunt of approval went around the table.

'All right. That's settled. I have briefed my colleagues concerning your weekend meeting with the authorities in Washington. How did it turn out?'

'Excellent in every respect. Most important, I received the assurance that you and your bank has the full, and I mean *full*, backing of the Federal Reserve Board. Robert Reston gave me his personal assurance of that. More important, yesterday he called me here in San Francisco to tell me that in their Monday morning meeting the Board of Governors approved a $5 billion standby facility which Bank of America can draw on at will if it should become necessary.'

This time it was a collective sigh of relief that went around the table.

For, in recent years, the American courts had demonstrated a growing tendency to hold the directors of banks *personally* liable for the damages inflicted on their customers and shareholders when the financial institutions which they were supposed to be running in a responsible and prudent fashion, went broke. A $5 billion credit line at the Fed might not eliminate that possibility where Bank of America was concerned, but it would certainly be of immense help in postponing that day.

George Pace responded, 'That's terrific news. I'm sure we all agree on that. But I also have good news: I don't think we will have to draw on that facility. Because I can assure you that already yesterday – in response to the article in *The Wall Street Journal* – the way the market views our bank has changed for the better. Bank Watch, which as you all know is the bank rating service in New York, has bumped us back up to a C rating from the C-D one we had before. Today we've already seen the results. E.F. Hutton has come back with a $100 million deposit this morning. The Kemper Financial people in Chicago have put us back on their eligible list and came through with $200 million about half an hour ago. So, thanks in a large part to your efforts, Paul, we're beginning to re-establish our commercial deposit base.

'But no one in this room should have any illusions,' continued B of A's Chairman. 'We are by no means out of the woods. The billion dollar writeoff is going to take care of *most* of our current problems. I say most, because it would be naïve for any of us here not to realize that every branch manager out there has at least two or three bad loans still stashed away in his desk.'

'Why not smoke them out?' interjected one of the members of the bank's Executive Committee. 'Then we'd have everything out in the open. Declare a moratorium. Tell our people out there that nobody here on California Street is going to come down on them if they come clean. Unless we do, the rumors are bound to start up again.'

'I agree with the idea, but we can't afford it,' answered the bank's Chairman.

'Why not?'

'Because you're talking about at least another half billion.

Maybe more. If we did what you're suggesting, everybody out there would believe that there was yet another half billion or more we still had hidden. Keefe Bryette's Bank Watch would drop us to a D rating, and the money would start leaving this bank again just as fast as it's starting to come in again.'

Paul Mayer was beginning to look a bit uncomfortable. 'Where are the remaining problems?' he asked.

'Shipping. Commercial real estate. Agriculture. We've got a glut of tankers, a glut of office buildings both here and in Los Angeles, and a glut of everything from grapes up in Napa Valley to cotton in the Imperial Valley.

'Real estate is the biggest headache. I just got the estimates this morning: Our non-performing loans in that area alone are going to be up by $400 million in the fourth quarter.'

'What about your energy loans?' Mayer now asked.

'They are all included in the billion dollar writeoff we're taking, Paul.'

'But what happens if the oil price drops another $5 a barrel next year?'

'Nobody here believes that it will. In fact, nobody here thinks we will see the price below $15 a barrel ever again.'

The room was now very quiet.

'Dr Mayer,' began another member of the Executive Committee, 'you have just met with those people in Washington. Was the oil price discussed?'

'It was.'

'And?'

'We all agree it depends on where the economy is heading next year.'

'And where is the economy heading?'

'Down.'

'You're certain?'

'Yes.'

'Could that drop oil $5 a barrel?'

'It could, yes. By even much more than $5.'

'Is that why the Fed agreed to that $5 billion standby credit?'

'That's partly the reason, I would think.'

'You say the economy is headed down, Dr Mayer,' the interrogator said, and then, turning his attention to George Pace, asked: 'What if it goes straight down, George? And what if that triggers precipitous decline in the demand for energy. Then oil will fall below *$10* a barrel. Maybe way below. Do you have a contingency plans for that? Will that $5 billion be enough?'

'That is not knowable,' Pace replied. 'And why so pessimistic all of a sudden? We've gotten rid of most of our problems. We've turned things around. I've just got done pointing that out. The big deposits are coming back.'

'Look,' continued B of A's Chief Executive Officer, 'if the economy turns ugly *everybody, every* money center bank, is going to be in trouble. What do you think will happen then? Do you really think that Keefe Bryette would then lower the Bank Watch rating of every money center bank in the United States to a D? If they did, then what? Where would the money market funds put their money? They've got $300 billion, and they've got most of it with money center banks like us. There would be no place left for them to put their money, would there? If they pulled out of our bank, sure we would have to draw on that $5 billion credit line from the Fed. But how many other banks would then need similar lines? Ten? Twenty? Do you see what I mean? Am I right or not, Paul?'

'I'm afraid you're right,' Mayer answered.

'Then let me ask you this, Dr Mayer,' asked the persistent interlocutor, who had only recently been asked to join the Board of Directors of Bank of America because he owned 4 percent of the bank's stock. 'Does the Federal Reserve, at least, have contingency plans for such a situation?'

'If they don't now, they will soon,' answered Mayer. 'In fact, I have just been asked to "counsel" the Fed on precisely these matters. All I can do is repeat what I have told you. The Board of Governors of the Federal Reserve has empowered me to assure you that it will stand behind Bank of America. Period.'

That calmed the waters. The discussion then turned to other matters, particularly the closing of further branch offices as a cost-saving measure.

While they talked, Paul Mayer's mind was busy. It appeared that things were in worse shape than George Pace had admitted in London. Maybe he had simply not realized it himself. Which raised a serious question: Was Pace really up to his job? Was anybody? It was certainly premature to assume that Pace would not be successful; after all, the bank was in better shape now than it had been when he had taken it over. With a little luck, he might be able to restore B of A to its former glory.

Mayer's mulling was interrupted when a secretary entered the conference room and laid what appeared to be a telex message in front of the bank's Chairman. As he read it, the weariness which Paul Mayer had seen on the face of George Pace in London returned in full force. Nobody in the room but Paul Mayer seemed to notice it. Or perhaps, Mayer conjectured, nobody wanted to.

Fifteen minutes later Pace adjourned the meeting. As had been pre-arranged, Paul Mayer remained behind.

'Let's stay here a few minutes longer, Paul,' George Pace then said. 'Something which may or may not be important has just come up.'

He handed Mayer the telex his secretary had brought in during the meeting.

'We are herewith informing you of our intention to invoke, within thirty days, paragraph 81 of the multi-year rescheduling agreement between the government of Venezuela and yourselves, dated February 18th, 1987.'

It was signed: 'José Martinez, Minister of Finance.'

'What's in paragraph 81?' Mayer asked.

'It's the *force majeure* clause.'

'What's it cover?'

'Earthquakes,' answered the CEO of the world's second

largest bank, 'and another drastic fall in the world price of oil . . . like the one you seem to feel is likely.'

'Who agreed to that?'

'My predecessor. After what happened in 1986.'

'I can't believe this,' Mayer exclaimed, his iron decorum finally slipping. 'How stupid can you get! Who else has the same clause?'

'Only two others.'

'*Only* two. *Which* two?'

'Mexico and Brazil.'

'At least you don't have to worry about Brazil,' Mayer said, calming down a notch.

'Maybe, maybe not.'

'Why?'

'They insisted on including a basket of commodities, their commodities, instead of oil. If coffee and sugar prices collapse, Brazil can trigger its *force majeure* escape clause. And as you full well know, Paul, if oil goes, as you are suggesting it will, coffee and sugar will not be far behind.'

'And everybody went along with all that?' asked Mayer.

By 'everybody' he meant the 600-odd banks which were members of the consortia which had lent money to Venezuela, Mexico and Brazil. When these loans had to be re-financed, a fourteen-bank advisory committee had been established and, since Bank of America was the lead bank in all three consortia, its CEO had been chosen to chair the committee and to conduct the negotiations on behalf of all the banks. The resulting new arrangements were governed by what bankers term 'Myras', or multi-year rescheduling agreements.

'They had no choice.'

'Have you heard anything from Mexico?'

'No, thank God.'

At exactly that moment, the banker's secretary stepped into the conference room once again. 'I thought you would want to see these right away,' she said.

After George Pace glanced at the two new telexes, he turned so ashen that Mayer thought he was about to keel over.

Mayer decided to step in before the situation started to slip out of control. 'Show them to me, George,' he commanded.

Pace pushed the two pieces of paper over to him.

The first began: 'We are herewith informing you of our intention to invoke, within thirty days, paragraph 92 of the multi-year rescheduling agreement between the government of Mexico and . . .'

'That's their *force majeure* clause?' asked Mayer.

'Yes.'

The second: 'We, the government of Brazil, are herewith informing you of our intention to invoke, within thirty days, paragraph 117 of . . .'

'This is going to finish us off,' Pace said.

'Easy does it, George,' Mayer said, eyeing the man thoughtfully.

Then: 'Look, George, the first thing you've got to do is respond immediately.'

'How?'

'Telex them that there are no grounds for invoking *force majeure* and that you want them to get their asses up to San Francisco pronto. Otherwise within thirty days, *you* are going to put *them* on the blacklist, just like you did Peru a few years ago.'

'Let's draft it right away.'

Fifteen minutes later similar telexes went out to Caracas, Mexico City, and Brasilia.

Half an hour after that, they had their first response, from Venezuela. Its finance minister, José Martinez, requested a meeting. He suggested Tuesday, January 10th, 1989, as the date, 9 a.m. as the time, and San Francisco as the place. He urgently requested a confirmation. The message from Venezuela closed with the suggestion that this matter be treated as extremely confidential by both parties.

'It's working,' said B of A's Chairman, now back in control of himself.

Fifteen minutes later, a similar telex came in from Mexico City.

'I'm afraid it's working too well,' said Paul Mayer this time.

'What do you mean?' asked Pace.

'Don't you have that sinking feeling that you – we – are being set up?'

When, ten minutes after that, exactly the same telex came from Brasilia, George Pace just looked at Mayer without saying a word.

'What's your exposure in Venezuela?' asked Mayer.

'Two billion.'

'Mexico?'

'Three billion.'

'Brazil?'

'Four billion.'

'How big a reserve do you presently have against that?'

'Five percent.'

'Jeezuz. If you had to write off those loans it would wipe out your entire capital.'

'And then some. I think we've got to keep this very, very quiet, Paul.'

'They seem to want it that way too.'

'Shall we agree to their proposal?'

'There's no choice.'

'You'll be here for the meeting?'

'Of course,' replied Mayer. Then: 'What about the other banks on the advisory committee?'

'They won't expect to be invited. At least not yet.'

'I'm not thinking about the January meeting. I am thinking about *right now*. Don't you have to inform them?'

'In all three telexes the Latinos say that they want to keep this thing confidential. I think we have no choice but to concur. You agree, don't you?'

Paul Mayer said nothing.

'It's not as if they have actually invoked the *force majeure* clauses. If they had, of course I would be on the phone right now,' continued Pace. 'But since they haven't, and since the odds are high that they're just bluffing like hell, I think it's in the interest of every bank in the consortia that we keep the lid on.'

'I guess you're right,' replied Mayer, reluctantly. 'But I *am* going to have to tell the Fed.'

'The whole Fed, or just Chairman Reston?'

'Just Reston.'

'And the Comptroller of the Currency? And the FDIC?'

'I don't work for them, do I,' answered Mayer.

George Pace grinned for the first time that day.

By now it was noon in San Francisco. 'How about lunch?' asked Pace.

'Let's go.'

They ate upstairs in the Bankers' Club at the top of the Bank of America building, which meant that they were in full view of most of the bank's top executives who normally lunched there. All of them were thoroughly familiar with the bank's condition, and, as a result, most of them had become very skittish of late. So, lest even the slightest hint of the new difficulties appear on their faces, George Pace and Paul Mayer completely avoided any further discussion of the looming Third World debt crisis. As they left, Pace introduced Mayer to half a dozen of his key men, making sure that the impression was left that Mayer was visiting the bank for the purpose of helping them re-build for the future now that the 'troubles' were behind them.

Downstairs on the 40th floor and inside George Pace's office, the façade was dropped.

'I'm going to need some details for the Fed, I'm afraid,' Mayer stated.

'You name it,' Pace replied.

'All three rescheduling agreements. And an item-by-item breakdown of B of A's exposure in Latin America.'

'You mean in Mexico, Brazil and Venezuela?'

'No. I mean in Latin America. All of it.'

'That's going to take a while.'

'Don't worry. I'll just sit outside in your ante-room and read the papers while you get some work done.'

Forty-five minutes later, Mayer rejoined Pace in his office. The Latin American documentation had been piled up on Pace's desk.

'You can hardly lug all that back to Washington,' Pace said. 'How would it be if I sent it out by courier?'

'Fine. I'll just keep the summary sheets.'

'When would be the best time to make delivery? And where?'

'Say around noon the day after tomorrow? At 3514 Dent Place.'

Pace wrote it down, and put the memo on top of the stack of dossiers.

'Are you taking the Red Eye back?' he then asked.

'No. The nine o'clock morning flight. United.'

'So what are your plans for this evening? Why not come with me over to Belvedere and have dinner with us. I'll call Annie and tell her you're coming. She'll be delighted!'

Mayer hesitated ever so slightly. 'Actually, I've already been invited to come to Belvedere for dinner,' Mayer then said, adding, 'by a lady.'

George Pace grinned for the second time that day. 'Do I know her?'

'No. I just met her very recently.'

'Is she presentable?'

'Very.'

'So why don't we pick her up and the four of us can at least have a drink together at our place.'

'All right. If it's OK with her.'

'You find out. I'll pick you up at the Clift at 6.30.'

It was 7.00 when the limousine pulled up in front of Azar Shahani's home on Madrona Avenue. Before Paul Mayer had even had a chance to ring the bell, the front door opened and the dark Iranian woman emerged.

'I hope this doesn't upset your dinner,' Mayer said.

'No, not at all. After you called I put everything on simmer.'

George Pace was standing beside the open door of the stretch Cadillac and was obviously taking all of her in as she and Mayer approached the car.

'George,' said Mayer, 'this is Azar Shahani. George Pace.'

'Delighted!' said the banker, and he obviously meant it.

Although she wore a mink coat, it was open, and both men were acutely aware of the fact that beneath it she wore a dark green dress that clung everywhere but at the neckline.

The Pace's lived on the other side of Belvedere Island, the better side since it faced San Francisco and where, therefore, the houses went for two million instead of just one. Annie Pace seemed to be as delighted as her husband to meet Paul Mayer's new friend. 'She's absolutely gorgeous!' she whispered to him, as her husband led the Iranian woman to the bar. 'Where in the world did you find her?'

'On a flight from London,' Mayer answered.

'But she's not English, is she?'

'No. Iranian.'

'Oh.'

'She's not one of *those* Iranians, Annie. Her husband worked for the Shah and with us. They killed him.'

'How awful!'

After that she went over to Azar Shahani and took her into protective custody. Two drinks later and it was 7.30 and the banker's wife and the Iranian refugee were already fast friends.

George Pace had kept the bank's limo waiting and insisted

that Paul Mayer keep it for the rest of the night and for the morning run to the airport as well. While they said goodbye, Annie Pace found out that Azar would be alone over the holidays and insisted that she join them and their friends for their annual New Year's Eve bash.

'I'll never be able to match her hospitality,' Azar said as they headed back toward the other side of the island. Once they were inside her house, she asked Mayer if he wanted another drink.

'No. That was enough for the moment.'

'Would you mind just sitting in the living-room alone while I get everything organized? I'll put on some music. And today's *Chronicle* is on the coffee table, if you haven't read it already.' Then she disappeared into the kitchen.

Paul Mayer picked up the *San Francisco Chronicle* and turned automatically to the business section. There was not much in it. He put the paper back on the coffee table and started to walk around the huge living-room. There were a couple of not very interesting modern American paintings on the wall; more impressive were two ancient vases which stood on either side of a rather large fig tree on the far side of the room; her *pièce de résistance* was no doubt the enormous, and obviously very valuable Isfahan rug on the floor. The view through the huge picture windows was that of the bay and the lights of Berkeley and the Oakland hills beyond.

Mayer looked at his watch. And then went through the door which he assumed led into Azar Shahani's kitchen. It did, and she was there, and she was busy.

'Excuse me, but would you have a Marin County phone book handy?' Mayer asked.

'Of course. It's on the table over there in the breakfast nook. And there's a phone there too.'

Mayer hesitated. Would it be impolite to ask if there was a phone somewhere else? It would, he decided. 'Would you mind if I make a local call?' he asked, mumbling, as an afterthought, 'If I can find the number.'

'Please go ahead.'

He went over to the breakfast nook and sat down, with his back to the kitchen.

The number was listed; the address not.

George Pace answered on the fifth ring, and the way he did indicated that he did not appreciate being disturbed at this hour at home.

'It's Paul Mayer. I hope you're not in the middle of dinner.'

'No problem.'

'Look, George, before you picked me up at the hotel I had time to take a quick look at the numbers you gave me. And they got me thinking.'

'And?'

'You – we – cannot give one inch to these guys. Your bank simply cannot afford any reclassification of your loans to any one of those countries, much less all three. If they formally invoke their *force majeure* clauses, all American banks loans to Mexico and Brazil and Venezuela will be automatically downgraded to "value impaired" by the authorities in Washington. That would require an immediate writedown of 15 percent. That amounts to $1.35 billion in the case of Bank of America. I repeat: *that* you simply cannot afford, George.'

'You're telling me! But who can stop them?'

'That's why I called,' Mayer answered. 'I'm going to lay this out before the Fed – and by the Fed, George, I mean Chairman Reston – and tell them exactly what I'm telling you. We've no choice but to play hardball all the way. We can first try it alone next month with those guys. But if it looks like we're striking out, I'll get Reston to come out to San Francisco on the next flight. Then they can hear it straight from the horse's mouth: either they forget about the *force majeure* crap, or the United States' government will cut off their financial balls!'

'Would Reston agree to that?'

'After I tell him what happened today, and after I explain your numbers, I would say the answer is a definite yes.'

'Jeezuz, Paul, make sure you and Reston keep the lid on this. Otherwise . . .'

'Don't worry. The Fed is probably the last place in Washington that's still leakproof.' Mayer continued: 'Sorry to have disturbed you, George, but I thought I'd better tell you about my thinking before I got on that plane tomorrow morning.'

'I appreciate it, Paul. I agree with every word you've said.'

'OK. I'll be in touch.' And Mayer hung up and went back to the kitchen.

'Sorry about that,' he said to Azar Shahani.

'Is Mr Pace's bank in trouble?' she asked, adding, 'I couldn't help but . . .'

'He does have some problems, yes.'

'But you are going to help him out?'

'Yes. I'll be back in January.' Mayer replied. 'We'll manage.'

'Mr and Mrs Pace are very nice people, aren't they? How do you know them?'

'He and Annie lived in Switzerland, in Zurich, for a number of years while I was still with the Swiss National Bank. He ran B of A's Swiss operations. I forget how we met. But after we did, we started to play golf together. Now that I think of it, it was at the golf course in Crans sur Sierre where we met. We were both on vacation there and for the same reason: Switzerland's best golf course is in Crans. Few people know how to golf in Switzerland, and very few play the game well, so it was not easy to put together a foursome. After we met, we ended up spending the rest of our vacation together.'

Azar just listened without saying a word.

'You might be wondering about that "foursome" bit,' Mayer then added. 'I was married back then . . . it was almost twenty years ago now. It didn't last very long.'

Now she spoke: 'And do you still play golf?'

'No.'

'So what do you do for fun?'

Now it was Paul Mayer who remained silent.

Then: 'I guess I have more than enough fun doing what I'm doing right now.'

'You mean what you're doing with Mr Pace?'

'Exactly. What we are doing is playing a very big, a very complex, and, believe me, a very exciting game. The risks are immense; the stakes are enormous. So who needs golf?'

'Maybe golf is less dangerous,' she said.

Paul Mayer thought about that for a few seconds.

'If you're worried about my dropping dead from a heart attack, don't. I had a physical a month ago, and the doctors at Georgetown said that I was as sound as the American economy.' And he laughed.

'That's a joke, Azar,' he then added.

'Oh,' she said. 'Sometimes I don't understand American jokes. Now we're ready. Would you mind opening the wine, Paul?' She had obviously noted his liking for Jordan wines, and thus had a bottle of both their Chardonnay and Cabernet Sauvignon ready to go.

The dining-room was small, elegant, and bathed in candle-light.

'At home, when we eat Persian, we do so on our carpets. We spread a leather cover on it, which we call a *sofreh*, which makes a firm base for the dishes, we put a white cloth on top of it, and then place the dishes on top of that. Then we surround the carpet with cushions for seating. And we eat from the fingers of our right hand.'

'Why not tonight?' Mayer asked.

'Because we are in America. Now please be seated.'

The food was already on the table.

'This first course is what we call *Sabzi Khordan*. That is a platter of green herbs – parsley, mint, tarragon, coriander leaves, *shahat*. . . I think you call that watercress . . . and more herbs whose names I don't remember in English. And over that is a plate of *panir*, our Iranian goat's milk cheese. And this is *nane lavash*, our bread. Now watch me.'

She tore off a piece of the flat bread, and with her right hand put a selection of the herbs and two pieces of the cheese on it. Then she took a spoon, scooped out a thick sauce from a bowl, added it on top of the herbs and cheese, and folded the bread.

'Try it,' she said, and handed the folded bread to Paul Mayer.

'Terrific,' he immediately said, after tasting it. 'What did you put on last? It's wonderful!'

'We call it *Mast va Vakhiar*. It's yoghurt with cucumbers and sultanas.'

The main course followed half an hour later. It was duck in a walnut and pomegranate sauce, served with steamed rice. The Persian term for their aromatic, hand-grained rice, she explained, was *chelou*, and the duck dish was known as *Khoreshe Fesenjan*.

By the time they had gotten to desert, a milk pudding called *Halvaye Shir*, which Mayer ate politely, they had, between them, killed off half of the Chardonnay and all of the Cabernet.

It was ten o'clock when they moved to the living-room for coffee. After serving him, she disappeared once more into the kitchen and returned, carrying what was obviously a fresh box of Partagas cigars. 'I noticed that you like these,' she said.

By this time Paul Mayer was feeling more comfortable, more coddled, better fed, and more at home than he had in years. Literally years. And as he watched her across the coffee table, an absolute vision of young desirable loveliness, he realized that he was not going to make any moves on her.

He knew that the mutual attraction was definitely there. He also sensed that there was a strong element of sexuality in this Persian woman. But it was evident in her body language, in fact very evident, that she was not ready to end up in bed with him. Or probably anybody else either. Yet.

This was confirmed when they got onto the subject of religion. It became obvious that Azar was a strongly moral person. It surprised Mayer to hear this modern woman, in her thirties, refer with such deep respect to her mother, as she explained to him how central the role of the family was in Islam.

The conversation then drifted to her boutique, to life in Marin County, to why she had settled down in Belvedere. She explained that the area was full of rich expatriate Iranians. In fact, the adjoining town of Tiburon had been nicknamed 'Little Teheran'. Their attitude toward the disciples of Khomeini who still ran the country? Careful, she answered. Why? Because most of them still wanted to go back. Did she? No. Then she abruptly switched subjects and asked about his life at the university. And at 10.30 he looked at his watch, got up from the sofa, and began thanking her for a lovely evening.

The effect on Azar Shahani was immediate. The restraint, the slight tenseness that had been there all evening, all of a sudden seemed to lift. And after she had opened the door for him, she suddenly took his face between her hands and planted a firm, lush kiss on the lips of the surprised man. 'You are a very decent, nice person, Paul.'

'Does that mean we will see each other again in January?' he asked.

'Yes. Call me. Please,' she said.

Azar Shahani did not go to bed after Paul Mayer had left.She just sat in the darkness of her living-room, looking at the lights across the bay, thinking. She liked this man. A lot. She wondered if, next time, they would end up . . . in bed. It had been a very long time. Too long.

But what if, after that, something happened?

At 2.00 a.m. the phone started ringing.

At 2.30 it began again.

At 3.00, she finally picked it up.

'*Schätzchen*,' he began, 'I hope I'm not interrupting anything.'

'He's gone.'

'I've got a tape recorder on,' the German then said. 'Tell me exactly what happened.'

She did.

When she stopped talking, the German asked: ' "We have no choice but to play hardball all the way." Are you absolutely sure those were the words he used?'

'Yes.'

'And you definitely heard him say that the Chairman of the Fed would come to San Francisco in January?'

'Yes. "To cut off their financial balls".'

'I'm sure you aren't making *that* one up, *Schätzchen*,' the German said, adding, '*Mensch*, they are not going to like hearing this one bit!'

'Do you mean that I did not get what you wanted?' she then asked.

'No. Quite the contrary.'

'Then my mother will be able to call me now?'

'That's up to my principals. I will certainly recommend it.'

'Are you coming here next week?'

'I don't know. From what I've heard you say, I would think not. It looks like it will all start to come down in early January. So I'm going to have to wait here until they figure out what they want me to do about it. When. And where. I'll let you know. With your mother, it will take a few days at least. One more thing: stay away from your Iranian friends. All of them.'

'But I was supposed to report regularly on them,' she answered.

'No more. That's over now. This will be the last thing we will be asking of you, *Schätzchen*. Then you can get your mother out of Iran, and live happily ever after. In the meantime, keep away from the Iranians, and keep your mouth shut. Very shut.'

When she got home from the boutique late the next day, a huge bouquet of flowers was in a box in front of her door. The note that accompanied them was from Paul Mayer. He thanked her for a lovely evening. He wrote that he looked forward, very much, to seeing her early in the New Year. And he signed it, 'Love, Paul'.

An hour later her mother called from Teheran. She was healthy; they were not hurting her. And they had told her that she would possibly get an exit visa and an airplane ticket to Zurich in January. They had told her that it all depended on Azar.

In the early evening of New Year's Eve, Paul Mayer telephoned George Pace at home. He briefly explained to him that it had taken two weeks, but he had finally been able to arrange for an extensive meeting with the Chairman of the Federal Reserve Board that afternoon. The Chairman had fully agreed to back them up *vis-à-vis* the Venezuelans, Mexicans and Brazilians in January. He thought this news would add to George Pace's New Year's cheer, and so he decided to call. Mayer then asked if Azar Shahani was at the party. She was, and when she came on, he told her that he had been thinking a lot about her, that he missed her, that he was greatly looking forward to seeing her in early January. She thanked him, but said little more.

Paul Mayer spent the rest of that New Year's Eve alone in his house in Georgetown, listening to the music of Bach and Mozart. At 11.30 he turned on the TV and watched the good-humored crowd on Times Square waiting for the ball to come down.

The TV announcers and their guests were sure that the joy of the masses in New York was well-founded. For six years now, America had prospered as seldom before. To be sure, some economic storm clouds seemed to be building up overhead. But, as the NBC spokesman concluded as time started to run out on the old year, with a new president coming into office bringing with him new ideas and new policies and new resolve, surely those clouds would quickly disappear in the New Year. And then, as so often in the past, America would again renew itself and plunge onward and upward into the future as its energy was unleashed as never before.

He might have something there, Paul Mayer reflected. 'Eighty-nine might indeed be the year when America will unleash an unprecedented amount of energy. But that energy release might come from a completely unexpected source: the onset of financial meltdown! A meltdown in the form of a cataclysmic financial blowout, where all of the paper that had fueled the great American economic machine in the 1980s – the junk bonds, the jumbo CDs, the interest-rate swaps, the stock market futures, the Mexican debt – suddenly went up in a huge puff of smoke.

He, for one, was not looking forward to the New Year.

At five minutes past midnight, on January 1st, 1989, Paul Mayer turned off the TV and turned out the lights.

PART III

Chapter 12

The first 'outsider' to catch on that something big was going to happen very early in 1989 was a Russian. His name was Grigory Ustinov. Grigory worked as an analyst for the KGB in their Western European department on the 3rd floor of the KGB's central office in Moscow. Commensurate with the fact that he had only been with the KGB for a year, despite the doctorate in economics which he had received from Moscow University in 1987, his rank was only the Soviet equivalent of a GS–11. And his salary was only half that earned by his counterparts at the CIA or DIA, meaning that he was paid just over 13,000 rubles a year.

Still and all, it was not bad for a guy who was only twenty-nine years old, who had a full career still ahead of him. Although he could not yet afford a car, he did have a color TV, a VCR, a Hi-Fi which he had just hooked up to a CD player, plus twelve discs, which a colleague had gotten for him in Finland.

When you came right down to it, Grigory Ustinov was a Russian Yuppie with all of the materialistic aspirations peculiar to this new class. And here lay Grigory's only big problem: there seemed to be very little scope for upward mobility in the immediate future since he had been given a very low profile job in the KGB, one that was not exactly career enhancing.

First, he was in no way connected with 'operations'; his was strictly a Moscow desk job which involved analyzing data, not delivering karate chops. Secondly, there was analysis and there was analysis. Lots of analytical action was to be found in those departments covering Central America or China: Ustinov, however, had been assigned to the Western European department which, by comparison, involved pretty tame stuff now that even the West Germans were bending over backwards to be nice to the Russians. Not only that, but the country 'desk' within Europe which had been given him was Switzerland, a nation that was about as low on the Soviet 'enemies list' as they come.

For months he had been trying at least also to get Sweden – a country whose territorial rights the Soviet Union were constantly violating with their mini-submarines, meaning that there was at least *some* potential for conflict and thus heightened visibility within the KGB for the analyst in charge. But he had been told just the prior week that Sweden rated at least a GS–13, and that there was no chance of his being promoted to that level for at least another year, maybe two.

So Grigory Ustinov was stuck with a very dull Central European neutral for the time being. But, being a pushy little bastard, he was determined to make the most of a bad situation. First, he developed his network of informed people. He was usually on the phone at least twice a week with one or other of the attachés – economic, military, cultural – in the Soviet Embassy in Berne, seeking further details on the reports which they regularly filed with the KGB in Moscow, reports which eventually ended up, usually in unopened envelopes, on his desk. He took the Moscow stringer for the Schweizerische Depeschenagentur, the Swiss newswire service, out to lunch once a month, using his Tass ID as a cover. He visited the man in charge of supervising the operations of the Zurich branch of the Soviet Foreign Trade Bank, the Vneshtorgbank, once a week, trying vicariously to keep in touch with what was going on in Swiss banking circles. And he read a lot. Being perfectly fluent in German, French and English, thanks to the foreign-language requirements for the completion of doctorate programs in social sciences at Moscow University, he read every page of every day's edition of the *Neue Zürcher Zeitung*, the *Schweizerische Handelsblatt*, the *Basler Zeitung*, *Blick*, the *Berner Tagesblatt*, the *Journal de Genève* – plus the *Herald Tribune*, and the European edition of *The Wall Street Journal*, for an American overall perspective of European and Swiss affairs – all of which arrived on his desk every day courtesy of Aeroflot. Twice a day, at 11.00 a.m. and at 5.00 in the afternoon, he tuned in to the broadcasts of the Kurzwellendienst of the Schweizerischer Rundfunk, the short-wave service of the Swiss national radio, to pick up news of potential importance.

The problem was: though Grigory was extremely well informed on what was happening in Switzerland where political, economic and financial affairs were concerned, none of it was of any significance to the Soviet Union. So nobody in the hierarchy of the KGB had ever had any reason to take notice of the existence of Grigory Ustinov.

Until January 4th, 1989, that is. It was the day before, on Tuesday January 3rd, when he received his first indication that, for the first time during his so-far short career with the KGB, something big was stirring in Zurich – something that just might have important global strategic implications for the Soviet Union.

It was the man responsible for the Moscow supervision of the Vneshtorgbank's branch in Zurich – the one he took out to lunch – who called him just before 5.00 p.m. that day. What he had told him was this: January 3rd was the first full day of business in Europe after the Christmas–New Year's holidays, and things were usually still pretty slow. But on this January 3rd, right from the word go somebody had started to short the dollar like crazy while, at the same time, somebody had also started to move very heavily into gold, by both making large physical purchases of the metal and taking large long positions in the gold futures market in Zurich. Since Zurich was the financial center where the Russians did most of their gold business and a lot of their foreign exchange transactions, they were very sensitive to shifts in the wind there. What the traders with the Zurich branch of the Soviet Foreign Trade Bank had sensed by closing time of the markets in that city on that January 3rd, 1989, was not just a shift in the direction of the heretofore prevailing financial wind, but an enormous increase in its velocity. Sticking to meteorological terminology, they had further said that the weather might be changing from fair and mild to stormy and cold. In Switzerland, they had explained, the warm wind is known as the *Föhn*: the cold as the *Bise*. What the Russians in Zurich had told him was that there was a *Bise* coming up that might be regarded as frigid even by Moscow standards. The chief trader had telephoned in their message on a scrambled telephone line, preferring that to even a coded telex message, since he knew the latter could be broken easily. That so impressed the man at the Vneshtorgbank in Moscow that fifteen minutes later he had phoned across town to the analyst at the KGB with the news. It was the first time he had ever taken the initiative and contacted Grigory Ustinov.

Ustinov, eager beaver that he was, decided to skip dinner that evening and to stay on at the office. Thinking. Pondering. Hoping that more information would be coming in. Every half hour he checked the Reuters' wire. Nothing. He called twice over to Tass. Nothing. Then, at 11 p.m., a telex came in from the cultural attaché in Berne. He had important news, and would be calling in at exactly 8 a.m. the next morning. Ustinov decided not to wait. He arranged for a high priority scrambled call to Berne. And he got his man just as he was leaving the building.

Once the KGB station chief had made sure that the line was indeed scrambled (you never knew about GS–11 analysts back at the head office) he got down to business. It seemed that the Swiss National Bank was in the process of organizing something very unusual. That morning, according to the cultural attaché, a flurry of telexes had gone out from that bank to the heads of the nine largest commercial banks in Central Europe. Three were Swiss: the Swiss Bank Corporation, the Union Bank of Switzerland and the Crédit Suisse. Three were German: the Deutsche Bank, the Dresdner Bank and the Commerzbank. The three remaining banks were Austria's largest, the Creditanstalt Bankverein, Netherland's biggest, the Amsterdam-Rotterdam Bank, and the Kredietbank of Luxembourg.

The message in each telex was the same: the Swiss National Bank was extending an invitation to attend a meeting, to be held in the offices of the Chairman on the fifth floor of the bank's headquarters at Börsenstrasse 15 in Zurich, to start at 9 a.m. on Monday, January 9th. Only one item would be on the agenda: the organization of a multiple-country collateralized sovereign credit facility. Due to the extremely sensitive nature of the transaction, only chief executive officers of the banks being invited would be allowed to attend. No substitutes, please. An answer was requested in no less than twenty-four hours.

It was signed by Dr Ulrich Huber, Chairman, Swiss National Bank.

Cryptic though the invitation was, acceptances started to come in within an hour. By 5 p.m. only Luxembourg had failed to respond positively.

Not only that, but all day long the Swiss National Bank had been engaged in a frenzy of activity in three areas: foreign exchange, gold, and interest-rate swaps. They were dumping the dollar as never before, and accumulating gold at a rate not seen since the late 1970s.

So Grigory Ustinov had now moved a giant step forward. He was getting a second source in-house confirmation of what he had been told by his man at the Vneshtorgbank. But now he knew *who* was behind the ominous action where gold and the dollar was concerned.

'But what is this about interest-rate swaps?' he asked the KGB's head man in Berne.

'They're swapping their floating rate obligations in dollars for fixed rates like crazy,' came the answer.

Now, though Grigory Ustinov had a doctorate in economics from Moscow University, and though, as already indicated, he read almost everything he could get his hands on regarding what was happening in Western financial markets, he never had quite understood what interest-rate swaps were all about. To his credit, Grigory decided that now was not the time to fake around. So he asked: 'What exactly does that mean?'

'What does what mean?' came the counter-question over the scrambled line which had more than a slight hum in it.

'What are interest-rate swaps?' he asked, coming right out with it.

'Agreements where two banks exchange interest payments on the same amount of money for the same period of time,' came the answer. 'No principal is ever involved.'

'I don't get it,' answered Ustinov.

'Look,' said the KGB man in Berne, who was a GS–21, 'say a bank, like the Swiss National Bank, has borrowed a lot of dollars at a floating rate. They usually tie the floating rate to LIBOR, or the London Interbank Offer Rate, which is the interest rate at which large banks lend to each other for three months in London. If LIBOR goes up, so does the interest which the Swiss National Bank has to pay out. If interest rates in general go down in London and New York, then the bank's interest costs go lower and lower. OK so far?'

'I think so.'

'Now, let's say the Swiss National Bank no longer wants to take a risk on floating interest rates because it thinks that interest rates are going *up*. What does it do?'

'Got me.'

'It swaps for a fixed interest rate. It goes to another bank and says: "Look, we have borrowed $100,000,000 for one year from General Motors at a rate of LIBOR plus one-quarter percent which means that right now we are paying 8¼ percent. How be it if you take over our *floating* rate interest payments to GM, while we agree to pay you a *fixed* rate of 8½ percent on $100,000,000 for one year?'

'But why should the second bank do that?'

'Because it thinks interest rates are going *down*. Then, if LIBOR goes down to, say, 7 percent, it will only have to pay 7¼ percent each month to GM, while the Swiss National Bank is paying it 8½ percent, as it agreed to do, no matter what, in the swap agreement.'

'Then,' said Grigory, 'if everything stays that way for the rest of the year, the other banks will make a profit equal to the difference in rates – or 1 percent of $100,000,000.'

'Plus change,' said the KGB man in English. He had spent five years with the Soviet Consulate General in San Francisco, and liked American slang.

'Then the Swiss National Bank obviously thinks dollar interest rates are going up. Probably way up. And probably very soon,' added Ustinov.

'You've got it, sonny,' came the answer from Berne. 'Which is interesting, but not very. What will be interesting is the answer to the question: *Why*?

'In fact, my dear Grigory, we are faced with a set of four very interesting questions. First: why is the management of the Swiss National Bank so sure that interest rates in the United States are going to skyrocket that it has given instructions to its swap team to get the bank out of its floating interest-rate obligations at almost any cost?'

'How do *you* know that for sure?' asked Ustinov.

'I do, sonny. Now don't interrupt.'

'Second: If dollar interest rates are going to skyrocket, why is the Swiss National Bank selling, not *dumping*, dollars? Shouldn't it be the other way around? After all, if interest rates go up in New York, money from all over the world will, once again, start to pour into the United States, driving the dollar *up*, not *down*.

'Third: Why, if interest rates are going up, are they buying gold like crazy? Gold pays no interest, does it? So why did the Swiss National Bank keep buying gold all day, bidding in essence against itself, with the result that it singlehandedly drove the bullion price up $12 an ounce? Nobody else seemed to be buying. Just them.

'Fourth: Could it just be a coincidence that, on the same day that all this was going on, Herr Generaldirektor Doktor Ulrich Huber was sending out all those invitations to all those other banks?'

'You mean there might be a connection between all four,' said Ustinov.

'Not "might",' said the KGB man in Berne. 'There *must* be a connection.'

'What is it?' asked Ustinov, spontaneously.

'How the hell should I know? I'm not the analyst, sonny. You tell me! Then I will know where to look next, what questions to ask next. It is important that *you* find out that connection, my dear Grigory, because something very, very important is starting to happen here. I smell it. Now what do you think? Venture a guess at least.'

Grigory Ustinov was faced for a second time with a decision: to bluff or not to bluff. He again decided to level: 'I frankly don't have a clue.'

'Well, find out and get back to me. Right away. Otherwise I'm going to have to go over your head, my dear Grigory, as much as I like you.'

'Yes. I'll get back. Tomorrow. Before noon. And thank you. Thank you very much.'

The scrambled line went dead.

Seconds later, Grigory was at his low-tech electric typewriter, drafting a report which he intended to have on his boss's desk within twelve hours. He had no sooner started than he stopped. How reliable was this information, especially that about the interest-rate swaps and that 'top secret' meeting that, supposedly, was scheduled to take place in Zurich in exactly six days? How could their man in Zurich know all this?

These doubts were being raised in Grigory Ustinov's mind because, being a lowly GS–11 class analyst, he hardly had access to the highly classified existence of Hanni Graber.

And who was Hanni Graber?

The answer to that involves a little back-tracking, in fact, going way back in the history of Swiss-Russian relations to World War I and Vladimir Ilyich Lenin. Lenin spent almost the entire war in Switzerland, in Geneva and Zurich. It was from there that he planned the Russian Revolution. And it was also from there that Lenin embarked on his famous trip in a sealed railroad carriage through Germany back to Mother Russia where he began to implement those revolutionary plans. That much is, of course, generally known. What is not so widely appreciated is the fact that *before* he left Zurich, Lenin developed a cadre of like-minded Swiss who, just a few years later, founded the Swiss Communist Party, the Partei der Arbeit, a party which was still alive and well in 1989. And Hanni Graber, though never a member, had, for two decades, been what might be best described as a 'social fellow traveller' . . . which meant that she attended most of the party's dances at the union hall, and often showed up at the Stüssihof restaurant for an evening of *Jass*, the Swiss card game similar to pinochle. The Stüssihof was a hallowed meeting place, because it was in that very restaurant that Vladimir Ilyich used to spend his Zurich evenings, sometimes drinking beer with the boys, at other times drinking white wine with his sweetheart, Inessa. Just as Inessa had joined Lenin and his pals on their mountain excursions, the Sörenberg being their favourite destination, so also, seventy years later, did Hanni Graber join Lenin's latter-day Swiss disciples in the Partei der Arbeit when they made their annual hike in the Berner Oberland.

Had she known about some of the statements and recommendations which Vladimir Ilyich Lenin had made in that very Stüssihof restaurant where she so often played cards, such as 'A republic of lackeys. That's what Switzerland is!' or 'Seize the banks right away! And Switzerland will then be a proletarian country!' it is highly doubtful that she would have continued such social activities. But, being a Swiss woman born thirty years before Swiss women were even enfranchised, Hanni Graber was totally apolitical.

How, then, did she get involved with these Communists? It happened back in 1959, the year she joined the Swiss National Bank as a lowly typist and also the year when she began dating, for the first time in her life. Her first love was an apprentice butcher who resented his status in life and was seeking to improve his potential upward mobility by fostering revolution through his membership in the Swiss Communist Party. He subsequently dumped the party and her and emigrated to Australia. Hanni stayed on in Zurich and, since she harbored no grudge against *them*, she kept on dancing and playing cards and hiking with the Swiss *Genossen*. These social activities, and the bank, of course, had become Hanni Graber's life . . . at least until 1985 when a third element was added. At the Christmas dance that year she met the cultural attaché of the Soviet Embassy. He became only the second man ever to bed Hanni. He did so just one hour after finding out that she was one of three girls in the secretariat of the Chairman of the Board of the Swiss National Bank. He bedded her weekly thereafter, always on Tuesdays, always at her place in Zurich, and always rather early, around 9 p.m., because Hanni had to get to the office at 7.30 each morning and prided herself on never having either missed a day or been late since 1959.

At 9.20 in the evening, on that Tuesday, January 3rd, 1989,

after an especially ardent session, Hanni Graber, as usual, started to spill the beans about what was new at the bank. There was a *lot* new that day, so the fifty-nine-year-old Russian cultural attaché kept stroking her, in the hope that she would remain aroused, and thus talkative. The alternative, he knew, would be that she would look at her clock and send him home. When he had squeezed all he could out of her, the Russian smoked one last cigarette, and sped back in his Volkswagen to his telex and code book at the embassy in Berne.

Why didn't the Swiss National Bank find out about Hanni's background and the fact that she consorted with the enemies of capitalism?

Very simply because she was a woman, a female, and therefore didn't really count, didn't matter much in the scheme of things. Swiss women might have gotten the vote in the 1960s, but that was about all. And even by the general Swiss standards where male chauvinism was concerned, the Swiss banks in particular were in a class of their own. At the beginning of that year, 1989, the number of vice-presidents in all the 400-odd Swiss banks was 3,457.

Not one was a woman.

Not one was a woman because one could hardly expect them to grasp the intricacies of world finance. Not that women do not have a place in banks! No Swiss banker would ever claim *that*. For as they, and all good Swiss *Bürger* know, Swiss girls are loyal, hardworking and, in general, neat. So they make good tellers and excellent secretaries . . . at least so long as they do not get any pushy ideas. Security risks? Impossible. Women were never involved in top secret matters, and if, somehow, they heard about them, they could hardly understand them, could they?

Hanni had never been pushy, and her reward was that she was now a member of the three-'girl' secretariat of Dr Ulrich Huber, and sat in an office right beside his office. She, or one of the other 'girls', took his dictation, sent his telexes, filed his correspondence, answered his telephone. So, in time, whatever he knew, she knew, and, in time, whatever he did, she knew about. And during that first Tuesday in 1989, she knew that her boss was personally organizing something very big.

Dr Huber had instructed her to get hourly reports from the chief traders in gold and foreign exchange, as well as from the head of the interest-rate-swap team. So every hour she collected them, and then, dutifully, she tiptoed into his office and placed them on the edge of his vast desk. It was also she who sent out those nine telexes to the nine chairmen of the nine banks being invited to come to Zurich the following week. But it was another girl in the secretariat who was given the responsibility for preparing the agenda for that meeting.

So although Hanni had a lot of pieces of information in her hands, she had not been able, as yet, to put together the puzzle. All that she could figure out was that the Swiss National Bank had been slipping, and slipping badly, of late. All this new activity, she then reasoned, was her boss's response.

Grigory Ustinov had the same pieces of information in his hands, and the more he thought about them the more he became convinced that he had no choice but to accept their validity. After all, the same information had come from the station chief in Berne, and from the Vneshtorgbank in Moscow, two independent and normally impeccable sources.

So back to the typewriter he went. And, at eight o'clock the next morning, his sixteen-page report was on his boss's desk.

At nine o'clock that same morning, Wednesday, January 4th, Sally Brown walked into the London office of *The Wall Street Journal*, took off her leather coat, got a cup of lousy English coffee, and sat down at her desk.

As usual, she picked up the phone and made a dozen calls.

Then she sat back in her chair and began to think. About Walter Wriston.

Walter Wriston had been, for many years, the Chairman of Citibank. It was he who had built that institution into the world's most powerful bank. After he retired, he spent much of his time lecturing and writing Op Ed pieces for the *New York Times*. One of his favourite themes related to the constant cries demanding a reform of the international monetary system, a return to the gold standard. Wriston's claim was that the world will never return to the gold standard because it had simply become outdated; it had been overtaken by the technological revolution, especially that which has occurred in the field of communications. We are now, he said, time and time again, on an 'information standard', where knowledge, facts, are disseminated throughout the world within seconds after something occurs. Something changes, something is said, something is denied. So anybody who has a vested interest in any asset, any country, any currency, any commodity, can be right on top of his situation even if he lives at the North Pole. All he needs is a satellite receiver, a computer with a modem, a clear telephone line, and a good heater. Information, then, not the barbarous relic, is what today determines the international value of the yen, the pound sterling, the franc, the dollar as well as the price of 100 shares of IBM stock in New York, or a ton of tin in London. The more perfect the communications system, the less the likelihood of error which could lead to violent fluctuations in international values, monetary and otherwise. So, according to the Gospel according to Citibank and Walter Wriston, the days of panic and crashes are over. As the efficiency of the world communications increases, so will the efficiency of all markets. No one will ever again have a reason to over-react. In summary, everybody will soon be able to know everything within fifteen minutes. It only requires that they be plugged in.

'Oh, yeah Walter?' said Sally Brown to the wall behind her

desk. 'Well, I'm plugged in and, true, I've got information coming out of my ears. But what that information *means* I haven't got a clue about.'

Her problem was that her dozen phone calls had been producing exactly the same information that was contained in Grigory Ustinov's sixteen-page report, which was now on the desk of his immediate boss within the hierarchy of the KGB in Moscow. Sally Brown was faced with exactly the same set of questions that he had posed. Why was somebody in Switzerland making big waves in the gold, foreign exchange, and interest-rate swap markets? Somebody obviously knew something *else*, something *extra* that nobody else knew. What was that something extra?

Walter Wriston had said that a situation like this was no longer possible.

She checked her notes to see if she was missing something: Gold is up another $9 an ounce, on top of the $12 move it made yesterday. The dollar continues to slip heavily against the Swiss franc, the German mark and the Japanese yen. Interest rates are up across the board in New York: Federal funds jumped a full percentage point this morning; the long bond fell well over a percentage point; the interest rates being offered on both three and six months' dollar CDs in London jumped 80 basis points. The Swiss, it was rumored, are continuing to dominate the swap action, and are getting out of variable interest-rate obligations in the United States as fast as they can.

She then wrote on her yellow note pad:

Conclusion: The Europeans, in any case the Swiss, are bailing out of the dollar, out of variable interest-rate commitments, and moving into gold because:

1. Somebody in Switzerland must see an immediate and major return of inflation in the US. Thus their move *out* of the dollar and *into* the classic hedge against inflation, gold.

2. If inflation goes up, interest rates always follow. *That* explains why the Swiss are rearranging their swaps, trying to lock in future payments at current fixed interest rates while they are still low.

'Makes sense so far,' she mumbled. Then she wrote:

Further Conclusion:

> If inflation is returning in full force in the United States, and thus, presumably, everywhere, (*see* 1 & 2 above), that will mean that the price of *all* real assets, not just gold, but *all* commodities, especially *oil*, will also move up.

Then she wrote: *Question*: Have they?

Sally Brown was rather pleased with herself. The mind was working. She turned on her computer, and logged on the Dow Jones financial news service. She asked it for oil. A second later the screen told her that oil was down $1.25 a barrel on both the spot market in Rotterdam and the futures market in New York.

That did not make sense. That was an anomaly. And anomalies usually represent potential clues. She did not remember who had told her that, but she believed it.

Think, girl! she told herself.

Then her phone rang. It was the head of Chase Manhattan's London interest-rate-swap team. Chase was the best in this business, and she had done a very flattering piece on them a few months ago in the *Journal*.

'This is Gerry Gohler over at Chase,' he began. 'I've got something that might interest you, Sally. Something very unusual. We don't know quite what it means. Maybe we can help each other out.'

'What is it, Gerry?'

'The Swiss, and particularly the Swiss National Bank, have

been very active, starting yesterday, but continuing full blast today in my area of interest-rate swaps. You've probably heard that already.'

'I have.'

'OK. What has cropped up this morning is this: the London brokers are asking around, looking for first-class addresses, preferably European banks, who might be interested in assuming some swap obligations of a major Swiss bank.'

'The Swiss National again.'

'The brokers aren't supposed to tell but, yes, you've got it.'

'Why are they doing that?'

'The logical reason would be that the Swiss National is worried that the counterparty to some of their swaps might default on its payments.'

'Has anybody ever defaulted before?'

'A couple of times, yes. But each time only about $20 million was involved. In other words, not much to worry about when you consider that the swaps outstanding right now must be close to half a trillion dollars.'

'While we're on that subject, are swap obligations included on the balance sheets of banks.'

'Of course not.'

And Paul Mayer had told her that there was absolutely nothing to worry about there. She made a note to call him. Right away.

'Now what is *really* interesting,' continued her informant at Chase, 'is which counterparty is involved in every case.'

'Go on.'

'Bank of America.'

That set Sally Brown back in her chair. After all, it had just been three weeks ago that she had written that upbeat story about B of A for the front page of the *Journal*. Had she been fed phony information? Had she been had? By Paul Mayer?

She now underlined her notation to call him, and added the word 'soonest'.

'Not only that,' the guy from Chase continued, 'but the

brokers tell us that the Swiss National is willing to pay a hell of a commission to anybody who can arrange such assignments, a commission which the brokers are more than willing to split with us if we can help them out. And you know the Swiss, Sally, they *never* offer deals.'

'So what does it mean?' asked Sally Brown.

'It might just mean that the swap team at Swiss National has gotten pissed off with B of A. Maybe the boys and girls in SF screwed them on a deal. All I know is that this sort of thing is unprecedented.'

'If they assign a swap, do they have to inform B of A in advance?'

'It would depend on the boiler plate in the original swap agreement, I guess. But my gut feeling is that not only would they have to inform B of A, but that B of A would have to give its approval. As I said, Sally, this sort of thing is really unprecedented. That's why I called.'

'I appreciate it, Gerry,' she said. 'If you hear anything more, call me. Even at home. Let me give you the number.'

She did, and then hung up.

She picked up the phone again, this time with the intention of calling Paul Mayer at home. Then she realized that she did not have his number and began instead to dial for directory assistance in Washington DC.

'Shit!' she finally exclaimed, realizing it was 4 a.m. in Washington DC, and slammed down the phone.

Then she decided to go and see her boss, the London bureau chief. She had an idea that would require his backing. If the Walter Wriston theory wasn't operative this week, with the result that the complete information she needed was not coming in, then Sally Brown would simply have to go get the information.

'Sally,' her bureau chief told her, after she had made her pitch, 'this is something that the Washington bureau can handle.'

'To hell it can. Look, I started this. I got the facts on Bank of

America when everybody else was striking out. I'm either *going* or I'm *quitting*.'

'OK, go.'

Just about the same time that Sally Brown was marching, triumphantly, out of her boss's office in London, the head of the political and economic analysis section of the Western European department of the KGB had almost finished reading Grigory Ustinov's sixteen-page report. It was then that one of his assistants did what he always did at this time of day: put a telex copy of the Reuters' roundup report on what was happening to oil that morning. What was happening on that January 4th, 1989, was that the price of oil was sinking.

Like Sally Brown, he spotted the anomaly. It did not make sense that the price of oil was falling. Not only that, but a drastic fall in the price of oil could have highly negative consequences for the Soviet economy. From that young Ustinov's report, it seemed that the Swiss National Bank and Consorts Unknown were on the attack against the dollar, and trying to make a buck on gold. Was the same gang in Zurich also now trying to rig the oil market?

This was getting to be serious.

He paged through the personnel directory until he got to U and then picked up his phone. 'Ustinov,' he said. 'This is Karpinsky. Get over here!'

During the next half hour they went through Ustinov's report. And Ustinov's boss asked the same question at least a dozen times.

'But are you sure?'

By noon both Grigory Ustinov's report, now with annotations added by his section chief, along with an updated Reuters' report on the oil situation were on the desk of Viktor Chebrikov, the man who had succeeded Andropov as head of the world's largest intelligence service. And it immediately produced the 'Aha!' effect. For Viktor Chebrikov knew that 'something extra' that neither Grigory Ustinov nor his section chief at the KGB, nor, for that matter, Sally Brown, nor her section chief, the head of the London bureau of *The Wall Street Journal*, knew.

He knew all about the Venezuelan and his visit in December to the Swiss National Bank. He knew about the bizarre proposition which that Venezuelan and the Chairman of the Swiss National Bank had made to Comrade Dolgikh. But when Dolgikh, unsure about what to do about it, had gone to his boss, Nikolai Ryzhkov, and when, subsequently, both of them had gone to Mikhail Gorbachev, what had been the response of the General Secretary?

'Forget it' he had told them. Imagine: 'Forget it!'

Well, he, Viktor Chebrikov, had not forgotten about it.

Because he – and Ryzhkov for that matter, because, he now remembered, he had told him about it – knew something that Comrade Gorbachev didn't. He knew about the *other* Venezuelan, Carlos. He knew about their meeting in Basel.

If Gorbachev had heard about *that*, maybe . . . But he didn't, because he had told Ryzhkov to 'forget it' before Ryzhkov had had a chance to tell him. Now, if he, Viktor Chebrikov, had been invited to that meeting as he should have been in the first place, in fact, as he *definitely* should have been, then . . .

Ah, Comrade Gorbachev, you have sorely misjudged this one!

Viktor Chebrikov pondered a few minutes. Then he called in his assistant and gave two commands:

— Tell our people around the Mediterranean to find out where Carlos is, and what he's doing. Immediately.
— Tell our station chief in Berne to find out what that meeting in Zurich is going to be about. Tell him to determine, soonest, if there is a 'Venezuelan connection'. And ask him if the loan which the Swiss National Bank is syndicating for us will be affected.

Then, as an afterthought, he told his assistant to get the chief of personnel section on the line.

'We've got an analyst in the Western European department, in the political and economic section: his name's Ustinov.'

'What's he done?'

'Nothing. What's his rank?'

'I will find out immediately.'

He did within twenty seconds.

'Grigory Ustinov, aged twenty-nine, graduate of Moscow University . . .'

'Just his rank, not his life's story.'

'GS–11.'

'He's now a GS–13,' said Viktor Chebrikov.

'Yes, sir.'

'One more thing: is there anything in his file that indicates in which direction he wants to go?'

'Let me see.' There was a long pause. Then: 'He has requested Sweden a number of times.'

'Give it to him.'

Normally nobody called Hanni Graber at the office. Her boss, Dr Ulrich Huber, hated it. But at 2.15 p.m., right before she got back from lunch, a man called. And left a number where she could reach him with one of the other two 'girls' who worked with Hanni – this one being a fifty-nine-year-old spinster who was known by some as the office gossip, by others as the office bitch.

When Hanni got back, she gave her the message. Which produced a very pronounced blush on Fräulein Graber's face. Which, in turn, induced Hanni's secretarial colleague, who was manning the PBX unit in their office that day, to listen in when Hanni returned the call. After all, it was a 031 number, so the call had come from Berne. Who could Hanni Graber possibly know in Berne? Especially a *man*. After all, she barely knew anybody, man or woman, in Zurich! Maybe he was the one she was always having those short, sneaky conversations with once a week, and always on a Wednesday morning, it seemed.

The office bitch was, of course, jealous. Because though Hanni Graber was fifty-one years old, she was still a very good looking woman. Her 132 pounds were perfectly distributed over her five-foot-five frame. Not only that, but wearing her long blonde hair in a ponytail as she did, made her look closer to thirty-nine than fifty-one.

The phone rang three times on the 031 number in Berne. Then a girl answered with the words:

'Botschaft der USSR'

'Ja, Fräulein,' said Hanni, in a very faint voice, *'Ich möchte gerne mit dem Kulturattache sprechen.'*

'Wenn darf ich melden?'

'Fräulein Graber.'

'Wie, bitte? Sie müssen etwas lauter sprechen.'

So she spoke louder. *'Fräulein Hanni Graber.'*

'Moment, bitte.'

When the Soviet cultural attaché came on the line he made it brief.

'Hanni, I need some help. Quickly. And I need just one small bit of information. That meeting next week, the big one on Monday morning. You know what I'm referring to?'

'Of course I do.' Hanni Graber's voice indicated her displeasure. 'But why are you interested in that?'

'I'll tell you that next Tuesday evening, Hanni. That is, unless you would rather not continue . . .'

'I didn't mean that.'

'Good. Now I need to know just one very small thing. Is that meeting being called next week in order to arrange for a large syndicated loan to Venezuela?'

'That's all?' she asked.

'Well, maybe you could help out on just one other little matter. What is the current status of the loan your bank is organizing for the Soviet Union? It's for $2 billion. It was planned for the end of January. Could you find that out?'

Hanni said nothing at first. Then: 'I'll try.'

'I will call you at home. At 7.00. And Hanni, I'll remember this.'

The Russian hung up. Then Hanni Graber hung up. And, finally, the office bitch hung up.

Without looking in the direction of Hanni, she then strode out of the office and down the corridor and, without even knocking, entered the office of the head of security of the Swiss National Bank.

Within two hours, the Swiss authorities already had a wire tap on the phone line leading to Hanni Graber's apartment.

At 7.00 on the dot that evening a call came in, and a man with a heavy Eastern European accent spoke.

'Could you get the information?'

'Yes.'

'And?'

'There will be two credit arrangements under discussion. One to Venezuela and one to Mexico.'

'Syndicated loans, you mean?'

'No. I mean credit facilities. Credit lines to be established by all nine banks. For a total of $15 billion. Mexico will get $10 billion; Venezuela $5 billion.'

'And the loan to the Soviet Union?'

'It will proceed on schedule.'

'Are you absolutely sure?'

'Yes.'

'Hanni . . . you are wonderful! I will never ask such a thing of you again. I promise. I must go.'

'Until next Tuesday?' she asked.

'Of course.' And he hung up.

Two hours later the Soviet cultural attaché crossed the border into France. At 8.00 the next morning he boarded the Air France flight from Paris back to Moscow. He planned on going directly from the airport to the office of Viktor Chebrikov.

At 6.45 that same morning, four officers of the Zurich *Kantonalpolizei*, one of whom was a woman, had knocked on the door of Hanni Graber's apartment. When Hanni answered in her housecoat having come directly from her bed, the woman cop informed her that she was under arrest, charged with economic espionage under Articles 272 and 273 of the Swiss Criminal Code.

The policewoman then took a small red-covered book out of her bag, and read the pertinent articles out loud. The final sentence of Article 273 stated:

'In schweren Fällen ist die Strafe bis zu zehn Jahren Zuchthaus.'

Hanni seemed not to hear.

'I'll repeat that sentence just once more, Fräulein Graber,' the policewoman said: ' "In serious cases the punishment will be ten years of hard labor." Do you understand?'

The Hanni Graber who finally answered no longer looked thirty-nine. In fact, she now looked a lot older than even her real age of fifty-one. *'Ja, Ich verstehe.'*

'Then get dressed,' the policewoman ordered, and sat on the edge of her bed while Hanni did just that.

'Now pack a suitcase. I suggest you include just the essentials.'

One hour later, Hanni Graber was locked up in the women's section of Zurich's central jail. It was well known to the local prostitutes, shoplifters and thieving barmaids as a place where they normally spent twelve hours before being sprung by their pimp, husband, or bar-owner. Nobody, however, was going to show up for Hanni Graber during the next twelve hours, nor, for that matter during the next twelve days. She would be held in solitary, and remain incommunicado with no recourse to a lawyer or anybody else. Including the Russians.

Hanni Graber was learning the lesson of her life: Don't fuck around with Swiss banks!

Viktor Chebrikov was also in the middle of a learning process. It looked increasingly as if his lifelong enemy, the fruitless pursuit of whom had been the main reason for his existence during the past five decades, was vulnerable after all. And what was amazing, in fact astounding, was that this vulnerability was of a nature that everybody had overlooked. Except for Karl Marx. He had very clearly predicted what would *inevitably* bring the Americans to their knees: their capitalistic system! It would blow *itself* up! But nobody read Karl Marx anymore, did they? Especially the young smart alecs surrounding Comrade Gorbachev.

Still, it would not hurt if the inevitable were helped along a little bit. As it now would be.

For soon, maybe very soon, the United States was probably going to get hit from three sides. One blow would come from Latin America. The next from Europe. This much had been re-confirmed by their man who had just returned from Zurich. And the final blow would come from the Middle East.

Bang, bang, bang!

The result will be chaos. The Americans will be numbed beyond action. Because, Chebrikov reasoned, they won't know against whom to retaliate. For all this is going to happen *without the Soviet Union having even to lift a finger!*

The final blow . . . that was what was so diabolical about the plan the Venezuelans had cooked up. And there was no doubt about the nature of it. No less than *five different sources* in the Middle East had reported back the same information: the word was out that Carlos and Abu Nidal were in Beirut, together. Carlos had flown in the night before in a Libyan jet. The plane was still parked on the tarmac at the Beirut airport, guarded by a dozen Palestinians.

They were recruiting assassins, it was said, in Sabra, Shatila and Burj al Brajneh, the three Palestinian refugee camps south of the city, those shacktowns which were full of desperate young men seeking their revenge against a world which had robbed them of their homeland and thus their future.

The target this time?

Nobody knew. But it was *said* that it must be a major one, since Carlos and Abu Nidal had lots of money to spend. Lots! Millions, it was said. Millions of dollars! At first it was thought that so much money meant that Gaddafi was behind it again. But others had quickly pointed out that with the oil price sinking once again, Libya's leader no longer had that kind of money to throw around. But if not Gaddafi, then who? Nobody in Beirut, nor in Damascus, nor in Tripoli seemed to know.

But Viktor Chebrikov knew.

Because he knew about that meeting between Carlos and the oil minister from Latin America in Basel. It was Venezuelan money. That's what that meeting in Basel was all about. Combine one's knowledge of that with what happened in Zurich in December, and then factor in what was scheduled to happen in Zurich next week and, *voilà*, it was clear.

The Americans were going to be blindsided:

— by the Latin American governments.
— by the European banks.
— by the suicide squad or squads being organized by Carlos and Abu Nidal with Venezuelan money.

Bang! Bang! Bang!

Although it was strictly against the rules laid down by Mikhail Gorbachev, the head of the KGB unlocked the bottom drawer of his desk and pulled out a large bottle of Stolichnaya.

'To the decline and fall of the United States,' he said aloud to his empty office, adding, under his breath, 'and the fool in the Kremlin who thought he could do business with Ronald Reagan.'

Then he placed a call to a colleague at the Defense Ministry. 'About Pakistan,' he said. 'I think the time may be soon ripe. Why don't you come over for a chat when you have time.'

Then Chebrikov called in his assistant. 'I want all of our people in Mexico to go on full alert. We may want to go into action there already next week.'

After his assistant had closed the door, Chebrikov took another slug of vodka. He had waited for this moment ever since 1962.

On the same day, January 5th, 1989, the intelligence services of the West began to stir. It was the BfV, the Bundesamt für Verfassungsschutz, West Germany's counterintelligence service, which telexed Interpol's central office in Paris that their informants had just told them that a certain Joachim Schmidt had disappeared from Frankfurt a month ago, and was thought to be abroad setting up some new terrorist activities. Schmidt, the message continued, was a leading member of the Red Army Faction. But his terrorist activities were not restricted to Germany. He had been seen twice in Beirut in the company of Abu Nidal and once in Tripoli with Ilich Ramirez Sanchez, otherwise known as Carlos. It was conjectured that, on occasion, he served as the 'on-the-ground supervisor' of terrorist acts undertaken in Western Europe and sponsored by both Nidal and Carlos.

Details on the man followed. He spoke almost perfect English with an American accent, learned when, as a young man, he had worked at the officer's club at the Rhein-Main Air Force Base. He also spoke almost flawless Arabic as a result of spending eighteen months in a terrorist training camp outside of Damascus in the late 1970s. He was six feet tall, blond, and the upper joint of the third finger on his left hand was missing.

The man was elusive and dangerous and, the BfV warned, he could surface anywhere from Rome to London to New York. So they asked Interpol to give their alert the widest possible global distribution.

That afternoon, Joachim Schmidt's credentials arrived on the telex of the anti-terrorist unit of the FBI, and were duly entered into that agency's central computer in Washington.

Chapter 13

Beirut, in 1989, looked like Berlin in 1945. It was a totally gutted city.

As Abu Nidal rode through its streets in the back seat of a Mercedes 300, with Ilich Ramirez Sanchez at his side, he looked out at the rubble with almost fatherly pride. For it had been he who had begun the process of destruction by arranging for the almost fatal attack on Israel's Ambassador to the United Kingdom, Shlomo Argov. It had evoked a massive Jewish response in the form of Israel's invasion of the Lebanon. And that had led to the destruction of the state of Lebanon in both the political and physical sense.

That alone, thought Abu Nidal, certainly established him as the premier terrorist of all time. Even greater than Carlos the Jackal, the man who was sitting, in silence, beside him. Sure, Carlos had dominated the 1970s. When he had stormed OPEC's headquarters in Vienna, and kidnapped no less than ten oil ministers to Algeria and Libya he became the most celebrated terrorist of the twentieth century.

But what had he done since? Almost nothing! Sure, he had bombed one of France's super-trains, La Très Grande Vitesse; he'd bombed the passenger station in Marseilles; he'd helped plan the assassination of some German bankers and businessmen with the help of the Red Army Faction in Frankfurt. But how many had been killed in all? A couple of dozen, at most.

And what had he, Abu Nidal, done? Since 1985 he had killed almost 700 people, that's what! And scared the entire world!

The 1970s had belonged to Carlos, yes, but there could be no doubt that the 1980s was the decade of Abu Nidal. In just one single year, 1985, he and his people had organized and implemented the hijacking of the *Achille Lauro* cruiseship in the Mediterranean; the destruction of that Egyptair 727 and sixty of its passengers on Malta; and the Christmas massacres of the Jews and the Americans at the Rome and Vienna airports. And those were just the highlights! If you included what he had done in the Middle East itself, especially in the Lebanon, and on the borders of Israel, in that single year Abu Nidal had managed to kill 181 persons, and seriously wound more than 200!

In the three years since, Abu Nidal and his Fata Revolutionary Council had massacred another 511 people. The body count arose from their bombing of the Pan Am lounge at the Charles De Gaulle airport in Paris, killing sixty-one people, principally Americans; their gunning down of the entire Israeli national soccer team as they were checking into the Amigo Hotel in Brussels; and, in their biggest coup of all, the shootdown, with the help of two portable Soviet missile-launchers, of the El Al 747 as it was in the process of landing at the Athens airport in the summer of 1988, killing every single Jew aboard. No less an authority than *Newsweek* had said of him that 'For sheer volume and casual viciousness he makes "Carlos", the top international terrorist of the 1970s, look like a choirboy.'

The Americans had tried everything to find him, and then to kill him. In vain! They had spread insidious lies about him: that he had died of cancer of the liver; that Yasser Arafat's men had assassinated him. That's how desperate the Americans were to have the world at least *believe* that it was rid of him. Sure, he was getting tired. And it was beginning to show. When he had looked in the mirror that morning he had had to admit to himself that his hair was receding further almost every day. But it was still black. Pitch black. And his eyes were clear. He was still Abu Nidal, 'the evil spirit which moves around only at night'.

But it was not yet night. It was a bright winter day in the Lebanon, where all blemishes were evident. Abu Nidal then looked over at his companion. Carlos's eyes were closed. *Newsweek* was wrong. He did not look like a choir*boy*: he looked like a tired, worn-out old man.

But, thought Abu Nidal, you had to give him credit: he at least knew where to come when he needed help. And help he definitely needed. For Carlos had no men of his own any longer, living as he had, in isolation, in Libya for so many years. He had to go to the 'outside'. That's why he was so close to the Red Army Faction in Germany. They could provide him with professional killers. But they couldn't help him this time. Because *this* time he needed professional killers of a very special and rare nature, a select breed that only he, Abu Nidal, could provide: terrorists who were both willing and ready to commit suicide.

And where else but here in Beirut could Carlos *buy* such people? After all, nobody *dies* for money, do they? Of course not. But money could buy Abu Nidal, and Abu Nidal could produce killers who were prepared to die: Palestinians.

He had proven that time and time again. All four of his young Palestinians who had kidnapped that Egyptair plane had been gunned down by the Maltese authorities. All three of his Palestinians who had massacred nineteen people as they were lined up at the El Al and TWA check-in counters at the Rome airport had also been killed. Ditto for the three Palestinians who had shot up the Vienna airport, the four who had bombed the Paris airport, the three who had massacred the Israeli soccer team in Brussels. All were dead, and all had been happy to die. For the Koran had told them that they would find their reward in heaven, a reward that would more than make up for the misery of the short lives they had spent in degrading exile on earth.

Why would young men be willing to die?

Because they were young men who were full of 'sacred rage', a rage beyond description, one that would only be calmed through the spilling of blood in the name of God. They took their directive from the Koran: 'Do battle in the path of God against those who battle you.'

And who were those battling them and all of Islam? The Jews and their protectors, the Americans. They had been told that, day and night, in the training camp in Iran. They were told that day and night in their refugee camps here in the Lebanon. Often by Abu Nidal himself. And they believed. For if Mohammed was their prophet, certainly Abu Nidal was His True Servant.

'Which one did you like best?' asked Abu Nidal, as the Mercedes continued north toward Beirut. Carlos opened his eyes, and, slowly, withdrew a notebook from his jacket.

'The tall one we saw in the Sabra district – I've got his name down here as Ben Ahmed Sharam. And the short, silent one from Shatila.'

'You mean Abdel Moussa.'

'Yes. That is one mean-looking bastard! How old is he?'

'Twenty-one.'

'Has he killed before?'

'Just once. An Iraqi Jew. He strangled him.'

Carlos did not seem to like that too much.

'But can he handle automatic weapons?'

'I'm told he plays a Kalashnikov like a violin.'

'What about an Uzi?'

'Not to worry. The Iranians have lots of Uzis. They buy them directly from the Israelis. And the Iranians trained Abdel Moussa.'

Carlos looked satisfied. 'Now, how do we get them there?'

'It is all arranged for,' replied Abu Nidal.

'They're not headed for Europe, you know. It will not be simple.'

'It's already arranged.'

'How?'

'Our people in Amman.'

'How?'

'Ever since you talked to me, after you returned from Basel, my people have known what would be needed. And we found two passports that exactly, and I mean exactly, meet your needs.

'Where did you get them?'

'They belong to two students – cousins, actually – who were returning to Amman from New York on Middle East Airlines. For their Christmas vacation. One of our people works the MEA check-in counter at JFK airport in New York. He spotted them right away.'

'But how did *you* get them?'

'We went to their parents in Amman. One of the fathers works with an American bank. The other for British Petroleum. We put it to them in very direct terms. Their children's passports, or their lives. It was a very simple decision.'

'And where are the students now?'

'Safe in their parents' houses in Amman. Where they will stay, until we let them know.'

'Where are the passports now?'

'Right here.' And Abu Nidal reached into his breast pocket for them.

Carlos, who had never travelled on anything *but* forged passports, looked very carefully at them. One was in the name of Mohammed Obeidat, the other Jaber al Ahmed. Both had student visas, valid until the end of June, 1989, the identical stamp having been put in both passports by the American embassy in Amman. One of the students was twenty; the other twenty-one.

'Perfect!' exclaimed Carlos. Then: 'Do you have pictures?'

Again Carlos reached into his breast pocket, and this time

produced a small envelope. Out of the envelope he produced two passport photos, one of the tall young thug they had interviewed at the Sabra refugee camp, the other of the short young murderer from Shatila.

Carlos kept looking at the second photo. 'God he looks mean!'

'He also looks twenty-one,' said Abu Nidal.

Then Carlos seemed to hesitate. 'But do they speak English?'

'The tall one from Sabra speaks it almost perfectly. The short one from Shatila . . .' Abu Nidal's hands moved back and forth to indicate that one could not expect too much there.

Then he added: 'There will be an element of risk when they go through immigration and customs in America. But the odds are very good that even the short one will get through. After all, they tell me that hundreds of thousands of foreign students go to America every year, and that a lot of them have only a limited knowledge of English. Remember, their passports and student visas are *authentic*. And the visas are for study at a school that takes a lot of Arabs.'

'Which school is that?'

'An old Jesuit University in Washington DC called Georgetown. The University has a special Arab Studies Program. Because of that apparently the University and Jordan, especially Hussein and Hussein's son, are very close. Both boys are studying under scholarships paid for by the Royal Family.'

'They won't like this,' commented Carlos.

'Too bad. They kicked me out of Jordan twelve years ago,' replied Abu Nidal. 'Then I went to Iraq. They kicked me out of Iraq eight years ago. So I went to Syria. Same thing. Now I am stuck in Beirut, like you are in Tripoli. I say fuck them all, Carlos.'

They were nearing the ocean front when the Mercedes pulled up in front of a large shack. Inside it was a restaurant, a Palestinian restaurant. It was therefore also a safe restaurant for men like Ilich Ramirez Sanchez and Mazen Sabry al-

Banna, alias Carlos and Abu Nidal. They ate a lamb stew while Abu Nidal's men were in a back room, switching passport photos in the two Jordanian passports.

'Are you organized in America?' Abu Nidal asked, as the meal neared an end.

'Yes. We have our best man on the ground there. You know him: Joachim Schmidt. And two safe houses, one on each coast.'

'And weapons?'

'Uzis, as I mentioned. We got an entire cratefull in through Mexico.'

Both men laughed. They appreciated the irony that Americans were going to be killed by Palestinians with Israeli-made weapons.

Carlos looked at his watch. 'I should be going to the airport.'

An hour later, the Libyan government-owned, German-made jet lifted off and, tracked all the way by the radars of the 6th Fleet, returned to Tripoli.

At 8.00 the next morning, Friday, January 6th, 1989 an MEA DC–8 lifted off, bound for London. Among its passengers were two students, returning to Georgetown University from their three week vacation at home in Amman. In London, they remained in the transit lounge at Heathrow for an hour before re-boarding, this time a British Airways' flight bound directly for Dulles airport.

Neither accepted food or drink from the unclean hands of the British stewardesses. Both read the Koran the entire way.

Seated just seven rows in front of them was an American journalist by the name of Sally Brown. She did not eat or drink much on that trans-Atlantic flight either because, typically, her mind simply would not stop working.

First it was Paul Mayer who preoccupied her. It was he who had gotten her into this thing in the first place. Sure, she'd been fishing around, hoping to come up with something juicy on Bank of America, but she'd found very little of substance until that lunch with Mayer in London. He'd even shown her the bank's computer printouts, which provided the basis for her story that B of A was not in such bad shape as rumor would have it. Now she wondered: Had Mayer led her down the garden path? Or had the bank's CEO, George Pace, set up both Mayer and the *Journal*?

She preferred to believe the latter. Because though Mayer was fifty-two, there was no doubt about it: he was a damn attractive man. And she wasn't exactly twenty-one herself.

Then she went back to the reason why she was on that plane, headed for Washington, and Mayer. Was she over-reacting? It had all been so clear on Wednesday: clear that the world was on the edge of a major financial crisis. The dollar had been plunging; gold had been soaring; and, once again, Bank of America seemed to be tottering on the edge.

But then the action had stopped.

It was as if there was somebody at the controls who had turned it on, and then, just as unexpectedly, turned it off.

Or was this just another case of paranoia, a disease which is very common among financial journalists?

Maybe *nothing* of any substance was going on.

If so, she, Sally Brown, was in trouble. She had convinced her bureau chief in London that she was onto something very big, something that could dwarf the crisis of August 1982 when Mexico was on the verge of defaulting; something that could make the latter days of July 1984, when Continental Illinois Bank was tottering on the edge of collapse, appear insignificant by comparison. She'd talked her boss into buying it, and his bosses, at 200 Liberty Street in New York, had agreed to pay for it.

Was she now going to just make a great big fool of herself?

She was depending on Paul Mayer to help her out, if she could find the son of a bitch.

José Martinez, Jr was uneasy, very uneasy, as he waited outside the immigration and customs area on the lower level of Dulles airport. His doubts had already begun to grow before Christmas, when he had spent the better part of a Sunday taking pictures of Professor Mayer and his visitors. Why did the German want them? Those worries had returned when, just six hours ago, the Nazi had shown up, uninvited, at his apartment in Georgetown. Sure, his uncle had told him to do whatever the guy said, but this was starting to get out of hand. The German had no sooner gotten into his apartment at 5.00 that afternoon than he had started to walk around the place as if he owned it.

'What the fuck do you think you're doing?' he had asked him.

The guy just kept sniffing around.

'You expecting any visitors this weekend?' the Nazi had then asked.

'Yeah. My girlfriend.'

'Well, call it off.'

'Why?'

'Because two people are going to stay here for a few days.'

'Does my uncle know about this?'

'Where do you think I got your address?' the German had answered. 'Now get on the phone and tell your girlfriend that you're busy this weekend.'

And now, here he was, at almost midnight, waiting for a plane from London to arrive, with the Nazi hovering in the background.

'What do they look like?' he had asked him.

'Like Arabs,' had been the answer, 'young Arabs. About your age. They go to the same school you do.'

'So why don't they take a cab back to campus like everybody else does?'

'Because they're special, that's why.'

'What's their names?'

The Nazi had had to pull out a slip of paper to get the answer, for Chrissake.

'Mohammed Obeidat and Jaber al Ahmed,' he had then read off.

At just before midnight, the passengers from British Airways' Flight 109 started to emerge from the customs area. And there they were.

José Martinez, Jr approached them immediately. 'You guys go to Georgetown?' he asked.

The short, vicious-looking one nodded. José Martinez Jr glanced back at the Nazi who was standing twenty feet away. He nodded.

'OK,' said José, 'let's go.'

They then headed for the parking lot, where the Nazi's BMW was parked. The German, who had kept twenty paces ahead of them, had the suitcases in the trunk and the Arabs in the back seat in record time. Minutes later the three Georgetown undergraduates, and their German driver, were on the expressway heading through the Virginia countryside toward the nation's capital.

'Are you guys in the School of Foreign Service, or what?' José asked, twisting around from the front seat to have a better look at them.

No answer.

'Business School?'

Still no answer.

'Leave 'em alone,' the German said.

'Don't they speak English?' José asked.

'Sure they speak English. How the fuck could they go to Georgetown if they didn't,' the German replied. 'They're just tired.'

Suddenly from the back seat, in perfect English: 'We are both with the Arab Studies Program. With Professor Michael Hudson.'

It was the tall one who spoke.

'So, where are you from?'

'Amman, Jordan.'

José, Jr started to relax for the first time that evening. Georgetown got them from all over the world, and a lot of them were really strange.

'You guys live on campus, or what?'

No answer.

José turned to the German. 'I mean, if they've got rooms in the dorms, why the fuck do they have to stay with me?'

'Enough,' said the German. 'Shut up, and I mean it. They are going to be with you for three nights. And you my smartass friend, are going to stay with them, in the apartment, the entire time.'

'Come *on*, man.

'And if you say *one* word about this, to *anybody*, you are going to end up in very big trouble. Like dead.'

Holy shit! thought José. The fucker means it!

So he shut up.

Half an hour later they pulled up in front of the Georgetown Arms on N Street, one of that exclusive area's most exclusive apartment complexes. It was not exactly where you would expect to find a safe house for terrorists.

The concierge was used to the late night comings and goings of José Martinez, Jr, usually in the company of fellow students of both sexes, and of diverse colors and tongues. Two Arabs, with suitcases, at 1.00 in the morning were, therefore, nothing out of the ordinary.

'Need some help?' the concierge asked.

'Yeah,' José answered. 'Could you take my two pals up the elevator and open up the door for them. I'll be right back.

The German was waiting outside in the BMW. José leaned down to speak to him through the open window.

'Did you really mean that about staying inside the entire weekend?'

'Yes.'

'So do you want us to starve to death?'

'I'll bring . . .' and then the German stopped. 'No, that won't work.'

He remained silent for a few seconds.

'OK. You go out and bring back food whenever you need it. But keep your mouth shut, and I *really* mean that, and keep those two guys in the apartment.'

'All right.'

'Here.' The German handed him an envelope.

'That should cover the food bill. I'll be in touch tomorrow. And he drove off.

Upstairs, the Arabs were waiting, still standing, in José's living-room.

'This bedroom will be yours,' he told them, as he led the way into his guest facility. 'You're supposed to stay here the whole weekend. OK? Otherwise it will be my ass. OK? Now you've got your own bathroom and shower and everything here. So I'll just let you guys take care of yourselves, and we'll see you in the morning.'

'Thank you,' said the tall one.

'You're welcome,' answered José Martinez, Jr.

An hour later he turned off his bedroom TV and went to sleep. His last thoughts were about his uncle. How in the world had he gotten involved with two young Arabs from Jordan? Especially the small one.

At 10.00 the next morning, the phone rang.

'I'll be over in half an hour. Wake up those two guys. I want to give them something.' It was the German.

The two young Arabs were still asleep when he entered their bedroom. Half an hour later, when the German arrived, they still looked very tired, and very wary.

The German spoke Arabic to them from the moment he entered José's apartment. He stopped for a moment to give José an order in English: 'Make some coffee. Black.'

When José returned with the first two cups, and placed them on the coffee table in front of the two young Arabs, he could not help but notice what was lying on his table. Photographs. Polaroid photographs. In fact, those pictures which he had taken with his new Polaroid camera before Christmas, the ones he had been worrying about ever since. He'd subsequently handed them all over to the German.

There was one of Professor Paul Mayer talking to his TA on the doorstep in front of 3514 Dent Place. There was also one each of the three men who had come for lunch that Sunday in December. And then two more pictures of them all leaving, as a group.

He went back into the kitchen to get a third cup of coffee for the German. This time, when he returned to the living-room with it, his hand was shaking. It was with difficulty that he placed it on the coffee table. The German, talking a mean streak in Arabic, pointing now and then at the Polaroids, took no notice of him.

Half an hour later, in his usual abrupt manner, the German left, leaving the two young Arabs sitting in José's living-room. The Polaroids had vanished.

'You guys getting hungry?'

'Yes,' came the answer, this time from both of them.

And I'm supposed to supply room service! José thought.

'What's your name again?' José asked the tall one.

'Mohammed Obeidat.'

'And him?'

'Jaber. Jaber al Ahmed.'

'OK Mohammed, now let me tell you my problem. I'm supposed to feed you guys here in the apartment, but I know fuck-all about cooking. The best I can do is to go over to the Roy Rogers on Wisconsin or the Burger King on M Street and pick up some lousy hamburgers, which will be cold by the time I get back.'

José paused.

'Or . . . or we can all go over to the Tombs and get something *decent* to eat. You guys must know the Tombs, right? So you know that they also have Heineken beer on tap.'

José paused.

'Oops. You guys don't drink, do you. Anyway, do you want to stay cooped up here for the rest of the weekend, or . . .'

'We'll go with you,' said the tall young Arab who claimed he was Mohammed Obeidat.

'Great. But you've got to promise me that you won't tell that fucking German. OK?'

It was noon on Saturday and the Tombs was packed. The Hoyas were playing St John's in the big sports arena in Landover later that afternoon, and a lot of students were stoking up with food and drink before heading out to Maryland for the game.

The Latinos, who disdained getting worked up over *anything*, especially sports, were installed at their *Stammtisch* at the back, obviously planning on spending the better part of the day there. When they saw José and the two guys with him, they automatically pushed together to make room for them.

'They're having a problem at the dorm. So they're staying with me over the weekend. They're in Arab Studies. He's Mohammed Obeidat,' José said, pointing at the taller of the two Arabs, 'and he's Jaber al Ahmed, or something like that.'

Everybody mumbled hello.

The two Arabs ate the hamburger, with the works, which José ordered; then another; then another. They drank milk, which José, with apologies all around, had also gotten for them. Neither of them participated in the conversation swirling around them, but nobody thought much of it, since most of the time the other students were speaking in Spanish. You could hardly expect an Arab to speak Spanish, could you?

Then around 1.30, one of the boys from Brazil, a pretty close pal of José Martinez, Jr, showed up. Once again, they pressed still further together to make room. And once again, José ordered another round of beer . . . and two milks.

'What's with the milk?' the newcomer asked José.

'It's for Mohammed and Jaber,' José answered.

'Jaber?' the Brazilian asked.

'Yeah. Jaber al Ahmed. My new pal from Amman, Jordan,' José replied, pointing at him.

The Brazilian looked at the short Arab and then back at José. Then he motioned with his head toward the exit. He had to do it three times before the son of the finance minister of Venezuela caught on.

A couple of minutes later, José said he had to go to the John. When the Brazilian caught up with him, out of sight of the *Stammtisch*, he grabbed his arm.

'What's going on?' he asked.

'What do you mean?'

'Where did you pick up those two guys?'

'Through a friend. What's wrong?'

'You said the short one is Jaber al Ahmed.'

'Right.'

'And he goes to the School of Foreign Service. He's in Arab Studies. And he's from Jordan.'

'Right, right and right.'

'Wrong, José. I know Jaber al Ahmed. This guy, my friend, ain't him.'

'What do you mean, you know him?'

'He rooms on the same floor I do in Village A.'

'Maybe there's two of them.'

'Come on, José.'

José Martinez, Jr fell silent. He *knew* that *something* phony was going on, in fact, *had* to be going on, with the Nazi involved.

Then he remembered the warning that the German had issued.

'Look, man,' he said to his Brazilian pal, 'don't say anything. OK? Otherwise I'm going to be in deep, deep shit. *Really* deep. Like . . .' and José Martinez, Jr's right hand made a cutting motion across his throat.

The Brazilian shrugged. 'No problem. It's no skin off my ass, is it? It's just that it kind of makes you wonder. What's happened to the *real* Jaber al Ahmed?'

'Look,' said José, 'we know that the Arabs are all screwed up. So they're playing some game. Sneaking some guys into the country, or something. That's the American government's problem, not ours. Right?'

'Sure. Just don't get involved, José,' his friend warned.

'Don't worry about me.'

Ten minutes later José left the Tombs with his two Arabs in tow. When he got back to the apartment, he turned on the TV, and got a re-run of *Gunsmoke*. They seemed to like it.

Dinner they all had in front of the TV. It consisted of pizza and chocolate milk shakes, delivered by Chicago Pizza on M Street.

At 10.00 the Arabs got up to go to bed.

'Thank you, José,' said the taller one. 'It was a very nice day. It was one of the nicest days we have had in a long time. Thank you.'

'Yes,' said the short one. 'My thanks, many thanks.'

They both smiled, and, for a moment, they both looked like what they might have been: two very young men who had been set down in a strange land and had, unexpectedly, been given food and shelter by a friendly native. They closed the bedroom door, leaving a perplexed José Martinez, Jr behind.

'What the hell,' he said to the empty living-room. 'They can't be *such* bad guys, can they?'

But when he woke up the next morning, he was not so sure of that assessment.

Why in the world had the German shown them those pictures of Professor Mayer and his visitors?'

José thought he knew.

He picked up the bedroom phone and dialed a series of numbers. His mother answered the phone in Caracas.

'It's José,' he said.

'What's wrong, José?' she asked immediately.

'Nothing, Mama. I want to speak to father.'

'He's not here. Why do you want to speak to him?'

'I just want to. Where is he?'

'In Mexico City.'

'Is my uncle with him?'

'Yes. Why?'

'Is nothing you should bother about, Mama. Do you know where I could reach him in Mexico City?'

'No. But the office will know.'

'It's Sunday, Mama.'

'What is so urgent?'

'Nothing, Mama. Look. I'll call dad's office tomorrow. How's the weather?'

'Warm and raining. What's wrong José?'

'Nothing, Mama. Look. I've got to go. Everything's fine, Mama. I'll call again next week.'

She said nothing.

'Bye, Mama. I'll call again next week.'

And he hung up.

'Shit!' he said. 'Now what?'

Ten blocks away, Sally Brown was also awake, and hungry. She had decided to treat herself and stay at the Four Seasons Hotel, right on the edge of Georgetown. After arriving at midnight on Friday, she had spent most of the time in her room, sleeping. Now she was ready to face the world again.

She called down for room service and ordered a real American breakfast – bacon, eggs, tomato juice, coffee – and asked them to send up both the *Washington Post* and the *New York Times*.

She decided to stay in bed for a while. She felt absolutely comfortable, but not just because of the luxury which the hotel offered. It was because she was back home in the good old US of A, back home among Americans. Europe was great, and she would never regret having gone over there for the *Journal*. But . . .

The problem facing Americans in Europe had been growing for years, but lately the increasing open dislike she had begun to encounter over there had started to get to her. She recalled an interview she had recently had with Britain's former Defense Secretary, Michael Heseltine, who was now poised to succeed Margaret Thatcher. She remembered it almost word for word:

> If the pre-eminent strength of America enables it to buy increasing sections of the European economy, changing the relationship between the United States and Europe from one of partnership to industrial subservience, then resentment against America will grow in Europe and anti-Americanism will become widespread.

And that from a British Conservative!

She had interviewed Willy Brandt in West Germany, now the *eminence grise* behind the Social Democrats who hoped to be back in power soon. His attitude towards the United States, the United States of Ronald Reagan in particular, had been one of open contempt. 'We don't need your missiles, nor your technology, nor your money. It is time that you Americans realize that and begin to mind your own business, and not ours.' And that had come from the man who had been

Regierende Bürgermeister of West Berlin, a city which had survived the Soviet blockade thanks only to an American airlift of food and fuel.

The young people were even worse. Throughout Central Europe a new generation had come to power, younger men and women who now looked at Americans not as the liberators of World War II, but as the aggressor of Vietnam. Americans were thought of as capitalistic predators, and the symbols of their power were the great multinational banks: Citibank, Chase Manhattan, Bank of America. They, not the Russian's tanks, were the enemy.

So are some of them out to destroy one of those symbols? she pondered, with the hope that it will set off a financial domino effect which would put America into retreat and rescue Europe from the economic 'subservience' which the Heseltines and Willy Brandts of the world had had enough of?

Breakfast arrived, and so did the papers.

The economy dominated the front pages of both the *Post* and the *Times*. The flash estimates for the first quarter of 1989 had been leaked. The boom, they said, was about to end. Gramm-Rudman, the papers concluded, would have to be suspended. The deficit, which everybody had hoped was finally getting under control, would start to soar again. The new administration coming into power in just two weeks would have no choice but to 'prime the pump' through massively increased government expenditures, lest unemployment soar to unacceptable levels. That pump-priming could only be financed by higher government borrowing, meaning that interest rates could go much higher again, perhaps very quickly.

The international consequences could be devastating, the *Times* suggested. Higher interest rates would mean that the cost of servicing the massive debt owed by the Third World could reach intolerable levels. And hit hardest of all would be those debtor nations which were also oil exporters, for if, in the pull of a sharp decline in business activity in the United States the demand for oil dropped in a market increasingly glutted again by supply, the price would plummet even further. And with it the income of some of the world's most heavily indebted nations . . . Mexico, Venezuela, Nigeria.

'And if they go,' Sally Brown thought, 'Bank of America goes. And if Bank of America goes, then . . .'

She had been right about her story! It was going to be the biggest one of her life. Unless . . . unless it all started to happen before she wrote it!

'Dammit!' she said, and kept reading. She struck gold in the business section of the *Times*.

In the lefthand column of the first page of that section, there were no less than *three* very peculiar little items. One referred to a meeting of the finance and oil ministers of Venezuela and Brazil and Mexico that was, apparently, going on in Mexico City over the weekend. The second said that it was rumored that the heads of the nine largest banks in Central Europe were getting together in Switzerland on Monday. The third said that the Swiss National Bank had, abruptly, called off the syndication of a $2 billion loan for the Soviet Union that had been scheduled for late in January.

She got out of bed.

'To hell with it,' she then said. 'I'll just barge in.'

An hour later, dressed fit to kill, she was pressing the buzzer beside the door leading into the house at 3514 Dent Place in Georgetown.

Paul Mayer was still in bed, reading the papers. He had just taken up the overseas edition of the *Guardian*, and was reading intently the front page editorial, entitled, 'I am not anti-American.' It contained some of the same worrisome thoughts that had bothered Sally Brown earlier that Sunday morning as she had read the papers in her hotel room just ten blocks away.

The article began:

> 'I'm not anti-American,' said Edward Heath. Nor is Mr Michael Heseltine, the former Defence Secretary, anti-American. Sir Raymond Lygo, head of British Aerospace, lived in America for many years, so he enters the now mandatory disclaimer with rare fervour. But they, and virtually every politician or businessman who ventures an opinion on anything these days, has first to chant in chorus: We are not, not, not anti-American.
>
> In a few instances, of course, the chant is simple hypocrisy. Some people simply do not like or trust America. But in 1989 it is necessary to pause over the ritual phrase because it is coming to have specific significance. The problem can be put crudely in business terms: because its multinational corporations can enter any market they choose, anywhere on earth, backed, as they are, by the giant American banking system, the United States is stripping Europe of its independent manufacturing capacity. And even more crudely in cultural, political and economic terms: We're willy nilly becoming the 51st state. On such perceptions frustration and discord flourish. For across so much of the continent there is now the feeling that the single giant engine of the American economy is beginning to win the battle against a bevy of nation states, too small to compete alone, too bemused to unite properly. There is rising fear and some desperation as the extremities of this dilemma dawn. Today, in January 1989, it is unfortunately all too easy to be anti-American as America increasingly comes to be viewed as future eclipse and present danger.

Paul Mayer's doorbell rang for a second time, and, finally, Maria opened the door.

It was hate at first sight.

'What do you want?' Maria asked.

'To see Professor Mayer,' Sally answered.

'Is he expecting you?'

'No.'

'Then you had better go away.'

Maria started to back into the house.

'Please give him this.'

She gave Maria her card.

'I'll wait,' she added.

Maria closed the door, leaving Sally Brown standing on the doorstep. Reluctantly, Maria went up the stairs and knocked on the door leading into Paul Mayer's bedroom.

'Come in, Maria,' he said. And after she did he asked, 'Was that somebody at the door?'

'Some woman,' Maria answered, and walked over to Mayer's bed, which was covered with newspapers, and handed over the card.

Mayer took one look and jumped out of bed. 'Get out, Maria, I've got to get dressed. And let that lady in. Give her a cup of coffee. And tell her I'll be right down.'

Maria fled as Mayer's pyjamas started to come off.

Ten minutes later, now impeccably dressed in a blue blazer and turtleneck sweater, he came down the stairs. 'Sally, what a pleasant surprise!' he said, and he went over to kiss her as she rose from the sofa.

'I'm sorry to burst in like this,' she said.

He waved his hand as if to dismiss even the thought that she was inconveniencing him.

'Are you free for brunch?' he asked.

'Yes, of course.'

'Good. We'll go to The 1789. We can walk there from here.'

'But first I'd like to talk,' she said.

'Then we'll need some more coffee,' he said, and called for Maria.

After the fresh coffee had arrived, Sally Brown began.

'Paul, I think we are on the edge of a major financial disturbance.'

'I see. Why?'

She explained, starting with the market action earlier in the week. All of a sudden speculation had mounted in Europe against the dollar. At the same time, a big play on gold had begun. Finally, though it didn't make sense, the price of oil in the futures market had begun to plummet.

Mayer interrupted her. 'Why doesn't that make sense? Didn't you read the papers this morning? The word's out: the good times are about to end. Recession lies ahead. So the demand for oil is bound to drop, as will its price.'

Sally Brown turned a little pink.

'So how did the Swiss National Bank get all the numbers a week ahead of everybody else?' she demanded.

'What do you mean?'

'I mean that the Swiss National Bank is the one that's been behind all the action – in gold, in the dollar, in the oil futures market. It's also the bank that's going after Bank of America. They started early last week, then they stopped. I'll bet you every nickel I've got that tomorrow morning, or Tuesday morning at the latest, all hell is going to break loose.'

Now she had really gotten Paul Mayer's attention.

'Back up a minute. What was that you said about Bank of America?'

'Don't you know what's been happening in the swap market?'

'No.'

She told him, and it obviously disturbed him.

'Are you absolutely sure about your information?' he asked.

'Yes. I got it directly from the Chase people in London.'

'Why do you think the Swiss National Bank is doing all this?' he then asked.

'To make money, obviously, on what now appears to be a sure thing. And to get even.'

'Why do you say it's a sure thing?'

'I won't tell you. I'll show you. Have you got the business section of the Sunday *Times* handy?'

'I'll get it.'

He was up the stairs and back in nothing flat.

'Here,' he said, as he handed the paper to her.

'Item one: the Venezuelan, Mexican and Brazilian finance and oil ministers are meeting in Mexico City. Item two: nine banks are meeting tomorrow in Zurich.'

'And?'

'They're going to pull the rug from under B of A. Venezuela and Mexico and Brazil are going to declare default on their American loans, and the European banks are going to step in and keep those countries solvent.'

'They wouldn't dare,' Mayer responded.

'Who wouldn't dare? Mexico and Venezuela?' she countered. 'You might have been right under normal circumstances. Because they have always known that if they default unilaterally, America would cut them off without one further dime.'

'Exactly.'

'Except now that won't matter. The Europeans will bail them out. Leaving the United States holding one big empty bag.'

'How do you know all this?'

She said nothing, bluffing.

'Look,' said Mayer, 'you're right about Mexico and Venezuela, and you can also add Brazil to the list. All three have already notified Bank of America that they are invoking the *force majeure* clauses in their loan agreements. The men who are meeting in Mexico City today will be meeting with us – and by us I mean Bank of America and myself, in my new capacity as a consultant to the Federal Reserve, and maybe a few others

– in San Francisco on Tuesday morning. How did you find that out?'

Having won on her first bluff, she decided to try again, and so she continued to say nothing.

So Paul Mayer continued: 'They threatened this before, at least half a dozen times. But nobody, including me, ever took them seriously because we knew that they could not get away with it.'

He paused, and got up, and, as he started to pace the room, he continued talking.

'But now, with the Europeans backing them financially, I don't know. When did this thing start?' he then asked.

'Remember I asked you about Venezuela in London?'

'Vaguely.'

'Well, we know for sure that Venezuela's oil minister, Roberto Martinez, was in Zurich in mid-December. At the Swiss National Bank.'

Paul Mayer looked at his watch.

'It's eight o'clock in the evening there now. I'm going to call him right now.'

The 'him' Mayer was referring to was Dr Ulrich Huber, Chairman of the Swiss National Bank, and former colleague of Dr Paul Mayer. He lived in Küsnacht, on the Lake of Zurich. Mayer had the telephone number on his computer. So he excused himself, and went upstairs to retrieve it. He also placed the call from up there.

A woman answered the phone.

'Bisch Du's, Heidi?' Mayer asked, in Swiss dialect. And he used the familiar *Du* since his friendship with the Hubers went way back to his post-university days in Basel.

'Jo. Wär isch am Telephon?'

'Do isch dr' Paul Mayer. Chasch du di no a mi erinnere?'

'Natürlig, Paul, bisch du in Züri?'

'Nai. I telephonier vo Amerika. Los, isch dr' Ulrich do?'

There was a long pause.

'I bi nit sicher, wart an Augeblick. I gang go luege.'

When she said she had to go look to see if her husband was at home – on a Sunday night in Switzerland when *everybody* was at home – he knew that she had been warned.

He was right. When Heidi Huber came back it was with the news that her husband must have stepped out, maybe for a walk to a local restaurant and a glass of wine. Could she give him a message?

Hardly.

Paul Mayer broke off the call as gracefully as possible, and then dialed again, the number of the Chairman of the Deutsche Bank in Frankfurt, the most powerful financial institution on the continent of Europe. This time a maid answered. She said he was not home, that he had just left on a short out-of-town trip. Mayer believed her. Probably at the very moment he was boarding a Lufthansa or Swissair flight, headed for Zurich.

He then tried Luxembourg. This time he got his man, the Chairman of the Kredietbank. He put it to him bluntly.

'Were you invited to attend a meeting in Zurich tomorrow morning?

'Yes.'

'Are you going?'

'No.'

'Can you tell me what it's going to be all about?'

'It's highly confidential, Paul.'

'Is the Swiss National Bank trying to put together an enormous credit facility for Mexico and Venezuela?' Mayer asked.

'So you know,' came the answer from Luxembourg.

'Why should any of you European banks risk such an exposure in Latin America when you know what a mess the American banks are in down there already?'

'Ah,' came the answer,' because *we* will be getting collateral.'

'I thought that we were talking about normal sovereign loans.'

'No, no, Paul. We Europeans are not *so* dumb, you know. These credits will be fully collateralized. By Mexican oil and by Venezuelan oil.'

'But those governments have always refused to even discuss such a thing.'

'No more,' was the answer.

'Then why isn't the Kredietbank going to participate?'

'Because we in Luxembourg are not interested in identifying ourselves with such a crass financial attack on America. Because that is what it is,' said the banker from Luxembourg.

'André,' said Paul Mayer, 'you don't know how much I appreciate your candor. I'll guarantee the confidentiality of this conversation. But I will also guarantee that when this is over, a few people in this town will be told where you and Luxembourg stood on this issue.'

Paul Mayer hung up, and then went down the stairs once again. Sally Brown was no longer sitting on the sofa in his living-room. Instead she was putting on her coat.

'So you're getting hungry,' Mayer said.

'No, I'd like to take a rain check on that brunch,' she answered. Then: 'Did it check out?'

'It did. You are right. All the way down the line.'

'That's why I've got to get going. I'm taking the shuttle up to New York, and will be writing the story up there.'

'Can't it wait a day?'

'It will take a day to put together. This is dynamite stuff, and our editors are going to want to verify every single detail before printing it.'

'So it will come out on Tuesday?'

'Yes. If they buy what I tell them in New York today, and turn everybody loose on it first thing tomorrow morning.'

'Everything we've discussed here is not for attribution. I

trust you realize that.' Mayer's voice now had a steely quality.

'I do,' and her tone of voice had now changed also.

'You know that you could do an enormous amount of damage with this story.'

'If we don't do it, the *Times* or the *Post* will. And, I suggest, they might do it in a manner that would be slightly less sympathetic toward the financial Establishment of this country. Remember: at the *Journal* we are all on *your* side, Dr Mayer.'

He saw her to the door.

'So you'll be going out to San Francisco for that meeting,' she said, turning back toward him from outside.

'Yes. And now so will you, no doubt.'

'For sure. Will it take place at the bank?'

'Yes. But they probably won't even let you in the building.'

'That's all right. We find ways.' Then: 'I usually stay at the Fairmont. I should be there late tomorrow night. If you have time for a drink, call me.'

'I'll do that,' Mayer said. Then he thought of Azar Shahani and added, 'if I can work it out.'

Sally Brown had one last word. 'By the way, there was an additional little item in the papers today. The Swiss National Bank, which seems to be our favorite subject this morning, did one other thing: it cancelled its syndication of a $2 billion loan for the Soviet Union. Could this also, somehow, tie in?'

'I don't see how,' Mayer replied.

And she left.

The next five hours Paul Mayer spent on the telephone, trying to get people, trying to warn them about what was about to come down, trying to line up support for standby arrangements in case they became necessary.

But it seemed that nobody was at home. Worse, it seemed that there was nobody left in Washington. For this was the time of interregnum. The President only had a couple of weeks left in office, and he was out at the ranch in California, working out final arrangements for the establishment of the Reagan Library on the Stanford campus, and receiving the California financial heavyweights who would be expected to finance most of it. All the President's men were back home, in Dallas and Oakland and Los Angeles, looking for jobs. And the lame duck Congress was in recess. All that remained in Washington were the bureaucrats.

And that Sunday afternoon, Paul Mayer lined up three of the most important ones for a quick trip to San Francisco, the three men who were in charge of America's banking system: Robert Reston, the head of the Federal Reserve Board; Roger Wells, the man who ran the Federal Deposit Insurance Corporation; and Charles Thayer, the Comptroller of the Currency.

All agreed to take the evening United flight the next day, the one which left Dulles for the West Coast daily around 5 p.m. The meeting with the Mexicans, Venezuelans and Brazilians was scheduled to begin at 9 a.m. the following morning, on a day which could prove to be a very critical one in the financial history of the United States: Tuesday, January 10th, 1989.

A fourth man, the Secretary of the Treasury, whom Mayer finally found in Houston, where, it was rumored, he would be taking over the chairmanship of that city's largest bank in early February, refused to join them. He said it was all bluff. And he warned Mayer. By going to San Francisco, the Fed – and the Secretary knew that Mayer was now advising the Fed, particularly its Chairman – would be adding credence to the story that something really serious was happening. He, the Secretary of the Treasury (at least for another two weeks), wanted no part of that. During the past four years, the Mexicans had repeatedly given him, the chief financial officer of the United States, their assurances that under no circumstances would they even consider default as an option.

'Remember the big scare back in early 1986?' he asked

Mayer. 'The price of oil, and I'm referring to the spot price, fell to $10 a barrel. Remember?'

Mayer said that, indeed, he did remember.

'And everybody said that by the summer of '86 the Mexicans would be broke and that they would have no choice but to default?'

Mayer remembered that also.

'Well did they? Hell no! And they won't this time either.'

With those words the lame duck Secretary of the Treasury had hung up.

Then around five o'clock that Sunday, January 8th, it was Paul Mayer who received a telephone call. It was from one of his colleagues over at Georgetown University's Center for Strategic and International Studies, the think tank that housed everybody from Kissinger to Brzezinski to Schlesinger to Mrs Kirkpatrick. This call, however, came from Sergio Dobrovsky, the man generally recognized as the foremost expert on terrorism in the United States. Each time a plane got hijacked, Dobrovsky was automatically on TV, being interviewed by everybody from Ted Koppel on ABC to either MacNeil or Lehrer on PBS.

'I just got back from Israel yesterday,' Dobrovsky began, 'and the people there told me a few things that may or may not have some bearing on matters of concern to you.'

Mayer then remembered. 'Sergio, I'm sorry. You left a message before Christmas, and now I realize that I failed to return the call. I left for London that day.'

'Don't worry. I understand. Now, what they told me in Tel Aviv is this. Apparently the terrorist Carlos – you remember him don't you, Paul?'

'Sure.'

'Well, he was seen in Beirut this past week in the company of Abu Nidal.'

He hardly had to ask Mayer if he knew who *he* was.

'They were recruiting some men, which is not that unusual.

What *is* unusual is that this time they *may*, I stress *may*, be going after a target in the United States. I say this because they were looking for at least one recruit who spoke excellent English, preferrably with an American accent.'

'How do the Israelis know this?'

'They've got informants all over the place in the Palestinian refugee camps.'

'But how could that possibly be of any direct concern to me, Sergio?' Mayer then asked.

'Let me explain. Rumors were also picked up by the Israelis that Venezuelan money is behind this. That's why Carlos is involved. The Israelis then tried to figure out why. And although this might sound absurd to you, Paul, they figured that Venezuela, which is today in a very serious financial bind with the oil price starting to go south again, might be trying to destabilize the American financial system, and somehow, as a result, be able to get off the hook where their debt payments are concerned. The Israelis also thought that the Russians might be in on this. What, they asked me, could be higher on the Soviet agenda than to encourage *anything* that might bring down the American banking system?'

'I still don't quite follow you, Sergio.'

'Well, to put it very bluntly, one of the hypotheses which the Israelis developed was this: what if, as part of a coordinated action on the part of some Latin American nations and the Russians, all aimed, as I said, at destabilizing the American financial system, they did something that would close down the American banking system?'

'You mean a terrorist act?' Mayer asked.

'Exactly. How would they go about it?'

'You've got me, Sergio,' Mayer replied.

'The Israelis were stumped too,' Dobrovsky said. Then: 'Do you know my colleague Robert Kupperman over here at CSIS?'

'I've met him.'

'He wrote a little brochure titled *America's Hidden Vulnerabilities*. That's why I called you last month. I wanted to get your opinion on it. It has to do with networks, strategic networks that could be put out of business by a few terrorist acts and paralyze important parts of this nation. His thesis is best exemplified by what could happen to electric power grids. If you recall, Paul, in both 1965 and 1977 New York City and parts of the Northeast suffered electrical collapses, *accidental* collapses, and the most densely populated area of the United States came, literally, to a halt during the next twenty-four hours. Kupperman's point is that if critical power nodes, in New York and Chicago and California and elsewhere, were attacked *deliberately* and *systematically*, then the ensuing blackout could not be lifted after a day, nor likely even after a week or a month. It would be a national disaster.'

As Mayer listened, he looked at his watch.

'Sergio, I follow you, and it all makes sense to me, but . . .'

'Do you know of that building on Water Street in New York? Where all the teleprocessing equipment is?'

'I've heard of it, yes.'

'That's where the computers are housed which process the data for the four Electronic Funds Transfer networks. As you know, these EFT networks link all the banks in the United States to each other, and also link the American banks to all the other banks that they work with around the world. I've been inside. The amount of equipment . . . it's staggering. What's more staggering is this, Paul: the computers in that *one* building process the equivalent of the federal budget every two to four hours! They handle *trillions* every week! Can you imagine if somebody blew that place up? Let me read to you what Kupperman concluded: "The most serious vulnerability of US banks may not be bad loans to Latin American nations, but rather a way of conducting business over networks that these institutions, and their investors, now take for granted."

What Kupperman says in plain English is this: Blow up Water Street, and you could bring all of the American and much of the world banking system to a halt for maybe as long as *two months*.'

Now Mayer was listening very, very carefully.

'That's one possibility: a terrorist strategy aimed at *physically* maiming our system,' Dobrovsky continued. 'The other would be a type of terrorist act that could create enormous *psychological* damage, with approximately the same results.'

'And that is?'

'They might try to target Paul Volcker's successor over at the Federal Reserve.'

'You mean Robert Reston,' Mayer interjected.

'Exactly.'

'Sergio, *that* sounds a bit far-fetched.'

'Oh, really? Well, I often heard that the head of the Fed is regarded by many as the second most powerful man in the world. At least they always said that about Paul Volcker. And I've checked around a bit, Paul. The Chairman of the Federal Reserve Board has got no Secret Service protection.'

'What good would killing him do?'

'In a time of a financial crisis? It just might tip the scales. And turn a financial crisis into a *panic*, a good old-fashioned nineteenth-century style financial panic. That's what good it could do!'

'OK, Sergio, what do you want me to do?'

'I've heard that you've become an advisor to Paul Volcker's successor . . .'

'Bob Reston,' Paul Mayer interjected, again.

'Please tell him what I've told you.'

'Why don't you call him directly?'

'Because it may be days before he has time to return my call. And there is some urgency involved.'

'I'm listening, Sergio.'

'The Israelis have just determined that two young potential

terrorists disappeared from Beirut two days ago. They *think* they might be on their way to the United States, potentially to Washington. They called me at home just half an hour ago. That's why I'm calling you now.'

'I appreciate it, Sergio. And I'll pass the word along to Reston. But shouldn't the FBI, or whoever takes care of these things, also be informed?'

'The Israelis have already done that. And I'll follow up.' Then Dobrovsky added: 'There's one other thing. While I was over there the Mossad, like every other intelligence service in the West, was informed by Interpol that an extremely dangerous member of West Germany's Red Army Faction is on the move. The man is thought to be used by both Abu Nidal and Carlos to "run" some of their operations. He might well be headed this way too. So please tell your friend Reston to be very careful during the next week or two. He should avoid parking garages. He should mix up the routes he takes from home to work. He should check out the street in front of his house now and then for funny-looking parked cars. He must know the drill.'

'OK, Sergio, I'll be seeing Reston tomorrow evening and I'll pass along what you've said. Thanks.'

After he hung up, Paul Mayer reflected upon what had been said for about thirty seconds. He had been told that Sergio Dobrovsky was an excitable man, one who got carried away rather easily. It probably came with the territory. Sure, he'd tell Reston about this on the plane. But if those two Arab terrorists, and their German leader, were real, and if they were indeed in Washington DC, that was basically the FBI's problem, not theirs.

Mayer's thoughts then moved on to more urgent matters.

The terrorist squad that Sergio Dobrovsky had been referring to was definitely real, and it had come to Washington. But it was no longer there. Nor was it on the way to New York, and that building on Water Street.

The three men were on United Airlines' Flight 87, headed for San Francisco, California.

The move had taken place very suddenly. At two o'clock on that Sunday afternoon, Joachim Schmidt had telephoned the Washington safe house where the two young Arabs had been parked, the apartment of José Martinez, Jr. He had told Martinez that his two houseguests were to be packed and ready to go within an hour. To where he had not said.

But young José had found out.

The tall Arab, the one who had said his name was Mohammed Obeidat, had left his flight bag – a British Airways' one – in the living-room and then returned to José's spare bedroom to finish packing. The other Arab stayed in there with him.

The coast being clear, José, nervous as hell, had decided to take a quick look.

There were only three items in the flight bag: what looked like a prayer book, in Arabic, and two unused airline tickets. The tickets had both been bought and issued in Washington DC. The names on them were Selim Aytul and Ugur Mumçu, hardly everyday names, but sounding more Turkish than Arab . . . and who ever takes notice of details like that at airport check-in counters in the United States anyway?

Both the dates and flight numbers had been left open, but the destination was clear: San Francisco, California.

And both tickets were one-way!

Just as he was about to put them back in the flight bag, José noticed something written on the back of one of the tickets. An address: 126 Madrona Avenue, Belvedere, California.

The next safe house. The German had probably written it down just in case they got separated on the other end. Which meant that they were going to disappear from his life and become somebody else's problem.

The German had arrived at 3.00 sharp. At 3.05 he and José's

two houseguests had already left. The Arabs had departed without saying a word, perhaps under instructions. But not the Nazi.

'Forget this whole thing,' he had said. 'Permanently. Otherwise not only you but your family back in Caracas, maybe your mother, will pay for it.'

After the door had closed, José Martinez, Jr went to his portable bar and pulled out a bottle of bourbon. He put a lot of it into a water glass and took a mighty slug. It made him feel better.

Then he thought of something that made him feel better still. Since yesterday, when he had seen those Polaroid pictures on his coffee table, his suspicions had been confirmed that there was a connection between those Arab thugs and Professor Paul Mayer . . . and his uncle. That's why he had called home.

But now he was less sure. After all *they* were going to San Francisco, while Professor Mayer was *here* in Washington. José Martinez, Jr knew that since Mayer would be conducting his seminar on international finance the next day. This semester the time had been switched to 4.00 in the afternoon. He intended to have a word with Professor Mayer afterwards – despite what that fucking German had said!

At 7.00 that evening José Martinez, Jr went to the Tombs for dinner with a few of his pals. But, for a change, his heart was not in it. The bizarre events had taken their toll, even on that twenty-one-year old. So he pooped out at 9.00, and by 10.00 was tight asleep, alone, in his luxury digs on N Street.

In another part of Georgetown, Professor Paul Mayer had also decided to go to bed early. It was going to be a tough week: first the flight to San Francisco, then the meeting with the Latin Americans, after which God knows what might happen. So the lights at 3514 Dent Place also went out shortly after 10.00 that evening.

Mayer's last thought before dozing off: to call Dean Krogh over at the School of Foreign Service. He would have to cancel tomorrow's seminar.

Chapter 14

Two hours later and it was already 6 a.m. the next day in Zurich, Switzerland . . . the time when Dr Ulrich Huber, Chairman of the Swiss National Bank, usually got up.

On this morning of Monday, January 9th, however, he was already in the back seat of his Mercedes limousine, being chauffeured through the dark and still mostly empty streets of Zurich. And he was still seething. At the Russians!

The unmitigated *gall* of those primitive Slavs! To think that they had had the *audacity* to plant a spy in *his* bank, and not only in his bank: in his *secretariat*. That KGB man at their embassy in Berne, the one who had already fled the country according to the authorities, had no doubt seduced her. *That* thought alone was disgusting. Not that she deserved any pity! She could rot in jail for the rest of the century as far as he was concerned.

The Russians would also pay. Even more than they now thought. They had needed that $2 billion loan that he had so generously agreed to raise for them. Now they would need it even more. Soon, within twenty-four hours, they would no longer be able to sell one more cubic meter of their expensive natural gas to Western Europe. All their customers would be immediately converting back to cheap oil. And even coal! Then where would the Russians get the hard currencies needed to buy food? Not from the Swiss National Bank: that was for sure!

And just a month ago, he had actually opened the door for the Russians, had offered to allow them to, in essence, join the club, the European club, or, in any case, the Central European club. It had been a big mistake. The Russians never had been, and never would be, *real* Europeans. He should have remembered that. And he should have stuck to his basic credo: never, ever, trust Communists!

Upon arrival at the bank on the Börsenstrasse, Huber's mind immediately shifted to the next subject, the private accounts of five ministers of state: two each from Venezuela and Mexico and one from Brazil.

The Swiss National Bank had advanced each account $10 million. The demand had been made by the Venezuelan oil minister, the greasy Roberto Martinez. And he had agreed to the payoff: to open a $10 million unsecured credit line for him, his brother, and for the three other ministers from Mexico and Brazil, $50 million in all. But these credit lines could only be drawn upon for employment as margin in the five investment accounts which were simultaneously set up for the Latin Five: no cash withdrawals were allowed. Nobody was going to be able to cut and run before they performed! And there was no risk otherwise. If the Latin Americans performed, and he now had no doubt whatsoever that they would do just that in San Francisco the next day, then their $10 million would be parlayed into $20 million, maybe even $40 million . . . and probably within less than a week! Once the operation was completed, the Swiss National Bank would take back the $10 million it had advanced in the first place to each of those Latin Americans. What they did then with the profits remaining in their accounts would be their business.

It was all working out exactly as planned. So far, half of these funds had been used as margin for three types of futures transactions: going long on precious metals, i.e. buying gold and silver, and establishing massive short positions in both the United States' dollar and oil in the hope of making a killing if the prices of both collapsed.

The Swiss National Bank had accumulated enormous positions itself, and had, in essence 'piggy-backed' the Latin Americans' accounts along the way. They had started the prior week. And then stopped.

Now, on this Monday, January 9th, they would resume the process. But, today, something new would be added. They would start to short stocks, essentially restricting their action to the thirty stocks which form the basis for the Dow Jones Industrial Average: IBM, General Motors, General Electric, du Pont, Exxon . . . the bluest of American blue chips. Why just these? Because most of them were listed on the Zurich exchange. Which meant that the Swiss National Bank could already start establishing their positions – for itself and the accounts of the five Latin American ministers of state – six hours before the exchanges in New York even opened. Zurich had another advantage: the rules governing short sales on that city's *Börse* differed from the rules in New York.

A short sale was known in Zurich as a *Leerverkauf*, German for an 'empty sale'. You were selling something you did not yet have for future delivery. What you hoped for, of course, was that you could *pre*-sell shares in IBM for $150 today, and, before you had to deliver them in Zurich a month later, you could cover yourself by buying IBM for only $100 a share, making a $50 per share profit in the process, and in a very short time. What was *different* in Zurich was that you did not have to wait for an 'uptick' to enter into a *Leerverkauf*, as you did in New York. That rule had been established in New York to prevent, or at least to slow down, any potential market collapse: the last sale of a stock had to involve the price 'ticking' *up* before a short sale could be executed. That meant that no avalanche of consecutive short selling could overwhelm the market.

Not that the Swiss National Bank did not intend to continue their short sales in New York when it opened. It might be more difficult, but their traders were instructed to sell as much as they could without creating a big stir. And in New York, their list would go beyond the Dow Jones component stocks. Bank stocks would be added: Bank of America, of course, and Citibank, and Manufacturers Hanover, and Chase, and Chemical and Bankers Trust. Why these? Because these were the six banks which had lent the most to Mexico, Venezuela and Brazil, the banks which had the most energy loans outstanding in the United States, and they were the banks which depended most heavily on huge deposits from abroad – from Europe and Japan – to finance these loans.

To paraphrase a concept from that professor of Georgetown University's Center for Strategic and International Studies: they were sitting ducks, and it was now open season.

Fifteen minutes later, in a highly unusual move, Huber gathered together the bank's chief traders in his office. And he personally gave them specific instructions as to what to do, and their limits. When, one by one, he gave them these limits, eyebrows, Swiss eyebrows, rose throughout the room. They were unprecedented. Huber was not talking tens of millions; he was talking *hundreds* of millions. Each. The bank was going to take enormous risks.

But then Huber added something to his instructions which lowered those eyebrows again. The bank would be at risk for only a very, very short time. Huber wanted all those short positions – be they in oil, the dollar, or IBM – to be covered just forty-eight hours later.

Sell short on Monday; cover on Wednesday.

Finally, he gave separate instructions to his bond dealers. They were to begin immediate liquidation of all dollar bonds: US government's and corporates' alike, and all Eurodollar bonds, be they straight, convertibles or zero coupon bonds. They were to sell at market, and then take the cash proceeds and convert the dollars back to Swiss francs. Without delay.

Then he dismissed his traders and dealers. Soon a more

prestigious group of bankers would be assembling in his conference room.

At 8.45 they began to arrive outside the Swiss National Bank's granite and marble monument to greed on the Börsenstrasse in Zurich: the men who controlled the banks which controlled Central Europe. First to arrive were the *other* three who ran Switzerland, the Chairmen of the Swiss Bank Corporation, the Union Bank of Switzerland, and Crédit Suisse; then came the heads of the Big Three from West Germany, the Deutsche Bank, the Dresdner Bank and the Commerzbank; finally the two men who ran the two banks which ran Holland and Austria, the Amsterdam-Rotterdam Bank, and the Creditanstalt Bankverein of Vienna, joined the others who had taken their seats around the oak table.

Luxembourg, inexplicably, had declined the invitation.

Dr Ulrich Huber brought the meeting to order at precisely 9 a.m. and, in his usual manner, came directly to the point.

'It is in the interests of each of our countries that we can be assured of a long-term supply of cheap energy. None of us has any domestic source of oil. We depend totally upon imports. Twice in the 1970s our continent was brought to the edge of disaster as a result of the massive price increases which our Middle Eastern suppliers forced upon us. During the 1980s we have had a respite. The reason why I have called you together today is to ensure not only that this respite continues, but that, at least during the next two years, we can have a *guaranteed ceiling* price on oil of $12 a barrel. All we will have to do is switch suppliers: from the Middle East, and Libya, to Latin America: Mexico and Venezuela. An assured supply of low-cost energy will allow our nations here in Central Europe to plan our economic future in an orderly manner, to greatly increase our economic growth, and to once again compete effectively in world markets. The rest of the world has mocked us during this decade of the 1980s. "Eurosclerosis" is the word they used to describe our condition. No more. The 1990s will again be a European decade.

'The *quid pro quo* for a long-term supply arrangement at this cost? Very simply this: an *initial* bridging credit arrangement, involving just $15 billion. For Mexico and Venezuela.'

The room, which had remained dead quiet, now began to stir.

'I know exactly what you are thinking, gentlemen. Why should we Europeans get involved in Latin America, which has proven to be a financial graveyard for the American banks? From a strictly banking point of view, for one reason and one reason only: we will have collateral! In contrast to the loans which the Americans made to them, these will not be sovereign loans in the classical sense. They will be in essence commercial loans fully collateralized by oil. It's never been done before. What do you think, gentlemen? And before you answer, I must telll you one more thing. I must have a commitment in principle from you today. Otherwise . . .'

The room fell completely silent.

Though the question, 'What do you think?' had been addressed to the entire group, everybody there knew that it would be Herr Generaldirektor Doktor Lothar Eisenstadt, boss of the Deutsche Bank, Germany's biggest, and Europe's finest, who would give the first response. For he was the *primus inter pares* of the group. Forgotten in 1989 was that fact that his bank had been the bank that had financed I.G. Farben, and Krupp, and Messerschmidt, the military/industrial complex of the Third Reich. His position as *primus* was based on the facts of life in 1989: as went West Germany, so would go Central Europe. And it was the Deutsche Bank which called the shots in Germany in 1989.

His response was short and came in the form of a question: '*Warum so dringend*?'

Why the hurry?

Dr Ulrich Huber's answer was not quite so short, but it certainly was direct. He explained what was going to happen in San Francisco the next day. The explanation ended with the word 'default'.

It was a word that, more than any other, struck terror in the hearts of bankers.

And, after Dr Huber had spoken that word, you could almost see how the other bankers in the room were calculating: adding up their exposures in Mexico, Venezuela and Brazil. Because they knew that their exposure in these countries was irrevocably linked to the exposure of the American banks there. Default on the American loans would automatically trigger default on their prior loans to Latin America. But they also knew that, after the dust had settled, things could probably be worked out, on a bilateral basis, without the Americans being involved, or even informed.

Not that it mattered that much. Except for Brazil, the European exposure in Latin America was not nearly that of the American banks, the European banks had *all* established massive reserves against possible future losses on their sovereign loans.

The man who ran the Deutsche Bank then asked about Brazil.

Dr Ulrich Huber had the answer ready. Venezuela and Mexico would get the full $15 billion collateralized loan; they, in turn, would take one-third of that and re-lend it to Brazil. This was not a new practice. They had done the same thing for Argentina in the early 1980s, although *that* time it had been American money which they had been passing around to each other.

That satisfied the representative of Deutsche Bank. 'Count me in,' he said.

After that, it was easy. Everybody else immediately fell in line behind the Germans. Then they started on the details. How much of the $15 billion would be trade credits; how much interbank lines; how they could be sure that the Americans would not seize their collateral.

'They can hardly invade Mexico, can they?' was Dr Huber's answer to the last question. 'Nor would they dare seize the cargo of the tankers of *our* oil companies on the high seas.'

Then came interest rates. They all wanted floating rates, and they all insisted on at least a full percentage point over LIBOR.

The biggest discussion centered on the price of oil, their collateral. It was agreed that $12 a barrel for Mexican Isthmus light crude would be the new benchmark, with an escalator built in related to the basic rate of inflation in Central Europe. Dr Huber suggested they use the GNP price deflator for West Germany, as calculated by the OECD for this purpose, and everybody agreed.

Why $12 a barrel? Because it was low enough to provide an enormous stimulus to the European economy . . . and, in the process, greatly bolster the fortunes of the most important industrial clients of every banker in that room. And it was high enough to supply Mexico and Venezuela – now that they would be *assured* of a market for their combined output of 3.5 million barrels a day for years to come – with enough income to survive. How was that possible, one of the men in the room asked, when everybody had been told for years that Mexico and Venezuela could barely survive even at $20 a barrel? Dr Huber also had an answer to that. Because Mexico and Venezuela will now be relieved of the burden of past debt: no more interest payments, no more repayment of principal on the billions of dollars which they owed mostly to the Americans. But what about Brazil? another asked. Answer: that country too would be relieved of any further cost of servicing its $120 billion debt *and*, like Europe, would now face much lower costs of energy. Brazil, like Central Europe, had to import much of its oil. It too would be able to do so at $12 a barrel, since the new benchmark they were now setting in Zurich would serve as the benchmark price for *all* crude oil, whether it came from Saudi Arabia, Nigeria or Libya. The prices for all grades of oil, from all sources, would inevitably fall in line, and stay there.

Finally, it was agreed that the Swiss National Bank would be the lead bank, and that its Chairman, Dr Ulrich Huber, would represent them all *vis-à-vis* the borrowers. He was also appointed as their spokesman *vis-à-vis* the Americans.

Then came the detailed drafting of the loan agreements with the Latin Americans. Lunch, which was served in the conference room, came and went. It was almost 5.00 p.m., Central European standard time, when each banker present signed an agreement in principle, subject in all cases to approval by their respective Board of Directors, to lend Venezuela and Mexico $15 billion. At 6.00 on the dot, Dr Huber adjourned the meeting. Half an hour later he sent a very long telex to the finance ministers of Mexico and Venezuela, informing them that they had a deal, and outlining very precisely the conditions of that deal.

One hour later he received telexes from Mexico City and Caracas. Both accepted his conditions *in toto*.

By the time the Germans got back to their banks in Frankfurt and the Dutch to their bank in Amsterdam and even the men who ran the Swiss Bank Corporation and the Union Bank of Switzerland back to their headquarters just a few blocks away from the premises of the Swiss National Bank on that Monday, January 9th, 1989, it was too late to *do* anything, based upon the startling information which had been given to them during the day. For Dr Ulrich Huber had literally closeted them in his conference room for nine straight hours. The markets, from Zurich to New York, were either closed, or about to close. The London branches of the American banks and brokers and investment banking houses, through which the Europeans conducted most of their business, had shut down for the day hours ago.

But, to a man, they knew exactly what they would be doing

at the opening of the financial markets the next morning. One of them, however, knew that he would be undertaking some serious business well before that.

The Russians had lost their 'man' inside the Swiss National Bank, Hanni Graber, but they still had more than enough informants inside Western European banking circles.

The most important of them, by far, was one of the participants in the Zurich conference, the Chairman of the Creditanstalt Bankverein in Vienna. Austria has had a 'special relationship' with the Soviet Union ever since the Russians 'gave it back' in 1954. Austria remains the only country ever to escape Soviet occupation. But there were strings attached, strings which the Russians yanked on regularly. The Austrians realized that one of the best ways to keep the Russians as happy as possible was to trade with them, and to bend over backwards to finance, very liberally, that trade. The Chairman of the Creditanstalt Bankverein, Austria's largest bank, had been the logical man to be put in charge of these financial arrangements. The Chairman's predecessor, and *his* predecessor, had had this responsibility and, in the process, they had gotten to know everybody who counted in Moscow.

That's how the current Chairman of the Creditanstalt Bankverein had gotten to know the current head of the KGB, Viktor Chebrikov.

Since the days of the Austro-Hungarian empire, the Viennese have been known for their laziness, their *Schlamperei*, but also for their highly developed sense of double-dealing. The banker from Vienna had sensed almost from the start in Zurich that here was an opportunity not only to make a lot of money, a full 100 basis points over LIBOR on a fully collateralized credit, but also to gain enormous 'credit' in Moscow. Ideology, East-West politics, played no role whatsoever in his Austrian mind. He just saw a truly golden opportunity to double-deal.

Already on his private jet returning to Vienna, the Chairman had placed a telephone call to Chebrikov's apartment, and alerted the person who answered the phone – it was either Chebrikov's wife or a maid – that he would be calling again at midnight, Moscow time, and that it was imperative that he speak to Chebrikov personally.

At midnight, when the Austrian banker dialed Viktor Chebrikov's home number direct, it was the chief of the KGB in person who answered the phone. By shortly after midnight he knew everything.

After he had thanked the Austrian banker profusely and then terminated the call, despite the hour Chebrikov did not hesitate for one minute before picking up the phone once again to call Chairman Mikhail Gorbachev at home on his private direct line.

Gorbachev was still up. He listened to Chebrikov and then said: 'I want you over here within thirty minutes.'

Chebrikov was elated! They finally had the Americans where they wanted them!

Chebrikov sensed that something was amiss when Gorbachev offered him neither food nor drink after he arrived. Not even tea!

It was 3 a.m. when Viktor Chebrikov emerged from that apartment. He was no longer jubilant. Quite the opposite. He was now a pale and shaken man.

Chapter 15

Right from the opening of the markets in New York on that Tuesday, January 10th, 1989, one could sense that this was going to be a bad one. Markets might like to 'climb a wall of worry' but the wall facing them that morning was, in the minds of many, simply too formidable to be scaled.

A lot of traders had already been getting jittery the day before. For in their minds were the figures that had been released over the weekend concerning the economy. The boom was over, the *New York Times* had told them. Recession in '89 now appeared to be a dead certainty. But that news had hardly been unexpected. Everybody knew, deep in their hearts, that the Reagan prosperity could not be extended *forever*. Upswings in business cycles always come to an end and usually after three years. This period of uninterrupted prosperity was now six years old, and its end long overdue.

So the markets had moved down in early trading on Monday. Then came the rumors, later confirmed, that the Europeans, particularly the Swiss banks, had begun to accumulate enormous short positions in everything from IBM to Citibank. That alone did not mean much: the Swiss were notorious for their inability to call markets, especially those in the United States. Nevertheless, it further dampened spirits on Wall Street, and by the close the Dow Jones was off 26 points. Bad, but hardly anything to get excited about.

But before the opening of this Tuesday morning, a new element had been added: the front page story in *The Wall Street Journal*, written by a certain Sally Brown. It told about two meetings: one involving nine European banks which had just taken place in Zurich; the other, involving Bank of America and the oil and finance ministers of Mexico, Venezuela, and Brazil which was scheduled to begin in San Francisco at 9 a.m., Pacific Standard Time, that day. What they added up to was this, the *Journal* said: 'Latin America was going to default on its outstanding debt, mostly involving American loans, and the European banks were going to step in and keep these countries solvent by providing new, *collateralized* loans. The collateral, oil.'

Reuters had confirmed all this. And also said that, as a result of the Zurich accord, the new benchmark price would be $12 a barrel.

At first, the market did not know what to do. After all, in 1985/86 the price of oil had collapsed from $31 a barrel all the way down to $10 a barrel, before it rebounded. Almost everybody had greeted this with total enthusiasm. Lower oil prices meant lower inflation, lower inflation meant lower interest rates, lower interest rates meant higher bonds. The ensuing bond market rally had produced a major stock market rally, and driven the Dow Jones to an all-time record high in 1986.

But then came the second thoughts.

These second thoughts had also been contained in the article in the *Journal* and had been expressed in a quote attributed to Professor Robert Lindner, a Latin American expert at John Hopkins University's School of Advanced International Studies. He recalled what he had said back in 1986: 'If oil prices *stay* substantially below $20 per barrel it will be a disaster.' Fortunately they hadn't, the Professor pointed out, and so a disaster had not occurred. Why? Because three more years of prosperity in the United States had kept energy demand growing, so despite an oversupply situation, the oil price had stabilized. But now, with recession looming, in 1989 you would be getting the effects of *both* a glut and a falloff in energy needs simultaneously. The oil price was going to be hit by both supply and demand factors at the same time. This was a totally new situation. So even *without* the deal in Zurich, $12 per barrel would have been inevitable. And now, with both Iran and Iraq both pumping oil at full capacity *that* 'benchmark' can hardly hold for long: the next step down will be to $7 a barrel. That, he said, will not mean just a disaster. Rather, it portends financial Armaggeddon for our banks.

Could all this be stopped? If so, by whom?

The *Journal* had answers to both questions. To the first, it was 'Maybe'. To the second: 'The only man who can head off this looming financial disaster is world's Lender of Last Resort, the Chairman of the Federal Reserve, the successor to Paul Volcker, Robert Reston.'

The *Journal's* article ended on a hopeful note. Robert Reston was apparently fully cognizant of the seriousness of the situation, and would be personally attending the meeting today in San Francisco, accompanied by his advisor, Dr Paul Mayer of Georgetown University, as well as the Comptroller of the Currency and the head of the FDIC.

But lots of bond traders never got to the end of the article. Rather than read further, they began to sell. Why?

Their first line of reasoning: Recession meant the suspension of Gramm-Rudman, which would lead to vastly increased federal borrowings which would lead to higher interest rates.

Result: They started to sell bonds.

Second line of reasoning: Mexico was pulling the rug from under the banks; $12-a-barrel oil, with perhaps $7 a barrel next, meant that the banks were going to have to pull the rug from under the domestic oil industry. Collapsing oil prices would bring down commodity prices across the board, meaning that the farmers would be in still worse trouble. At best, this meant that the banks were going to have to pull in their horns dramatically. Bank credit would dry up. Interest rates would go still higher.

Result: The bond market sank further.

The confluence of bad news, and the collapse of the bond market, was soon too much for the traders on the stock market.

So they also started to sell.

After the first hour of trading, the Dow Jones was off 66 points. If it stayed there, it would set a record for the largest drop in one session. A generation earlier, a similar record had been set on a Tuesday, one that became known as Black Tuesday: October 29th, 1929.

The malaise was not restricted to the New York Stock Exchange, however. On the New York Futures Exchange, where the NYSE Composite Stock Index was traded, on the Chicago Mercantile Exchange where the S&P 500 was listed, the story was the same: the biggest drops in history.

Then the commodity futures:

pork bellies:	limit down across the board.
cotton:	limit down across the board.
copper:	limit down.
lumber:	limit down.
lead:	limit down.

Almost every single commodity traded on every futures exchange in the United States was limit down – meaning they had dropped in price by the full amount allowable in one trading session. The prices for March delivery, where no such limits applied, were plunging almost out of sight.

But some moves were more important than others that day.

gasoline:	limit down.
heating oil:	limit down.
crude oil:	limit down.

It was upon these prices that Mexico and Venezuela depended for their future national income.

coffee:	limit down.
soybeans:	limit down.
soybean oil:	limit down.
soybean meal:	limit down.

It was upon these prices that Brazil depended for much of its future income.

And then there were the interest-rates' futures.

Ginnie Mae's:	limit down.
Treasury Bonds:	limit down.
Eurodollars:	limit down.

Which meant that interest rates were climbing across the board. Interest on most sovereign loans floats, up or down, with interest rates in general. What the futures markets were telling Mexico and Brazil and Venezuela on that day was this: while your income from your exports of oil and coffee and soybean meal is going to sink rapidly, your interest expense is going to soar rapidly: i.e. you are going broke!

With default now growing in credence, with bonds collapsing, with stocks falling out of bed, the wisdom of remaining invested in the American dollar was now starting to be questioned by an increasing number of foreigners holding assets in the United States. So some decided to get out of dollars while the going was good.

Soon the currencies started to go wild too. In the interbank market, the German mark, the Japanese yen and the Swiss franc moved up 5 percent against the dollar in the first hour. Even the pound sterling was up 3 percent.

That's what prompted the New York Fed to call Robert Reston in San Francisco. That institution is the one responsible for intervention in the foreign exchange markets, acting in essence as the agent for the United States' government when it decides that it is necessary that action be taken to stabilize the international value of the dollar. What they wanted to know from Reston was: Should they now start selling marks and yen and francs and begin mopping up the dollars that were being sold in increasingly large quantities? If so, in what amounts?

Robert Reston was shaving in his suite at the Clift Hotel in San Francisco when the call came in.

After the people in New York had told him what was happening – not just to the dollar, but also to stocks and bonds and commodities during the first hour of trading on the exchanges on the East Coast, with the ones in the Midwest just now phasing in, and moving in the same direction – Reston authorized an initial intervention of $1 billion.

Then he called Paul Mayer, who was in the suite next door, and the Comptroller of the Currency and the head of the FDIC who had adjacent suites on the floor below. They had arrived very late the night before since their flight from Dulles had been delayed for more than two hours because of weather. They had gone straight to bed.

Twenty minutes later all had assembled in Reston's suite, and were watching the action on television. The Clift carried the Financial News Network on Channel 10, and, on that Tuesday, January 10th, before the day was over, it would achieve the highest ratings in its history, beating out even KGO-TV, which had always been the hottest station in town.

By 7.45 the Dow was down 73 points, and still heading south. Reston's phone rang. It was the New York Fed again. Reston authorized another billion dollars.

And everybody in his room realized that this might be an exercise in futility: the United States' government, through the Federal Reserve Board, could intervene to prop up the value of the dollar in the foreign exchange market. But there was no power in the land, public or private, which was able to intervene on the New York Stock Exchange to prop up the value of IBM or General Motors.

'What do you think, Paul?' Reston asked, after he hung up on New York.

'It's getting out of hand. The price of *everything* is collapsing, except for gold.'

'What else can I do?'

'Nothing. Ride it out for the next couple of hours. And hope that, in the face of this, the goddamn Mexicans and Venezuelans and Brazilians will come to their senses!'

As if on cue, the Fed Chairman's phone rang again.

This time it was the Chairman of Bank of America. 'They want to change the venue,' he told Reston. 'In fact, they insist upon a venue change. To a neutral site.'

'No problem,' said Reston. 'Where?'

'The Fairmont Hotel. They've got a conference room already set up and ready to go. I'll be by with the bank limo in about an hour and pick you up.'

'We'll all be in the lobby waiting for you, George.'

'One other thing. They've scheduled a press conference for 10 a.m. at the Fairmont.'

'Sons of bitches,' Reston said, and hung up.

'What's wrong?' Mayer asked.

Reston told him, and the two other men in the room.

'That doesn't sound at *all* good,' said the Comptroller of the Currency.

Then each went back to his respective suite, agreeing to re-convene at 8.45 a.m. in the lobby of the Clift.

At the Fairmont, the oil minister of Venezuela had just placed a call to Switzerland, a person-to-person call to the Chairman of the Board of the Swiss National Bank, Dr Ulrich Huber.

Although nobody else was in his room, Roberto Martinez somehow felt compelled to speak in a low voice. After the initial exchange of courtesies, he came directly to the point.

'How are we doing?'

'So far, even much better than we expected.'

'How much better?'

'I would say that we have already doubled your money, at a minimum. In fact, it is good that you have called. Some of our people feel that we should start taking profits in New York. What do you think?'

Now the Venezuelan's voice rose to full power.

'Under no circumstances! Do you hear me?'

'I do. But if not now, when?'

'Tomorrow. Just as was originally planned.'

'Why are you so adamant?' asked the Swiss banker, in his prissy manner.

'Because I am much closer to this situation than you,' the Venezuelan answered. Then he asked: 'What time is it in Zurich?'

'Almost 5.00 p.m.'

'You normally close at 5.00, don't you?'

'Yes. Why do you ask?'

'Because I think you will find it worth while to stay late at the office today,' came the enigmatic reply from the Venezuelan. 'I must go. I will call you at the same time tomorrow morning.'

And he hung up.

At exactly this time, Azar Shahani's car was backing out of the carport onto Madrona Avenue on Belvedere Island. Joachim Schmidt of the German Red Army Faction was sitting beside her in the front seat of her Mercedes; two young Arabs sat in the back.

The German looked at his watch: 'Are you sure it will only take half an hour?'

'Are *you* sure you are supposed to go to the Fairmont?'

'That's what the man said.' The man, the Venezuelan oil minister, had telephoned the night before.

'What are we going to do at the Fairmont?'

'Just meet some people.'

'If that's all, why did you want me to describe the hotel in such detail?' He had even asked her to draw a diagram of the lobby.

'Don't worry, *Schätzchen*. This is the last thing we will ever ask of you. We shall go to the Fairmont together, and then we will disappear from your life.'

After that, as Azar Shahani drove down Madrona Avenue toward Tiburon Boulevard, which would then take them to US 101, the freeway leading south to San Francisco, the German maintained a steady patter of conversation.

'I like your house. It's quiet. How long have you had it?'

'Seven years.'

'Is your mother going to live with you here?'

'Yes. If you keep your word and let her out of Iran.'

'We keep our word. Don't worry, *Schätzchen*,' he answered. 'Say, did you ever get that Georgetown professor in bed with you?'

She didn't answer at first. Then: 'Why do you ask?'

'Just wondering.'

'You are not going to hurt him, are you?'

'No. We have nothing whatsoever against him. He's not important. I'm sorry I even brought the subject up.'

After that, she appeared to relax. She knew that Paul Mayer was in San Francisco. He had promised to call her . . . and hadn't. She also knew that he always stayed at the Clift. So whatever it was that these people were planning to do after they got to the Fairmont, it would not involve him.

'What do they call that?' the German now asked, pointing to his left at the body of water they were just skirting. It had been dark when the taxi had taken them from SFO to Marin County on Sunday night. And since then, none of them had left the safe house on Madrona Avenue.

'Richardson Bay. It's a bird sanctuary,' Azar replied.

'Really? I like birds. In my country the forests are all dying. From pollution. If the trees die, so will our birds. It's terrible.'

Five minutes later they got onto the freeway. It was the height of the morning commuter hour, and the traffic was moving very, very slowly. It therefore took another fifteen minutes before they finally got on the north end of the Golden Gate bridge and another five minutes after that before they got to the toll plaza at the other end.

The German was getting more and more nervous. 'You've got ten minutes to get us there,' he said to Azar.

As if on cue, on Doyle Drive, which leads from the bridge in the direction of both the Marina and Lombard Street, the two alternative routes to downtown San Francisco, the traffic finally started to move again at high speed.

'We'll be there in ten minutes,' she told him.

The Federal Bureau of Investigation is the law-enforcement agency responsible for dealing with the problem of terrorism in the United States. It has a special section devoted exclusively to such activity, headquartered in Washington DC. Most of its information comes in from Interpol, from the CIA, the DIA, the NSA and the State Department – all of which monitor terrorist activities abroad, and alert the FBI if anybody or anything seems to be moving toward American soil.

In the 1980s nothing of any import ever did. But that did not mean that the anti-terrorist unit of the FBI was not constantly busy. Every other kook in America, it seemed, was regularly spotting suspicious-looking Libyans at New York airports, Lebanese entering the Washington monument, Syrians outside a Los Angeles synagogue. They checked most of them out. And in nearly 100 percent of cases it involved a total waste of effort. So it was natural that over time they began to regard outside tips about pending terrorist strikes in the United States with increasing suspicion.

Between late Sunday afternoon, January 8th, 1989 – the incoming telex from the Israelis was clocked at 4.56 p.m. – and exactly 11.35 a.m. two days later, on Tuesday, January 10th, four things happened which radically changed that attitude.

First was the telex. It was hardly in the 'outside tip' category, since it came directly from the Mossad, the world's most experienced intelligence service where terrorism is concerned. The problem with the Israelis, from the FBI's point of view, was that they developed *too* much information. It gradually became a wheat and chaff problem.

In retrospect, it is obvious that they put this telex in the 'chaff' category. They had called the security people at Dulles and Kennedy. Had two suspicious young Arabs arrived during the past day or two? Not that they knew of, came the answer. It was Sunday at the airports. It was also Sunday at the FBI. So the telex message was entered into the computer, 'filed' among various other reports of known terrorists who had recently 'disappeared from view' in Beirut and sundry other places such as Damascus and Tripoli and were, potentially, headed for targets unknown, in Israel, Western Europe, or – though the possibility was remote – in the United States.

The telephone call from Professor Dobrovsky the next morning had caused them to retrieve it from the computer. Yes, they had told him, the Israelis had warned us that two or more Arabs may be heading our way. Yes, they had subsequently checked with the security branch of the Immigration Service out at the airports and, no, nothing had turned up. What about Joachim Schmidt? Yes, they had also received the Interpol warning about him. But there was no reason to believe that he had come to the United States.

The Professor had told them about the theories of his colleague, Robert Kupperman: about the building on Water Street in New York, and about the Chairman of the Federal Reserve. The FBI had heard them at least a dozen times before, both of them. But they promised Dobrovsky, who was known to them as a nice, competent, academic, though a rather excitable man, immediately to contact the security people over at the Federal Reserve buildings.

Which the FBI did, and, again, went on to more pressing matters.

The security people at the Fed had nothing whatsoever to do most of the time, so, after they heard about the call from the FBI, they spent most of the rest of the day speculating on how each of them would respond if a pickup truck full of dynamite drove in the front door. When their chief heard that Robert Reston was going out to San Francisco that evening, he contacted the Chairman's secretary and told her about what the FBI had said. She told him to get hold of the security chief at Bank of America in San Francisco, just in case.

He did. And was assured that security out there had already been beefed up considerably in anticipation of the meeting which was scheduled to begin in the Boardroom of the bank, on the 40th floor, at 9 a.m. on the next day, Tuesday, January 10th, 1989. Now they would increase it even more.

So that was where the matter rested. Until 11.35 a.m. Eastern standard time, on Tuesday, January 10th, 1989.

That's when a call came into the switchboard of the FBI headquarters in Washington. The caller, and he had a young voice, asked to speak to someone who dealt with terrorism. He said it was urgent.

Special Agent Joseph McGrath took the call. 'I understand that you are calling in regard to a terrorist act?'

'Yes, sir,' came the answer.

'Please explain. I'm going to tape this, if you agree. Do you?'

'Yes, sir.'

'Then proceed.'

As the Special Agent took notes, José Martinez, Jr began to tell his story. About the German, about his surveillance of Professor Mayer's house in Georgetown, about taking the pictures with his Polaroid, about the arrival of the two Arabs, about his discovery that they were phonies, about his seeing their two airplane tickets for San Francisco, and about the address: 126 Madrona Avenue, Belvedere, California. And, finally, he had told Special Agent McGrath that they had left his apartment for good on Sunday afternoon.

Up until this point, the FBI man had just let him talk without interrupting even a single time.

'How did you get involved with these people in the first place?' he now asked.

'I can't tell you that, sir.'

'Fair enough. Then can you tell me this: Who is Professor Mayer?'

'He's a professor at Georgetown. He's the reason I'm calling. I'm afraid they're going to kill him. Professor Mayer teaches international finance. He's a very big man in international financial circles. He used to be Managing Director of the International Monetary Fund. He . . .'

Now the bell started to ring.

'Hold on a minute,' said the FBI man, 'and please don't hang up.'

Putting his hand over his phone he yelled across the room, 'George! George! Get the Federal Reserve immediately. The Chairman's office. Ask if they know a Professor Paul Mayer. And find out where the Chairman is. Right now!'

He went back to his phone. 'Now I want you to give me as precise a description as you can of the German, and the two young Arabs. Take your time.'

José, Jr was still talking when a voice yelled from across the room.

'Joe!' It was George. 'Listen. I've got Chairman Reston's secretary on the line. Mayer's an advisor to Chairman Reston. Both went to San Francisco for a meeting at the Bank of America. It's scheduled to begin at 9 a.m. West Coast time. That's exactly fifteen minutes from now.'

'Holy shit! Keep her on!'

Joe McGrath yelled at another colleague. 'Pick up line five!'

Then he interrupted José Martinez, Jr. 'Listen, and this is very, very important. I am going to act immediately on what you've told me. It's imperative that you stay with us. A colleague of mine is now on the line and he will be taking over on this end.'

Then Joe McGrath put the anti-terrorist unit of the FBI on total alert.

'What line are you on, George?' he yelled.

'Seven.'

McGrath cut in. 'Now listen very carefully,' he said to the secretary of the Chairman of the Fed. 'Where is Mr Reston right now?'

'At his hotel, I presume.'

'Which hotel?'

'The Clift in San Francisco.'

'Its number?'

She had it immediately. '415–775–4700.'

'Thanks. Now stay on the line. OK?'

'Harry,' he said to one of the special agents that had gathered around his desk. 'Get our San Francisco office.'

To another agent: 'George, get the Captain of Intelligence of the San Francisco PD. His name's Chris Sullivan.'

To another: 'Get the head of security of Bank of America in San Francisco.'

To another: 'Call Chairman Reston at the Clift Hotel in SF. Here's the number.' He tore it off his notepad and handed it over.

That's when the confusion started.

Azar Shahani had just parked her car in the underground garage of the Fairmont Hotel. She had been right. It had taken exactly ten minutes to get there from the Golden Gate bridge.

There is a long ramp which leads from the garage of that

hotel to a row of elevators. You press L and it takes you two storeys up to the main lobby. When the door opened on the elevator which had brought the German, the Iranian woman, and the two young Arabs up from the garage, the doors of the adjacent elevator also opened, spewing out a dozen guests who had come down from their rooms, some with suitcases, most of whom went directly to the cashier's windows which were situated at the rear of the lobby to their right.

The German, followed by the two Arabs, with their suitcases, and Azar Shahani, walked straight ahead toward the circular, deeply upholstered red bench which sat exactly in the middle of that hotel's vast lobby. The German motioned with his head toward it, and, while he kept walking, the other three did not.

Azar Shahani sat down, directly facing the main entrance to the Fairmont. The two Arabs took their places, one to her left, the other to her right. They each had placed their suitcases on the floor beside them.

The three now sat, silently, watching the people come and go through the two sliding glass doors about thirty feet in front of them. To the casual observer they were nothing more than three hotel guests who had checked out and were waiting to be picked up by somebody, probably headed for the airport.

It was 8.45 a.m. exactly.

The Bank of America limo, carrying its Chairman, George Pace, had just pulled up in front of the Clift Hotel. Pace had been going over the proposal he intended to make to the Latin American debtors ever since leaving his home on Belvedere Island. His daily morning trip to the city was one of the only times he could ever be assured of peace and quiet, of total privacy, time he needed even more to prepare the defence of the world's second largest bank which was under pressure, it seemed, from all sides. Deliberately, he had refused to install a phone in his limo lest even these thirty minutes a day of quietude be lost.

That proved to be a mistake.

The Chairman of the Federal Reserve, Robert Reston, and his newly-appointed chief advisor, Professor Paul Mayer, were waiting in the lobby along with the Comptroller of the Currency and the head of the Federal Deposit Insurance Corporation. None looked too happy.

Pace greeted them all, and without any further words they left the hotel and piled into the black stretched Cadillac, three on the back seat, two on the jump seats. The car pulled away from the curb, and then swung immediately right off Geary Street onto Taylor, headed for Nob Hill.

'Dammit,' said the Chairman of the Fed.

'What's wrong?' asked George Pace.

'I forgot my cigars,' Like his predecessor, Paul Volcker, Robert Reston smoked cigars under pressure.

'No problem. Dunhill's is just a few blocks down Post Street,' said the head of San Francisco's largest bank.

Then George Pace looked at his watch. 'They're probably not open yet. But the St Francis's newspaper shop is, and I know for sure that they have a full supply of cigars.'

He then turned around on the jump seat, and, pulling open the sliding glass which separated him from the front seat, said, 'Pat, take a right on Post and pull up beside the side entrance to the St Francis.'

The car pulled up *exactly* in front of the place where Squeaky Fromm had taken a shot at President Gerald Ford back in 1975. The mark of the bullet, which had missed by quite a bit, could still be seen on the Post Street wall of the hotel.

It was 8.47 when the Chairman of the Fed disappeared through the side entrance of the St Francis. Four minutes later, at 8.51, he emerged, triumphantly bearing half a dozen Partagas Rounds. The limo then swung back onto Post Street, and turned left onto Powell Street headed toward California Street which lay four blocks up the hill. At the intersection of Powell and California, where the driver wanted to turn left once more, the limo got stuck behind a cable car, which had stalled there for some reason. The front entrance to the Fairmont was just one block further up Nob Hill, at California and Mason.

The FBI had called the Clift Hotel at 8.45. Robert Reston did not answer. It then took a full minute to get the operator back on the line, to get her to connect them to the assistant manager, and to then explain to him that the FBI wanted to speak to Robert Reston and that it was a matter of extreme urgency. Thirty seconds later, the assistant manager was back on the line. He told them that the Chairman of the Federal Reserve, and three other guests, had apparently all just left in a limousine. What did he mean by 'just left?' Maybe two or three minutes ago.

On another line another special agent had gotten to the head of security of Bank of America. It had taken a full minute to do so. In fact, the agent just caught him as he was about to leave the garage of Bank of America with half of the bank's security force. He explained what was happening. The Chairman's secretary had left a message for him, which he had received just ten minutes ago when he had arrived for work. Her boss had called about half an hour before that: the venue of the meeting had been switched from the bank to the Fairmont Hotel. He was now in the process of making the appropriate adjustments in the security arrangements.

He was a deliberate man, and it took him almost a full minute to get all this out.

'Jeezuz Christ, man,' said Joseph McGrath, finally, 'get off the phone and get your ass up to the Fairmont. And then get your Chairman and everybody else out of there! Everybody! I'll explain later. Get going!'

He hung up.

'Hold everything!' McGrath then yelled at the room containing the core of the FBI's anti-terrorist unit.

'Who's got our San Francisco office?'

'Line eleven,' somebody yelled.

McGrath pushed the line-eleven button.

'What were you just told by our people?' he asked.

'To get Reston. Either at the Clift Hotel or at B of A,' came the answer. 'Two of our groups are already heading down toward their cars.' The FBI's San Francisco office is on the 18th floor of the Federal Building at 450 Golden Gate Avenue.

'Forget that. The venue's been switched. Reston just left the Clift Hotel three minutes ago, and he's headed toward the Fairmont.'

'OK. Our men will be there in five or six minutes.'

Then McGrath yelled: 'Who's got the SFPD?'

'Line two.'

McGrath told the Captain of Intelligence at San Francisco's Hall of Justice of the change of venue.

'OK,' came the answer. 'We've got two Tac Squad cars on the street, and both are headed toward B of A. I just spoke to the one that's going down California Street. I'll turn it around. It should be at the Fairmont in two minutes. We'll be going in through the back.'

'Get me the Fairmont Hotel!' McGrath then yelled.

At 8.54 the cable car which had stalled at Powell and California finally started to move again, and the B of A limo was able to swing left on California and, one uphill block later, right on Mason. The driver pulled the Cadillac onto the circular drive and then stopped in front of the steps which led immediately up to the doors leading into the main lobby of the Fairmont Hotel.

The SFPD's unmarked car which had been going down California, bearing three members of the city's Tactical Squad, had turned around and had entered the Fairmont Hotel from the rear, having pushed its way around the intersection of Powell and California, where a cable car was stalled, by jumping the curb. They screeched to a halt in the same garage where Azar Shahani's Mercedes was parked. The three uniformed policemen grabbed their weapons, AR–14 automatic rifles, which were always laid out and ready to go on the back seat, and raced up the ramp for the elevator which they knew would take them directly to the Fairmont's lobby.

When they emerged from the elevator it was to see, to their right, the manager of the hotel talking urgently to two hotel security people in front of the reception desk, and pointing toward a circular, deeply upholstered red bench, which was positioned directly in the middle of the vast lobby.

On that bench sat three people, all of dark Middle Eastern complexion: two young men, exactly as they had been described on the Tac Squad's car radio, and an older, very beautiful woman.

Then it happened very quickly.

A man – the German, Joachim Schmidt – who was standing at the front entrance, looking out, suddenly turned, gave a hand signal toward the Arabs, and then started to move away very quickly.

The two Arabs immediately leaned down to open the two suitcases beside them. The woman between them just sat there, staring straight ahead, as if in a trance.

The sliding glass doors leading into the Fairmont lobby began to open and, one by one, in came George Pace, the Chairman of the Bank of America, Robert Reston, the Chairman of the Federal Reserve, and Professor Paul Mayer, advisor to them both.

The three members of the Tac Squad were already on the move, running toward the circular bench in the middle of the lobby. Then, all three began to scream at the top of their voices.

For a full second it seemed that everything and everybody

stopped. Even the two Arabs who had now risen to their feet, their Uzis in hand, seemed to pause. So did the three men who had just entered the lobby and who now stood twenty feet in front of the muzzles of their guns.

Then the Tac Squad opened fire.

The bullets from their AR–14s almost cut the two Arab boys in half. The head of the beautiful woman, who had remained seated between them, seemed to explode.

Three other men, all wearing badges and coming from a breakfast meeting of their trade association, had just entered the lobby from the north, and were thus directly behind the circular bench when the shooting started. The spray of bullets caught all three in the neck. Blood erupted in all directions as they fell, and continued to flow onto the red carpet after they were down. One of them let out a piercing, pitiful shriek, before his body shook in a final death spasm.

Paul Mayer's eyes recorded all this in a sort of speeded-up slow motion, while his mind was providing the running commentary. The focus of both his eyes and his mind was on Azar Shahani. First, just noticing her sitting there, and wondering why. Then, seeing the two men at her side rise, with submachine guns pointed at *him*, and knowing why: she had set him up and they were now going to kill him! But instead, somebody else opened fire, and it was her head that exploded, not his.

It was too much. He fell to the carpet of the Fairmont Hotel, retching.

The two cars full of FBI agents arrived one minute later. Within thirty seconds, amidst absolute chaos, they quickly and quietly removed Robert Reston, and the other men who were with him, from the building. There might be more of them around, was their explanation.

Reuters had arranged to have a stringer cover the press conference which the Latin ministers of state had scheduled for later that morning; he had arrived early, and was drinking coffee in the breakfast nook just off the side entrance to the lobby of the Fairmont, when the shooting started. After it ceased, he waited for three minutes and then made a dash for the lobby. The police were already then in the process of fully clearing the lobby, and they were being very aggressive about it. Before they, literally, shoved him out the door, he managed to get a clear view of the entire lobby . . . and a body count. Although he stood fifty yards from the middle of the lobby, he could definitely see six bodies lying there, five men and one woman.

'Who are they?' the Reuters' man asked the nearest cop.

'Bankers,' he answered. 'Now get the fuck out of here.' And that's when the shoving started.

That bit of misinformation was what turned a building financial crisis into a financial panic.

For three minutes later, at exactly 9 a.m. Pacific Standard time, the Reuters' man was in a telephone booth in the lobby of the Mark Hopkins Hotel, just across California Street from the Fairmont, phoning in his report. He wanted to be first, and he was. Seconds later, the word was flashed around the world, via satellite, to every bank, to every brokerage house, to every exchange from Frankfurt to London to New York to Tokyo, that the Chairman of the Federal Reserve, the Chairman of Bank of America, and three other men, including the Comptroller of the Currency of the United States and the head of the Federal Deposit Insurance Corporation had been massacred in the lobby of the Fairmont Hotel in San Francisco. An unidentified woman, probably an innocent spectator, had also been gunned down. The identity of the assailants was not known.

It was 12.00 noon on Wall Street when word of the contents of the Reuters' 'flash' from the West Coast spread around the floor of the New York stock exchange, and everybody reacted the same way. Let's get the hell out! During the final hour of trading in New York, the Dow plummeted, and by the close was down 112 points. The reaction on the commodities markets was the same: instant collapse. The price of oil sank with everything else, and by the end of the trading day it had reached the lowest level since 1973: $5 a barrel.

During that same hour, something new developed which turned what had up to then been a domestic crisis involving a mass liquidation of financial assets into a full-blown international monetary crisis. Foreigners, beginning with those in Central Europe, concluded that there was nobody left at the financial rudder of the United States. The joke had once gone around that the world was no longer on a gold standard, but on a Paul Volcker standard. Robert Reston has assumed that mantle. And now he was dead. The President of the United States, with only ten days left in office, was at the ranch. The lame duck Congress had been recessed. Nobody was left to run the store known as the United States of America.

Forty-five per cent of the deposits of Bank of America were controlled by foreigners. All were institutional deposits; all were in amounts larger than $100,000; therefore none was insured.

Twelve billion of those deposits were yanked out during the next three hours, representing almost 10 percent of the bank's total deposits. An additional $32 billion were withdrawn from Citibank, Chase Manhattan, Manufacturers Hanover, Bankers Trust, Morgan, First Chicago, Chemical, Security Pacific and First Interstate. These funds not only left the banks; they also left the country. All this was done by means of wire transfers so the money was here one minute, and, literally, gone the next. Despite massive intervention by the New York Fed the dollar collapsed.

It didn't matter that at noon, West Coast time, Robert Reston went to the San Francisco studios of ABC on Front Street in San Francisco, under the heaviest police escort seen in years in that town, and went on live national TV to explain that he was alive.

A run, once started, feeds on itself. Because all of a sudden people start crowding to get through the door, more precisely to get *out* the door of the bank with their money in hand, before it slams shut. The Germans call it *Torschlusspanik*, closed-door panic.

At three o'clock that afternoon, the Chairman of the Federal Reserve, his advisor, Paul Mayer, the Comptroller of the Currency, and the head of the FDIC all flew in an Air Force jet to Santa Barbara. A helicopter would then take them to the President's ranch.

Initially, very little was being said among the four men after takeoff. They were all still stunned by the enormity of the situation that had developed in such a short time. They were also awed by the security arrangements. No less than twenty secret service men and FBI personnel were on the plane. And they had been told why. The leader of the terrorist attack, a German by the name of Joachim Schmidt, had been seen by the Tac Squad immediately before they had opened fire. During the chaos that followed, he had disappeared.

But then, fifteen minutes into the flight, Robert Reston and Paul Mayer moved to the back of the plane, and went into a huddle. They stayed that way during the entire trip, with Paul Mayer doing most of the talking. When the helicopter landed in the pasture adjacent to the ranch house, the President himself came out to greet them. A storm was just coming in from the Pacific, and it had turned windy and cold. So the first thing the President did, once they were inside his living room, was to offer them coffee. They all accepted.

'My Chief of Staff is on the way,' he said, 'but I don't expect him to arrive for at least another hour. Shall we proceed or shall we wait?'

He addressed the question to Robert Reston who, as Chairman of the Federal Reserve, was the senior man among his visitors.

'I think this is a matter of extreme urgency,' Reston said. 'So I'd suggest we get going.'

'All right. What are our options?'

'We don't have any,' Reston replied immediately. 'It's either close the banks, or face unknown consequences of such proportions that we cannot afford to risk them as a nation.'

The Comptroller of Currency interrupted. 'I disagree. This whole thing started with Bank of America, and we can end it with Bank of America. Had we moved in to audit Bank of America, as I suggested, this never would have happened in the first place.'

'Charles,' interrupted the President, 'let's not rehash the past. Do you have an alternative proposal?'

'I do. Two years ago, Congress gave the Federal Deposit Insurance Corporation the authority to take over any bank in this country that is insolvent and to run it for as long as necessary. I say, let's do it. Let's move into B of A right now. The Fed can re-finance it overnight. And tomorrow morning we'll open it up as usual. After that, things will settle down just as they did in 1984 after we re-financed Continental Illinois and in 1987 when we did the same with the First National of Texas. What I'm saying, Mr President, is that there is no need to over-react.'

Robert Reston cut back in. 'I think we should hear Professor Mayer's opinion, Mr President.'

'Go ahead, Paul,' the President said. They had met maybe a dozen times in the past, while Mayer was still running the IMF.

'Thank you. I will be blunt. I totally disagree with Charles Thayer. This is not a one-bank crisis. The problem we are facing is *systemic*. The credibility, the solvency, of the whole American banking system is being questioned. We must come up with answers to those questions. While we search for them, we have two choices: stay open, such as Charles suggests, but doing so in the full realization that the Federal Reserve is not going to have to re-finance just *one* bank, but *all* of them. If we are not prepared to re-finance the banking system on a monumental scale, then we have no choice but to close down all the banks before *they* close them down for us.'

'Who are "they"?' the President asked.

'The Germans, the Swiss, the Japanese . . . they've got hundreds of billions of dollars on short-term deposit with our banks, Mr President. They've already yanked out $50 billion. Tomorrow, if allowed them, they'll pull out another $100 billion. That would result in the insolvency of every money center bank in the country. The problem may have started with Bank of America, but now Chase, and Citibank, and Security Pacific – all of the big banks – are in the same boat.'

'He's right,' said Roger Wells of the FDIC. 'If it were just Bank of America, we could handle it. Barely. But as Paul just pointed out, the problem is systemic. And what he didn't mention is that tomorrow it's not just going to be the foreigners; Americans, domestic depositors, are bound to join the run. Then the little banks are going to get into trouble. As Bob Reston said, we've got no choice other than to close them *all* down. Now.'

'All right,' said the President, 'so I close the banks down. Then what?'

Bob Reston answered, 'We must immediately address the problem that triggered this whole thing in the first place: the open default by the Latin Americans on their foreign debt.'

'Does anybody here know how to solve that problem?'

Nobody said a word. Until Paul Mayer spoke up.

'Yes, sir. I think I do.'

'Go ahead.'

'We are going to have to go back to some fundamentals, Mr President. First, the United States must seek to peg the crude oil price at $20 a barrel. I'll explain both why and how in a minute. Then . . .' Mayer spoke for fifteen minutes, and nobody interrupted him.

Just as he finished, the President's Chief of Staff arrived. The two of them excused themselves and, after donning their raincoats, went outside. After they returned, both moved in front of the fireplace, facing the four men who sat before them.

'We agree with you,' the President said, addressing the head of the Federal Reserve. 'We're closing the banks. We want both of you and Professor Mayer to stay out here "for the duration", as we used to say, to work out a plan to solve this mess. Then, let's hope the Latin Americans buy it. If they stonewall, well,' and he shrugged his famous shrug, 'at least nobody will be able to blame us for not trying.'

The helicopter took the four men back to the Santa Barbara airport. It landed beside a second military helicopter that was being frantically loaded with television equipment, as the TV crew that would use it stood around impatiently. The Comptroller of the Currency and the head of FDIC re-boarded the Air Force jet that had brought them down from San Francisco, and minutes later were headed back to Washington DC. Robert Reston and Paul Mayer were driven to the Biltmore Hotel, and installed in one of the cottages on the grounds of that magnificent hotel by the sea.

An hour later Ronald Reagan went on television to issue a proclamation declaring a three-day national bank holiday. All the exchanges would also remain closed. It was the first time a president had been forced to take such action since March 4th, 1933.

Despite the grimness of the situation, Ronald Reagan appeared calm, presidential, sovereign, and eternally optimistic. He closed his brief remarks with the statement that a solution was already in the making.

His political advisors, who had been streaming into Santa Barbara, were less calm. In fact, they were mad as hell. The foreigners were raining on their boss's parade, the very last parade of his political career. They were ruining the last two weeks of his presidency. And, of all people, it was the Mexicans and Venezuelans and the Brazilians who had pulled the plug. The goddamn ingrates!

Chapter 16

The Mexicans, the Venezuelans and the Brazilians had holed up in their suites on the 16th floor of the Fairmont Hotel after the shootout in the lobby. There were more hotel security people than guests up there. Initially, the Latin Americans had been as confused as everybody else. The press conference they had scheduled for 10.00 that morning had been cancelled out of respect for the five American high officials who had been slain. Then, as the day progressed, it became apparent that the only dead were the terrorists, two young Arab men and an Iranian woman, and three innocent bystanders. As they watched television, listening to the speculation as to who was behind what was now known as the 'Fairmont Hotel Massacre', it became apparent that no one, absolutely no one, was attempting to make any connection between their presence in San Francisco, and the attempts on the lives of the Chairman of the Federal Reserve and the four men who had been with him.

The press, however, had them under siege. For it was obvious to all of them, and the rest of the world, that it had been the intention of the Latin Americans to default on their outstanding debt to the American banks which had triggered what was now being called 'The Panic of '89'.

After the American President had appeared on television declaring a national bank holiday, Roberto Martinez, now nervous as a cat, talked the situation over with his brother.

Both quickly agreed that they could no longer remain silent. It was best to state their position to the Americans, and then to get out of the country. Quickly. Very quickly.

Mexico's oil and finance ministers agreed to this immediately, as did Brazil's finance minister. They also agreed that Roberto Martinez would be their spokesman.

Sally Brown of *The Wall Street Journal* asked the first question. 'In view of what has happened today, do you still intend to stick with your decision to default?'

Martinez's answer: 'What has happened today, aside from the unfortunate incident earlier today in this hotel, has only *reinforced* our decision to evoke the *force majeure* clauses in our loan agreements with the American banks, with the International Monetary Fund, and with the World Bank.'

Then he went into something that closely resembled a tirade. The oil price at the close of the day had sunk to $5 a barrel. The coffee price had sunk to 98 cents a pound. Interest rates had soared a full 200 basis points. Add that all up, and it would mean poverty in Latin America on a scale not seen since the nineteenth century!

But didn't they realize that they had caused financial havoc? Didn't they know that with the closing of the American banks, for which they had been at least partially responsible, they would now be cut off from any further American financing? How could Mexico survive?

The Mexican finance minister decided to answer. 'We will survive very nicely, thank you.'

'How?'

'With the help of our European friends. The banks there are still open, you see. And after what has happened today, I think even you people of the American press are smart enough to realize that they are now bursting at the seams with money.' He paused for effect. 'We don't need you Americans. *You* need *us*.'

The *Schadenfreude* was so evident on his face that some of

the reporters actually began to hiss. And the questioning now began to turn ugly. So, fifteen minutes later, Roberto Martinez abruptly adjourned the press conference.

Sally Brown had one last comment to make as she filed out of the conference room with a colleague, Warren Hinkle of the *San Francisco Examiner*. 'I think they know that they've got us by the balls. And they are going to keep squeezing no matter what happens.'

Hinkle's answer: 'It's like the Iran hostage crisis all over again. Only this time it's our banks. I never thought that Reagan would let anybody do anything like this to us.'

A Venezuelan government-owned Gulfstream–III was waiting at San Francisco airport. It would carry twelve passengers in total luxury, but for this trip it only needed to hold four. The Venezuelan finance minister, José Martinez, Sr, would not be boarding with the rest. He had received a desperate call from his son who was attending Georgetown University, and would instead be taking a commercial Red Eye flight to Washington DC to find out what was wrong.

The G–III was airborne at 9 p.m. The flight plan was to proceed to Mexico City, where the Mexican ministers would report in to their president who would be waiting for them at the airport, to refuel, and then collectively to proceed on to Caracas where they intended to prepare for an emergency meeting of *all* Latin American debtor nations, from Argentina to Peru, from Chile to Ecuador. The purpose: to present a totally united front *vis-à-vis* the Yankees and the IMF and the World Bank. Now that they had them on the run, it would not be hard to gain total Latin American unity.

It was midnight when they landed at Mexico City, and while the Mexican oil and finance ministers conferred with their president, and while the Brazilian finance minister had a drink, the Venezuelan, Roberto Martinez, placed a call to the Swiss National Bank.

When he got Dr Ulrich Huber on the line, he could not restrain his jubilation.

'I told you, didn't I. To wait until Wednesday. And you see what happened!'

The response from Zurich was irritatingly unenthusiastic. 'There will be no Wednesday. Nor Thursday. Nor Friday. Everything is closed.'

'What does that matter?'

'How can we take profits when all the markets are closed? Even in Europe, this morning, there is no trading in *any* American securities, stocks or bonds, governments or corporate issues. Our commodity exchanges are also closed and won't open until the American ones do.'

'So what? We must have huge profits locked in!'

'We have huge *paper* profits, yes.'

'But what can happen now?'

'I don't know. But I don't like it,' was the reply of the Swiss banker. 'And now I have other things to do. Goodbye Señor Martinez.'

At 1.30 a.m. the Mexican crew had finished refueling the G–III and tidying up its cabin. The four Latin American ministers re-boarded, and half an hour later the plane lifted off the runway, headed for Caracas.

At 15,000 feet it exploded.

Chapter 17

What followed throughout all of Latin America was fear and loathing. And a revival of respect for the Yankees.

Memories were evoked of what the CIA was said to have done, successfully, to Lumumba and Dag Hammarskjøld in the Congo, about what they had tried to do to Castro on numerous other occasions, though unsuccessfully. Jimmy Carter had put a stop to that sort of thing. But now the CIA was obviously back in business. And this time they had outdone themselves: they'd pulled off a total wipeout.

As much as all this was appreciated in Langley, Virginia, the fact of the matter was that no one at the CIA knew a thing about it!

So it was with a clear conscience on Wednesday, January 11th, the day after the 'Panic of '89', that, already at dawn, messages of condolence were issued from the Western White House in the hills behind Santa Barbara. They ended with the hope that if a tragedy of such proportions could have any meaning, it might be to serve as a catalyst for a reconciliation of the interests of all peoples of the Americas. The President of the United States invited the presidents of Mexico, Venezuela and Brazil to join him, immediately, in California to achieve that end.

The Chief of Staff of the President of the United States woke both Robert Reston and Paul Mayer with a 5 a.m. phone call, informing them about what had happened in Mexico City and about the President's intention to convene a meeting with the three Latin American heads of state as soon as possible. The two men went to work immediately.

Paul Mayer's first move was to mobilize his colleagues at Georgetown University's Center for Strategic and International Studies. He called it a full back-channel press. He started with Dr Henry Kissinger by calling him at home. 'This is Paul Mayer,' he said. 'I hope I didn't wake you.'

'Somebody else woke me about three hours ago with the news from Mexico City. I assume that is why you are calling.'

'It is. We feel it represents an opportunity to solve the bank crisis. The President has invited the presidents of Mexico, Venezuela and Brazil to come to Santa Barbara. We want them to reverse their decision of default. As part of our *quid pro quo*, we are going to propose reactivating the International Energy Agency, Henry. And the President has asked me to ask you to help us do that.'

That agency had been established back in 1973, at the instigation of Henry Kissinger. Its purpose then had been to provide protection for the oil-consuming nations against any future oil embargoes. Under its provisions, each of the twenty-one signatory nations had agreed to buy up and store sufficient oil to allow them to bridge a new energy crisis. The United States had subsequently established the Strategic Petroleum Reserve, and had bought and then stored 500 million barrels of oil in the underground salt domes of Louisiana. In spite of the fact that the storage of a full billion barrels had been originally authorized, the entire process came to an abrupt halt when a huge world oil glut developed in 1986. Paul Mayer wanted to change that, just as abruptly. Only this time the mechanism would be used for exactly the opposite reason: not to combat the dangers of an oil shortage, but to alleviate the world economic effects of an oil glut that had produced a price drop that had simply gone way too far. The objective: to establish a floor on the world price of oil, one that both Mexico and the United States could live with. He explained all this to Kissinger.

'Ja. I see what you're after, Paul. And I'll help, of course. I'm sure that you realize that if we can convince the Germans and the Japanese, all the others will fall in line. At least that's what happened in '73.'

'I agree. Would you call Chancellor Kohl?'

'Sure. What do you want me to tell him?'

'That the President is prepared to begin to buy in the additional 500 million barrels for the Strategic Petroleum Reserve. We want the Germans to reactivate their program simultaneously, and buy in another 100 days' supply.'

'Ja. But at what price, Paul?'

'Twenty dollars a barrel.'

'Why $20. Why not $15, or $25?'

'Twenty dollars a barrel was the last price at which the SPR bought oil from Mexico back in 1985. If it was acceptable to them then, there is no reason to believe that it will not be acceptable now. Especially in the light of the current price of crude oil in the open market. Before we closed the markets it had gone down to $5, Henry.'

'I realize that. But why should Germany go along with us on this? After all, it's *our* banks that are closed because of the Latin Americans, not *theirs*.'

'Yes, Henry, but it is our *troops* that are keeping the Russians on the other side of the Elbe, not theirs.'

'Maybe you should have David Abshire remind them of that before I call,' Kissinger responded. David Abshire was on a leave of absence from Georgetown. Reagan had appointed him as the American Ambassador to NATO, and he still held that post in Brussels.

'I'll arrange that immediately,' Paul Mayer said.

'I think you had better work on Kohl from inside Germany also,' Kissinger added. 'You must know Lothar Eisenstadt at the Deutsche Bank. You should call him right away, Paul. He should be receptive. I hear he was involved up to his ears in that deal the Europeans tried to put together with the Latin Americans. Tell him we are all very pissed off at him.'

'May I quote you, Henry?'

'Absolutely.'

'One other thing. In addition to what we want to do on oil, we're going to have to put together some new bridging financing for Mexico, Venezuela and Brazil, and probably a few other Latin American countries who will be riding on their coat-tails. We want the Germans and the Japanese to chip in.'

'They won't like that idea either.'

'We know. And that's why I'd like to ask another favor, Henry.'

'That is?'

'Could you have a word with David Rockefeller? He's got a lot of influence in both Bonn and Tokyo.'

'Sure.'

'And Walter Wriston. You must see him fairly often.'

'I'll do it,' Kissinger responded. 'How much are you after?'

'We think that Japan should come in with $5 billion. And that the Germans could arrange for, maybe, $3 or $4 billion. We'll get Constable at the World Bank to kick in $5 billion, and my successor at the IMF will be good for another $3 billion. That should do it.'

Kissinger grunted his approval. Paul Mayer was obviously thinking big, just as *he* always did.

'One other idea,' Kissinger then added. 'Are you on speaking terms with Paul Volcker?'

'I am, although I'm not sure Bob Reston is.'

'If I were you, I'd call him up right away. Ask him to get to work softening up Pöhl at the Budesbank, and Sumita at the Bank of Japan. Volcker still carries an enormous amount of clout with those guys, Paul.'

'I know. It's just that Bob Reston's a bit touchy on that subject. No matter. I'll work something out.'

'Most of the people I'll be talking to are certainly going to want more details. Where can they reach you, Paul?'

'I'm at the Biltmore in Santa Barbara. So is Bob Reston.'

Then Kissinger said, 'Paul, I'd appreciate your doing one thing for me. Could you have the President give me a ring? That way I can tell everybody it's coming directly from the Oval Office.'

'Certainly, Henry. His Chief of Staff is staying over at the Sheraton. I'll have him call you immediately and set up a time for the President to call you.'

'The sooner the better.'

'I agree. And thanks, Henry.'

'A pleasure, Paul. We must see more of each other.'

Mayer called the White House Chief of Staff and was assured that the President would make that call to Kissinger within the hour.

Then Mayer started to work on Tokyo. He put a call through to Mike Mansfield, the American Ambassador there, and caught him just as he was on the way to bed. Again he explained what they were proposing to do to solve the American banking crisis. Where oil was concerned, their hope was that Japan would buy in 250 million barrels during the next seven or eight months, at $20 a barrel, and store them in tankers around their islands, taking advantage of the glut of ships which had reappeared on the world scene. They were also expecting the Japanese to help out with some bridging financing for Latin America.

'How much, and in what form?' the Ambassador asked.

'Five billion in the form of a direct loan to Brazil.'

Mansfield reacted with the same question Kissinger had, 'But why should they?'

'Because that $5 billion is peanuts compared to what they already have at risk. *We* owe *them* almost as much as Latin America owes *us*. They've got over $300 billion invested here, in US government securities, in bank deposits, in stock and bonds. You've got to put it to them bluntly, Mike. The United States is to Japan what Mexico is to the United States: a debtor which simply cannot be allowed to go down the drain.'

'I'll need all the backup I can get,' Mansfield then said.

Mayer told him about the back-channel pressure which Kissinger was in the process of supplying. And if he could get hld of Paul Volcker, he was sure that the former Chairman of the Fed would soon be doing the same.

'That's terrific. I'll go see the Prime Minister right away in the morning, our morning, which means in about eight hours. If the President called him about the same time it sure wouldn't hurt.'

'I'll arrange it,' Mayer replied. He called the White House Chief of Staff once again.

Mayer then looked at his watch. It was barely 7 a.m., West Coast time. He decided to walk over to the cottage next door, where Robert Reston was staying. Reston was, of course, on the phone when Mayer walked in. He was working on the domestic side, while Paul Mayer was working on the international side.

After Reston hung up he said, 'That was Carl Reichart, the Chairman of Wells Fargo. His bank's in terrific shape, but even he fears what could happen if we can't make a deal with the Latin Americans. So I gave him the same message I've already given the people at Bank of America, Chase, Citibank, and Chemical. Now I've got to talk to the rest.'

He went back to the phone. Reston's message to the nation's money center banks was this: The Federal Reserve stood prepared to fund, without limitation, any American bank that got into trouble. The Fed's discount window would be wide open, all day and all night if necessary. No American bank would go under due to lack of liquidity.

After Reston had finished speaking to the Chairman of Manufacturers Hanover Bank, Mayer said: 'I was just talking to Henry Kissinger. He's going to help us out a lot by softening up the Germans and Japanese. He'll get David Rockefeller and Walter Wriston to do the same. But he did suggest we enlist the help of somebody else. Paul Volcker.'

Reston said nothing.

'I could call him, Bob, but I'm sure he'd rather hear from you.'

'OK. I'll do it. What do we want him to do?'

Mayer explained. Then he went back to his cottage, and went back to work on the oil-price problem, this time from the supply side. He did not know Sheikh Yamani personally, but knew that he was a good friend of a former US Ambassador to Saudi Arabia, who now lived in Virginia. The Ambassador and Mayer saw each other for lunch once a month in Washington. Mayer called him and, again, explained what they were trying to do.

'Tell Yamani that we need his cooperation if this is going to work. And tell him, if he cuts back Saudi Arabia's output by 10 percent, we'll get both Britain and Norway to do the same.'

'Have you got their commitment on that?' the voice at the other end asked, incredulously.

'No. But I'm about to get it. And tell Yamani if he wants a call from the President, he'll get it. It seems that everybody else does.'

Next, Mayer again called the Sheraton Hotel, situated just a mile up the beach from the Biltmore. It was where the President's men always stayed when he was at the ranch. This morning the hotel was jam-packed with lame duck Cabinet members, and staff, who had been summoned by their commander-in-chief the day before. Mayer made two appointments: one with the Secretary of State, the other with the Secretary of the Treasury.

Half an hour later, Bob Reston and he were driven over in a limousine, protected by two Secret Service cars. They saw the Secretary of State first. They told him what they wanted from Mrs Thatcher. No money; just a 10 percent cutback on North Sea oil production. He promised to get on it immediately.

Then they went to the suite of the Secretary of the Treasury. It did not prove to be an easy session. He had wanted to leave office a hero, leaving the next administration a budget that was as close to being balanced as any the Reagan administration had been able to produce since taking office eight years ago. Now it was all falling apart. And now, *they* were asking *him* to commit an additional $25 billion?

'We've no choice, Jim,' Mayer pointed out. 'We've got to help the banks. Right now. With big money.'

Mayer's proposal was for a new, $25 billion, Latin American Debt-Relief Fund which would have the purpose of purchasing Lesser-Developed-Country loans from American banks, relieving them of at least part of the burden of carrying impaired sovereign loans on their books. Once the new Federal agency had taken over these loans, it would be open to a discussion with the Latin American debtor nations of both a rescheduling of the repayment of principal and a temporary moratorium on interest payments.

Mayer concluded with the words, 'The President wants it, Jim.'

'All right. As long as you people make it clear that this was *your* idea, not mine. But you had better make sure of one other thing before you go public on this.'

'That is?'

'That the President-elect and his men are willing to go along with this.'

'That's precisely what is next on the agenda,' Mayer replied.

By 9 a.m. West Coast time, Reston and Mayer were back at the Biltmore. They jointly called the head of the President-elect's transition team and briefly explained what they were trying to put together to solve the national financial crisis. He agreed to get the next plane out to Los Angeles, and to meet them at the Century Plaza Hotel at 8.00 that evening.

'I think we're getting there,' Reston said, after they had hung up.

'Did you get hold of Volcker, by the way?' Mayer asked.

'Yes. He couldn't have been nicer.'

'Terrific,' Mayer said, and left it there. Then: 'I've got two more phone calls to make, Bob, and then I suggest we take a long coffee break.'

'I agree. I'll meet you in the coffee shop in half an hour.'

The first call Mayer made was to Lothar Eisenstadt in Frankfurt. He was still in his offices at the Deutsche Bank.

'I thought I might be hearing from you, Paul,' were his first words.

'Henry Kissinger sends his greetings, Lothar. He also told me to tell you that we are all very pissed off at you.'

'Ja, I understand. Anyway, that's all over and done with now. But remember, it was Ulrich Huber who organized that, not me.'

'Really? I understood that the German banks had committed $7 billion.'

'Maybe.'

'Well, we're only going to be asking for half that much. The difference is that it will involve a straight sovereign loan to Mexico. No collateral.'

The German banker gave a very non-committal response.

So Paul Mayer put it to him in very blunt terms. He might try to push all the blame off onto the Swiss, but everybody in American financial circles knew that the German banks had played a key role in the 'Zurich Agreement', which was now as dead as the four passengers on that airplane that had gone down outside Mexico City. If the United States did not now get full cooperation from the German banks in solving the financial crisis which they had been instrumental in creating in the first place, there would be retribution, serious retribution.

Lothar Eisenstadt got the message.

'You can always count on your German friends, Paul,' he now said. 'I will go personally to the Chancellor on this. This evening. Now give me all the details.'

After the German banker had repeated his pledge of support, he returned to the subject of the Chairman of the Board of the Swiss National Bank.

'If the Latin Americans cooperate, and if you can open up the markets again next week, all hell is going to break loose on the upside. The word over here has it that Huber's bank currently has the short position of the century. When they try to cover, they are going to get slaughtered.'

'Wouldn't that be just too bad,' Mayer said.

'I have the feeling that Ulrich Huber will soon announce his early retirement,' the German banker said. Then he added: 'Paul, next time you come to Frankfurt, you must dine with us at the bank.' The German had already caught on to where Paul Mayer now stood in the American hierarchy of power.

Mayer assured him that he would. And hung up.

Mayer's final call that morning was to the CEO of Bank of America, George Pace.

'I think we'll soon be out of the woods, George,' he told him, and then explained what had been happening since before dawn.

'Are you sure the Latin Americans are going to show up?' Pace asked, the anxiety apparent in his voice.

'We'll soon know. But I'm convinced they will,' Mayer replied.

'Reston called me this morning, you know,' Pace then said. 'From what he told me, even if they don't show up, the Fed is going to bail out all of us.'

'It will never come to that, George. By the way, the Comptroller of the Currency was of the opinion that such Fed action was not really necessary. He proposed that the FDIC should immediately – and I mean, last night, George – move in on your bank, and take it over. That action alone, he said, would end the crisis.'

There was a tremor in Pace's voice when he asked, 'Who knocked that idea down?'

'All of us.'

'Will it stay knocked down?'

'I'm sure.'

'Paul, you don't know how grateful I am for your support during the past month.'

'That's what pals are for, George. Now relax. Enjoy the bank holiday while it's still on.'

During the coffee break, Bob Reston and Paul Mayer agreed on a further division of labor. Reston would work on the finance ministers of both Japan and West Germany, while Mayer would make his moves on the World Bank and the International Monetary Fund in Washington.

Reston was paged as they were about to leave the coffee shop. A few minutes later he returned with the good news. The call had come from the President's Chief of Staff: All three Latin American presidents had accepted the President's invitation to come to Santa Barbara. The meeting with them was scheduled to take place at the Biltmore Hotel, to begin at 4 p.m. the next day, Thursday, January 12th.

At eight o'clock that evening, Paul Mayer, Robert Reston, and the Secretary of the Treasury met with four members of the transition team of the President-elect at the Century Plaza Hotel in Los Angeles.

After the 'Mayer Plan', as it was now being called, had been thoroughly explained, the discussion turned to what the budgetary ramifications would be in 1989. The cost of buying in that oil would be tremendous; then there was the funding of the $25 billion, Latin American Debt-Relief Fund.

Would the old administration be prepared to share the 'blame' for this?

Did they have any choice? was the reluctant response of the Secretary of the Treasury.

Then Paul Mayer steered the discussion in another direction. Maybe the American people would understand that all this was just what the country needed. The economy was sinking into recession. The injection, directly or indirectly, of massive amounts of government funding into the banking system, would certainly lead to more liberal domestic lending policies by the nation's banks. If Gramm-Rudman remained suspended, or was repealed by the Democrats, much higher across-the-board government spending would follow. That Keynesian stimulus, combined with the revival of the banks' ability to lend, might stop the slide, and turn the economy around very quickly. The lame duck Secretary of the Treasury winced at Mayer's words. But the Democrats in the room all liked it.

At 1.00 a.m. that morning, the President-elect gave his endorsement to the Mayer Plan.

The author of that plan got back to the Biltmore in Santa Barbara at 3.00 a.m. Three hours later, he was up again. The responses were coming in from Bonn, and London, and Tokyo, and Riyadh, and they were all completely positive. Mayer then started to put his plan to paper. The President would submit it to the three Latin American heads of state at four that afternoon.

The meeting did not begin well. After the President had presented the Mayer Plan, each of the Latin American presidents went into his declaration of independence. None of them could or would simply accept a program which had been developed unilaterally by the United States. One could begin to discuss it, yes, but it would take weeks and probably months before a solution could be developed.

After they were done, the President let them have it. If they wanted to learn how to live with $5-a-barrel oil, it was fine with him. And if they also wanted to live without any further credit or financial aid from the United States' government and the American banks, that was also fine with him.

Take it or leave it, is what he told them.

They took it.

What 'it' amounted to was this: The United States, Germany and Japan, combined, would be buying 5 million barrels of oil a day, for at least the next seven months. All other members of the International Energy Agency would be strongly encouraged to join in their effort to stabilize the world oil price by increasing their strategic petroleum reserves also.

Where supply was concerned, the exertion of American pressure, of 'moral suasion' on the Saudi Arabians and the British had paid off. It had been the price war between these two producers of petroleum which had led to the oil-price collapse in 1986. Now, responding as much to the 'carrot' of an American-sponsored floor price for crude oil as to the political pressure that had been exerted, both nations had agreed to cut back their output immediately by 10 percent; thereafter the Saudis would put a ceiling of 4 million barrels a day on their output, the British 2 million. It was felt that following the Saudi's lead, the other OPEC members would also lower their output, and, for a change, stick to their revised production quotas. Non-OPEC producer Norway had already committed itself to that course.

The net result of all this: Venezuela and Mexico would have an assured market for their entire combined output of 3.5 million barrels a day, at $20 a barrel minimum.

What about Brazil? In a last minute flurry of activity, Paul Mayer had been able to add something to his plan that addressed one of Brazil's most serious problems: the United States' government would immediately undertake joint talks with the Brazilians aimed at reactivating the International Coffee Organization, a commodity pact designed to stabilize the world price of coffee. It had been up for renewal in 1989, and it had been feared that the United States, the leading consumer of coffee, would pull out . . . hoping that a collapse of the agreement would lead to a collapse of coffee prices.

Now, as with oil, it was recognized that establishing a floor price – in the case of coffee, $1.35 a pound – would be as good for Brazil as $20-per-barrel oil was for Venezuela and Mexico. And what was good for Brazil, Mexico and Venezuela was, of course, good for America's banks, and thus the country.

Finally, there were the financial arrangements. The World Bank had agreed to establish a new $5 billion credit, to be divided up among the three countries, with *no* conditions attached. The International Monetary Fund was committed to establish new $1.5 billion lines of credit each, for Venezuela and Mexico. The Japanese had pledged $5 billion in direct loans to Brazil. The Germans had agreed to make a direct loan of $3.5 billion to Mexico. The United States' government promised the establishment of a $25 billion, Latin American Debt-Relief Fund. The Latin leaders were told that the President-elect had given his assurances that the funding of this program would be very high on the priority list of his new administration.

And what did the three Latin American nations have to do in return? To desist, permanently, from any further talk of default. And to resume, immediately, their interest payments on their outstanding international debts.

At 9.00 p.m. the agreement was signed, and the Mayer Plan was in place. The press conference which followed was held in the ball room of the Biltmore Hotel under very heavy security, and it lasted untill 11.00 p.m.

Paul Mayer, who had fielded most of the reporters' questions, caught up with Sally Brown of *The Wall Street Journal* on the way out.

'How about a nightcap?'

'Sure,' she answered. 'And this time it will be on me. But first I've got to file my story. I'll meet you at midnight in the bar.'

When she arrived an hour later he was waiting for her, alone, at a small table. Her first words after they sat down were, 'You were absolutely spectacular tonight, Paul. And I said so in my story.'

Then she told him what else was in her story. Two Scotches later, he broke in. 'Say, would you like to see my cottage?'

She looked at him for about five seconds and said, 'Sure. Why not?'

Fifteen minutes later, as he turned out the the last light in Cottage 3A, she suddenly sat bolt upright in his bed, holding the sheets primly in front of her. 'I just thought of something. Was luring me to your cottage part of the Mayer Plan?'

'Yes. Although I just added it at the last moment. I hope it works out to the satisfaction of all parties involved.'

It did.

On Monday, January 16th, 1989, the banks were back in full operation, as were the exchanges from New York to San Francisco.

The money that had poured out of the banks, and out of the country, just six days earlier, now came pouring back in on a scale never seen before. The dollar climbed to the highest level in eighteen months! Gold collapsed. Oil prices soared. Now all the benchmark crude prices, from Arabian Light to West Texas Intermediate to Brent North Sea to Mexican Isthmus Light, were clustered around the $20-a-barrel mark. Oil prices had been buoyed not only because of the terms of the Santa Barbara Accord, but also due to the fact that Iran and Iraq were at it again. In a surprise air attack, the Iraqis had taken out Karg Island, Iran's main oil export terminal on the Persian Gulf. And the stock market! By the end of the day it was up 151 points. The biggest percentage gainer on the Big Board was Bank of America.

For it was now universally agreed: The 'Panic of '89' had acted as a catharsis. It had forced a cure to some of the world's most serious economic problems. The banks were now back on a solid footing. Most important of all, it had demonstrated that the American government could respond to financial crises in a magnificent fashion, even under 'lame duck' circumstances. The looming recession, it was now agreed, would be dealt with next.

Four days later, on January 20th, 1989, the new President was inaugurated. And Professor Paul Mayer and Sally Brown, who was down from New York for the week, had decided to go to Pennsylvania Avenue and watch the parade. A quarter of the way through, it started to get very, very cold, so Mayer suggested they take a cab to Georgetown and watch the rest of it on television.

They were barely inside the taxi when he said, 'I've got an idea. Why don't we go by the Four Seasons Hotel and pick up your things?'

'Just like that, huh?' she answered.

'Not exactly. Anyway, you'll only be here for a week.'

'Little do you know, buster. The *Journal* has just made me their Washington bureau chief. Next time I'm back, it won't be for just a week.'

'I think I could live with that,' Mayer responded.

'We'll see,' she answered.

Then Mayer added: 'By the way, I might get a new job too. The President-elect asked me to drop by the White House next week.'

Then Mayer re-directed the cab driver to the Four Seasons.

When the two of them walked through the door of 3514 Dent Place in Georgetown, he carrying her suitcase, it was to a chilly reception. Maria's eyes went immediately to the suitcase.

'I'll take it up to the spare bedroom,' she said.

'No, Maria. Take it to *my* bedroom.'

After she had disappeared, Sally said, 'Are you sure your maid isn't going to poison my coffee in the morning?'

'No. I've already thought of that. I've given her the night off. Don't worry, she'll get used to it.'

Then he turned on the television to watch the rest of the inaugural parade. Five minutes later there was a knock on the front door. At first Mayer appeared concerned. But when he opened the door, it was José Martinez, Jr.

'José,' Mayer exclaimed. 'Come in before you freeze.'

The young man looked beyond Professor Mayer, and saw Sally Brown.

'No, I don't want to disturb you.'

'Come on in. Just for a few minutes. We'll have something to drink.'

He introduced José, Jr to Sally Brown as one of his star students, and then asked Maria to bring in a bottle of champagne and three glasses.

'I'm here to thank you personally, Professor Mayer,' José Martinez, Jr then said.

'José, it is nothing, and on top of that, it is the very least I could do. After all, you saved our lives.'

What Mayer had done was to establish a small scholarship fund for José, one which would enable him to study at Georgetown, or anywhere else, for as long as he chose. He had found out that José's family was no longer in a position to do this. His father, who had been forced to resign from his ministerial post in Venezuela, had apparently become involved with a Swiss banker in a speculation which had gone badly wrong, and he was now deeply in debt. The banker, it seemed, had shot himself.

'If it hadn't been for a call that this young man made to the FBI,' Mayer explained to Sally Brown, 'it would have been Bob Reston and I who would have ended up dead on the carpet of the Fairmont Hotel, instead of those two young terrorists. And Azar Shahani.'

This was the first time he had used her name with Sally.

'You knew her, didn't you.'

'The Iranian woman?'

'Yes.'

'Was she a terrorist?'

'Absolutely not. At first, when the shooting started I thought she had set me up. But I found out later that they were holding her mother, in fact her whole family, hostage in Teheran. The last time she visited them, she was told: Help us, and they will be allowed to leave. This was to be the last time.'

'How do you know that?'

'The authorities searched her house in Belvedere. It was all there. The letters, her diary . . .'

'Poor woman.'

'Yes.'

Maria arrived then with the champagne, and suddenly the mood changed. Their attention shifted to the television set where the bands were still playing. Half an hour later, José, Jr rose to leave, and Paul Mayer took him to the door.

When he returned to the living-room, Sally said, 'He's a very nice young man.'

'Yes he is.'

'It took a lot of guts to do what he did. I have a feeling that you had a lot to do with it, Paul. The kid obviously thinks you're great.'

Paul Mayer said nothing more on the subject. His attention returned to the television set, and for a while he just sat beside Sally Brown on the sofa, watching the parade and the camera shots of the President, old and new. Maria had lit a fire. The champagne and the warmth started taking their toll.

Then Sally Brown sat up straight, as he remembered her doing in his bed in that cottage at the Biltmore Hotel.

'There's one other thing we've never discussed, Paul,' she said, adding, 'beside that Iranian woman.'

'Don't you ever stop thinking?' he responded.

'No I don't.'

'OK. What is it?'

'Did the CIA *really* bomb that plane?'

'Who knows,' Mayer answered, 'I certainly don't.' He could

have added that he had his suspicions, especially after the phone call from George Pace of Bank of America the night before. But he didn't.

'Well,' she said, '*somebody* must know.'

In Moscow, Mikhail Gorbachev and his wife, Raisa, were also watching the satellite transmission of the inauguration on their television set. The new head of the KGB was with them.

When it was over, Gorbachev also broke out a bottle of champagne, Crimean champagne.

'In a way, it's too bad his eight years are over,' he said. 'I got to like him. You could do business with him. He knew that it was in our mutual interest to protect each other's position of co-hegemony. As long as we both remain strong, we both remain safe.'

He told his wife about the offer that had come in that morning from Bank of America: to organize a $3 billion loan for the Soviet Union. Now that the oil price was back up to $20 a barrel, Russia was once again considered a good credit risk.

Then he said: 'Let me show you something else that arrived today, by courier.'

Gorbachev went over to his desk and removed a handwritten note from the middle drawer. With a wink and a nod at the KGB man, he handed the note to his wife. It read:

'Dear Mikhail: Thanks!'

And it was signed: 'Ron'.

'Thanks for what?' his wife asked.

'For a little something his people', and he nodded again toward the new head of the KGB, 'did at Mexico City airport.'

Raisa Gorbachev thought that one over.

' "*Pyka Pyky Moet*," ' she said, citing an old Russian saying.

'Exactly,' her husband replied.

' "One hand washes the other." '